Applied ICT

GCSE

Stephen Doyle

First published in 2002 by:
Nelson Thornes Ltd
Delta Place
27 Bath Road
CHELTENHAM
GL53 7TH
United Kingdom

02 03 04 05 06 / 10 9 8 7 6 5 4 3 2 1

A catalogue record for this book is available from the British Library

ISBN 0 7487 5747 3

Cartoons by Geoff Waterhouse
Illustrations by Derek Griffin and Alex Machin
Page make-up by GreenGate Publishing Services, Tonbridge

Printed and bound in Italy by Canale

Thanks are due to the following for permission to use material reproduced in
this book:

AOL; Amazon.com, Inc. (All rights reserved); Arts Management Support;
Blockbuster; Britannia Airways; Bromcom Computers plc; BMW (picture
courtesy of Thatcham Media Services, 1995); Call centre picture courtesy of
Locate in Kent; Dr Jo Christophers for the GP's surgery photo; Crown copyright
material [page 307] is reproduced with the permission of the Queen&rsquos
Printer for Scotland; Dental Design; easyJet airline company limited;
Environmental Images; Flytecomm.Inc; GreenGate Publishing Services; Heinz;
Library card courtesy of Kent County Council; LloydsTSB Bank plc 2002;
Napster; The Dental School, Newcastle University and NCCPED; NHS DIrect
Online; Nokia; Royal Mail Book of Stamps © Consignia plc 2002, reproduced by
kind permission of Consignia, All Rights Reserved; Seatem UK Limited for use
of First Call theatre tickets; Taxi computer courtesy of Taxitronic; Tesco; Touch
screen picture courtesy of GNC, Tonbridge; Toyota GB plc.

Microsoft screenshots reprinted with permission from Microsoft Corporation.
Microsoft and its products are registered trademarks or trademarks of Microsoft
Corporation in the United States and/or other countries.

Introduction   iv

Acknowledgements   v

UNIT 1   2
ICT tools and applications

Using ICT applications   4

Presentation of information using
wordprocessing, publications and
presentation software   5

Communication, searching and
selection of information using the
Internet   32

Organisation and analysis of
numerical information using
spreadsheet software   39

Organisation and analysis of
structured information using
database software   65

Organisation and presentation of
information using multimedia
software   101

Getting the message across –
developing your business
documents   113

Investigating how ICT is used in
organisations   120

File management and standard
ways of working   123

UNIT 2   128
ICT systems in organisations

How and why organisations use ICT   130

Main components   177

Graphical representation of systems   192

How ICT systems are designed and
implemented   201

UNIT 3   224
ICT and society

Available technologies   226

How ICT is used in business   247

How ICT has affected work styles   260

Legislation   267

How ICT has affected personal
communications   279

How ICT is used in community
activities   293

ICT and people with special needs   300

Glossary   310

Index   318

Introduction

Welcome to the GCSE in Applied Information and Communications Technology (Double Award). On starting this course, you will already have had plenty of exposure to ICT and ICT systems. I have tried to present all the information that you will need in order to do well on the course, in an easy-to-understand way. Where a term is used for the first time, it is clearly explained.

All the examples are based on Microsoft applications. Microsoft Office XP has been used throughout. If you have a previous version of Office, then most of the instructions in the exercises will work. Microsoft Word XP and Excel XP are very similar to the previous versions, but the database software Access differs more.

If you do not use these Microsoft products then do not worry as the tools and facilities are available in other applications although the techniques of using them will be different.

How this book is organised
The book covers all the material in the three units that you have to study according to the specification, which are:

Unit 1: ICT tools and applications
Unit 2: ICT systems in organisations
Unit 3: ICT and society.

Unit introduction
Each unit has an introduction which will give you an overview of what is covered in that unit.

Jargon Dragons
Jargon Dragons in each unit define terms and words that you may be unfamiliar with and that are important for you to understand.

Research Tasks
The research tasks involve finding out about something for yourself. You may have to collect material, look things up in books or use the Internet. The purpose of these research tasks is to build up your experience in finding out information. The material that you look up and write about can be useful reference material for when you do your assessments.

Find It Out
This 'Find it out' feature is used to suggest ways in which you can do your own research and investigation.

Think It Through
This feature is designed to develop your research and investigation skills further and will allow you to gain higher grades. Using this

feature will also help you to develop your analytical, discussion and
evaluation skills.

Activities

Activities are groups of short questions at the end of a section on a
series of topics. These questions ensure you have understood the
work covered in the section.

Case Studies

The Case Studies outline how real businesses and organisations use
ICT in a way that is covered by the material in the unit. Most of the
case studies are followed by some questions designed to reinforce the
points made in the case study.

Exercises

Unit 1 involves learning a lot of skills in order to use various types of
software. It is assumed you already have some basic skills, and these
skills will be developed by a series of exercises in which you have to
follow a set of instructions. After completing the exercises you will
learn how to do various tasks using the software, and eventually you
will use the skills you have acquired for the production of assessment
work in this and the other units.

Glossary

The Glossary, which is at the end of the book, contains all the words
defined in the Jargon Dragons, along with definitions of other ICT
terms.

How will your work be assessed?

There will be a mixture of internal and external assessment. Some of
the work is assessed through portfolio and some via an assessment
taken under examination conditions.

The exact make-up of the assessment varies depending on the
assessment board that your school/college is using. Your
teacher/lecturer will be able to explain your assessment in more detail.

Acknowledgements

The author and publishers would like to thank the following people
for their valuable advice and assistance in the development of this
resource.

Ian Carey, ICT Coordinator, Irlam and Cadishead Community High
School, Lancashire
Val Ford, Deputy Headteacher, Mildenhall Upper School, Suffolk
Ann Montgomery-Smith

Thanks also to Rick Jackman and Louise Watson at Nelson Thornes,
and Katie Chester at GreenGate Publishing Services, for their help and
encouragement in producing this book.

This unit will help you to:

- learn and make use of ICT tools in the way that they would be used in the workplace
- understand how ICT tools and applications are used by different organisations
- develop relevant knowledge and understanding of ICT applications such as:
  - wordprocessing
  - publications and presentation software
  - spreadsheets
  - databases
  - multimedia
  - web browsers and e-mail
- demonstrate understanding of file management and standard ways of working.

You will also learn how to use ICT tools and applications to:

- develop documents for different purposes
- find, store and manipulate data.

In addition you will learn how ICT tools and applications can be used to develop business documents to meet communications needs, and how standard ways of working are used in ICT.

You will also find out that some organisations use more specific ICT tools and applications, such as CAD/CAM or control technology, and that they use them for particular purposes, such as monitoring data or image creation.

ICT tools and applications 1

In this unit you will learn about:

Using ICT applications   4

Presentation of information using wordprocessing, publications and presentation software   5

Communication, searching and selection of information using the Internet   32

Organisation and analysis of numerical information using spreadsheet software   39

Organisation and analysis of structured information using database software   65

Organisation and presentation of information using multimedia software   101

Getting the message across – developing your business documents   113

Investigating how ICT is used in organisations   120

File management and standard ways of working   123

Using ICT applications

Different applications have different tools and facilities. As part of this course you will need to learn what needs are met by these kinds of applications software, and when and how to use their different features. Here are some applications you will need to develop skills in:

- presentation of information using wordprocessing, publications and presentation software
- organisation and analysis of numerical information using spreadsheet software
- organisation and analysis of structured information using database software
- organisation and presentation of information using multimedia software
- communication, searching and selection of information using the Internet.

In this section we will look at each application in turn and give you some practice in using the software to build up your skills. You must work through this material carefully and thoroughly since you are required by the specification (i.e. the syllabus) to know about all the software facilities outlined, as in the list above.

The assessment in this unit will require you to understand the different types of applications software available. As well as knowing about the software, you will also need to know how to use it in a business context.

The programs that enable a computer to do a useful job are together called '**software**'. Software can be the **operating system** (e.g. Windows XP, Windows 2000, Windows Millennium Edition, etc.) or applications software (e.g. wordprocessor, spreadsheet, database, etc.). Applications software is software that performs a specific task.

Here is a list of the types of software that you should be able to use:

- desktop publishing
- spreadsheet
- database
- multimedia.

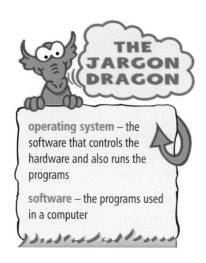

THE JARGON DRAGON

operating system – the software that controls the hardware and also runs the programs

software – the programs used in a computer

You may also wish to find out about and use:

- computer-aided design/computer-aided manufacture (CAD/CAM)
- software for monitoring data
- software for creating images.

Presentation of information using wordprocessing, publications and presentation software

Software used for presenting information is the most familiar type of software. Wordprocessing, desktop publishing and presentation software are all used for presenting information. These types of software have similar features, and it is sometimes difficult to decide which one to use. An important factor is which is the *easiest* to use, and many people will choose the one they are most familiar with.

If you are using Microsoft Office, you will be using the following software packages:

- Wordprocessing: Microsoft Word
- Desktop publishing: Microsoft Publisher
- Presentation: Microsoft PowerPoint.

By the time you start your GCSE course, you are likely to be quite familiar with the use of wordprocessing software. Rather than start from the basics, this book will therefore assume some prior knowledge and will concentrate on the less widely used features.

Entering text

Most text is entered via the keyboard by typing it in. This is not the only way of entering text. If there is a lot of text to enter, perhaps from a book or newspaper, then you can scan it in and use optical character recognition (OCR) software (which usually comes free with a scanner) to put the text into the application you are using.

If there is some text on a web page or website that you want to enter and edit then this is easily done as follows. Highlight the text you want to enter (you can include the diagrams as well if you like) and then click on Edit and then Copy. This will put the text plus any pictures onto the clipboard. You then start your wordprocessing software, go to a new document or one created already and position the cursor where you want the text to be inserted. Then click on Edit and then Paste. The text will now be inserted. You can now edit (i.e. alter) the text in some way if you want to.

Selecting, cutting, copying, pasting and moving text

You will often have to move a block of text from one place to another. Sometimes you will just want to move a section from one place in a document to a different place in the same document. Other times you may want to move it to a different document.

Selecting text

To select text, move the cursor to the start of the text. Then click on the left mouse button and, keeping your finger on the button, move the cursor across the text. This process will leave the text you have selected highlighted.

Cutting text

Cutting text takes a block of text out of the current document and stores it in an area of memory called the clipboard. When you cut text it is no longer in the current document. If you want the text to remain in the document then you should copy the text rather than cut it (the next section explains how to do this).

To cut a block of text you follow these steps:

1 Select the block of text to be cut by highlighting it.
2 Click on Edit.
3 In the pull-down menu, select Cut. The text is removed from its current position and stored on the clipboard.

Copying text

A block of text can remain in its current position while it is copied to another position, either in the same document or a different one. Copying text involves storing the text on the clipboard.

To copy a block you follow these steps:

1 Select the block of text to be copied by highlighting it.
2 Click on Edit.
3 In the pull-down menu, select Copy. The text is stored on the clipboard and also remains in its current position.

The block can now be pasted in the way described in the next section.

Pasting text

Pasting text involves using text that has first been stored on the clipboard. You could *copy* a section of text onto the clipboard with the original block of text remaining unaltered, or alternatively you could *cut* a block of text by taking it from the document and transferring it to the clipboard. Note that you can have only one item on the clipboard at any one time. Copying or cutting an item to the clipboard deletes any item that is already there.

To paste text means taking an item from the clipboard and putting it into a document. You could put it into the same document or a completely different one. To paste text you must first have some text on the clipboard. You then follow these steps:

1 Move to the document where the text is to be pasted.
2 Make sure that the cursor is positioned where you want the block of text to be inserted.
3 Click on Edit.
4 In the pull-down menu, select Paste. The text should appear in its correct position.

Moving text

Text can be moved by cutting it from its original position and pasting it to a new position. If you make a mistake, then there is an Undo command in the Edit menu which will 'undo' the last action.

Formatting text

Text is formatted to make it stand out. Here are the three main styles you can use:

Bold B   <u>Underline</u> U   *Italics* I

To format text, select it and click on the relevant button.

There are other ways to format text. First, select the text you want to format and then, in the Format menu, select Font... from the list. You will then be presented with the following screen from which you can format text in a number of different ways.

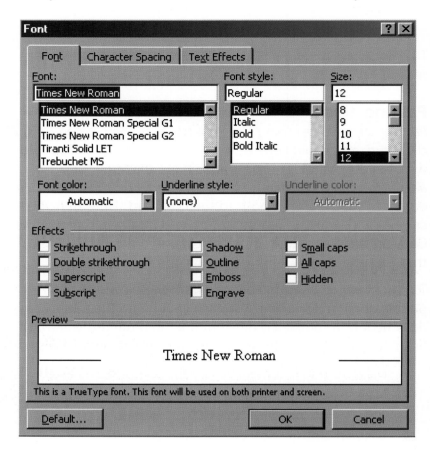

From this menu you can do many other things, such as:

- alter the colour of the text
- produce many other text effects (emboss, engrave, etc.)
- use different styles for underlining text.

Justifying text

Justifying text means aligning (lining up) the text in some way. The main buttons for justifying text are shown below.

- **Align left (also called left justified)**
  This lines up the text with the left margin but leaves the right-hand side ragged. This alignment is the most common and is the one used by wordprocessors unless you specify another type.

- **Align right (also called right justified)** ≡
  This lines up the text with the right margin but leaves the left-hand edge ragged.
- **Centre** ≡
  This lines up text with the centre of the text.
- **Fully justified (also called justified)** ≡
  This lines up text with both the right and left margins.

Fonts

Changing the font alters the appearance of the characters. Fonts are given names and you can change the font by selecting the text and then clicking on the part of the formatting toolbar shown opposite. Notice also that there is a section for altering the font size (i.e. how big the characters appear).

When the arrow pointing down (correctly called the 'down scroll arrow') is clicked, the following list of fonts appears for you to choose from. Click on any one to make your choice.

Click here to alter the font size

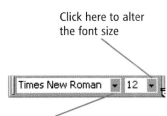

Click here to alter the font (each font is given a name. In this case the font is called Times New Roman)

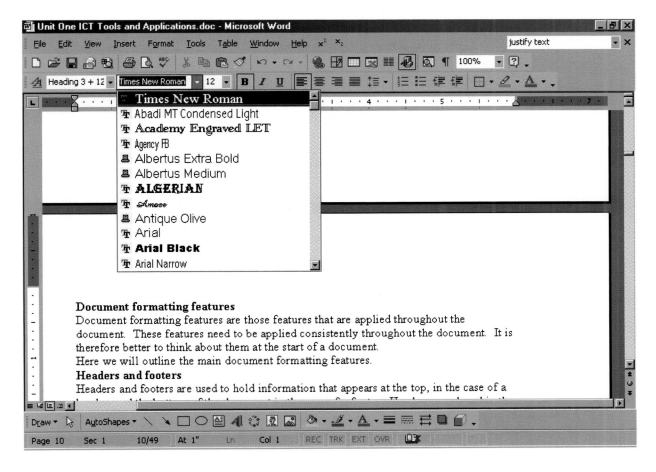

Document formatting features

Document formatting features are those features that are applied throughout the document. These features need to be applied consistently. It is therefore better to think about them at the start of a document.

Here we will outline the main document formatting features.

Headers and footers

Headers and **footers** are used to hold information that appears at the top of each page in the case of a header, and at the bottom of each page of the document in the case of a footer. Headers are placed in the top margin and footers are placed in the bottom. You can choose whether they are included on every page or just some of the pages.

Here are some types of information that are commonly put into headers and footers:

- Page numbers
- Today's date
- The title of the document
- A company logo (it can be a graphic image)
- The author's name
- The filename of the file that is used to hold the document

footer – text placed at the bottom of a document

header – text placed at the top of a document

This multi-page document has headers and footers throughout, except on the first page

Bullet points

Bullet points can be used to:

- make several points
- make each point separately
- emphasise each point.

You can choose from lots of shapes for a bullet. In the list of points above, spots were used but you can have triangles, arrows, diamonds, etc. You can even design your own.

The screen shown below illustrates some of the different types of bullet points available.

THE JARGON DRAGON

bullet point – a paragraph or section of text that has a symbol placed in front to make the section of text stand out

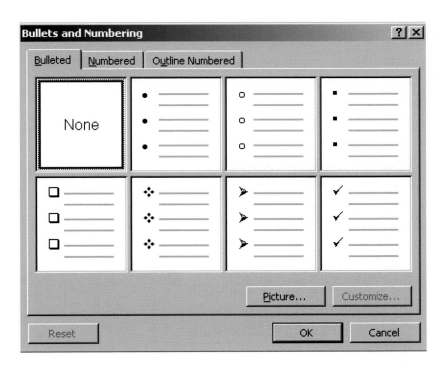

Incorporating tables into a document

Putting data, especially numerical data, into a table makes it look neat and professional. It also makes it easy to read. Tables may also be used to summarise information. In Word, there are many different table types you can insert into a document.

NOW DO EXERCISE 1

exercise 1

Using a table to provide a summary

In this exercise you will learn how to:

- insert a table into a document
- adjust the column width and row heights
- input data into a table.

We are going to produce a table to show two of the main differences between a wide area network (WAN) and a local area network (LAN).

1 Load Word and start a new document.

2 Click on Table on the menu toolbar and select Insert and then Table. The following menu appears, where you can specify the number of columns and rows. Change the number of columns to 3 and the number of rows to 3 and click on OK.

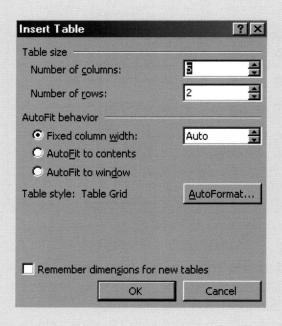

3 The following table will appear at the cursor position. Notice that it spans from one margin to the other.

Adjust the width of the columns and the height of the rows in the following way. Move the pointer onto the lines and you will notice that the cursor changes to two parallel lines (either vertical or horizontal). Press the left mouse button and drag until the widths of the columns are similar to those shown in the following diagram.

	LAN	**WAN**
Difference 1	Confined to a small area, usually a single site.	Cover a wide geographical area spanning towns, countries or even continents.
Difference 2	Usually uses simple cable links owned by the company.	Uses expensive telecommunication links not owned by the company.

4 Type in the data shown in the table above. You can centre the headings 'LAN' and 'WAN' by typing them in, highlighting them and then clicking on the Centre button on the toolbar. This will centre the headings in the columns. Also, embolden the words 'LAN', 'WAN', 'Difference 1' and 'Difference 2'.

5 See how neat this now looks. Save your document using the filename **The differences between a LAN and a WAN**. Print out a copy of your document.

Selecting a table

The table created in Exercise 1 was the simplest type of table you can produce in Word. There are some pre-stored tables you can use. Once you have selected the number of rows and columns in the Table menu click on Table AutoFormat... and the menu on the following page appears. By flicking through the sample formats you can select one that will work well with the data you need to present.

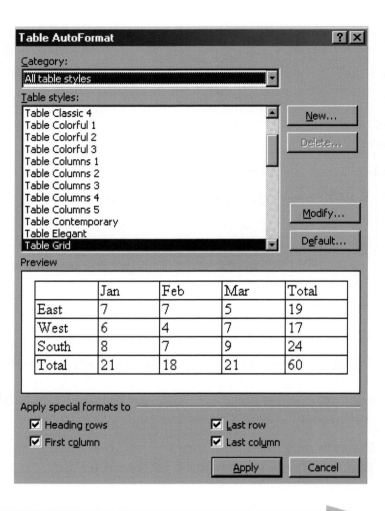

NOW DO EXERCISE 2

You have been asked by your dentist to design and produce a poster to encourage young children to take care of their teeth. The poster is to be placed on the wall of the surgery and it is to be produced on an A4-sized piece of paper and in colour.

Produce three draft designs for the dentist to choose from.

Consider using the following:

- different fonts
- different-sized text
- clip art.

exercise 2

Incorporating clip art or graphic images

A document's appearance can be improved by adding clip art or graphic images.

In this exercise you will learn how to:

- search for clip art or graphics images
- insert clip art or graphics images into a document.

To insert clip art, follow the following instructions:

1 Open a new document or a saved one.

2 Position the cursor where you want to insert the clip art.

3 Click on Insert.

4 In the pull-down menu, select Picture and then Clip Art... .

5 The screen will now be split into two. On the right is a search facility that will help you find suitable clip art.

6 Suppose you want some clip art about looking after your teeth. Type **dentistry** in the Search text box and then click on the Search button.

7 Thumbnails (small pictures) of the clip art are shown.

Use the scroll bar at the side to look for a suitable piece of clip art.

8 Double click on one of the pictures to place it into position in your document.

You may be asked to insert a CD with the clip art on. Alternatively, the clip art may be stored on the hard disk so that it can be accessed immediately.

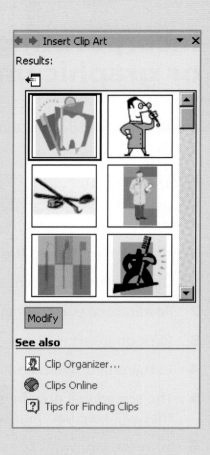

wrap – the process by which a computer automatically starts a new line

Using word-wrapping facilities around images/objects

When an object (e.g. a table, clip art, spreadsheet, photo, etc.) is inserted into a document, the text can be made to flow ('**wrap**') around the object in different ways.

NOW DO EXERCISE 3

Wrapping text around an image

In this exercise you will learn how to:

- wrap text around an image.

1 Open a new document and type in the following text:

Getting cash from your supermarket
It is common to see cash dispensers in the walls of out-of-town supermarkets. It is also possible to get cash at the same time as paying for the goods using the EPOS terminal.

The service is called 'Cashback' and to get cash, the customer needs to have a card called a Switch card or a similar debit card. Debit cards can be used as an alternative to paying by cheque. When the customer pays for their goods they will be asked if they want 'cashback'. The customer details are read off their card using a card reader and a voucher is produced that the customer then signs for the goods. For cashback the customer also signs for the amount of cash they have received. When a debit card is used, the money is transferred from the shopper's account to the store's bank account. This process takes place immediately.

2 Move the cursor to the gap between the two sections of text.

3 Insert an item of clip art or another suitable image into this space. The text with the image should now look as shown below, but yours will contain a different image (preferably something to do with cash dispensers or supermarkets).

Getting cash from your supermarket
It is common to see cash dispensers in the walls of out-of-town supermarkets. It is also possible to get cash at the same time as paying for the goods using the EPOS terminal.

The service is called 'Cashback' and to get cash, the customer needs to have a card called a Switch card or a similar debit card. Debit cards can be used as an alternative to paying by cheque. When the customer pays for their goods they will be asked if they want 'cashback'. The customer details are read off their card using a card reader and a voucher is produced that the customer then signs for the goods. For cashback the customer also signs for the amount of cash they have received. When a debit card is used, the money is transferred from the shopper's account to the store's bank account. This process takes place immediately.

4 Select the image by clicking on it. You should see some small squares appear.

5 Click on the Format menu and then on Picture. The Format Picture screen will appear.

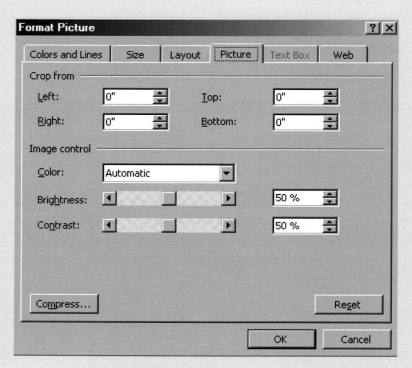

6 Click on the Layout tab. The screen will now change to this:

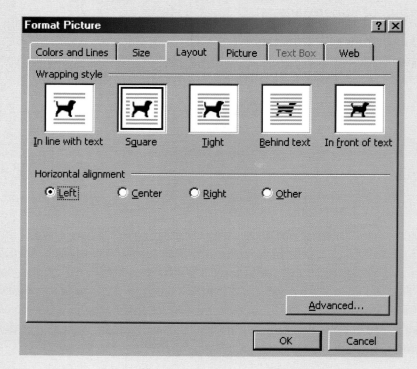

Select S<u>q</u>uare for the wrapping style and <u>L</u>eft for the horizontal alignment.

Click on the OK button.

7 The text will now flow around the image like this:

Getting cash from your supermarket

It is common to see cash dispensers in the walls of out-of-town supermarkets. It is also possible to get cash at the same time as paying for the goods using the EPOS terminal.

The service is called 'Cashback' and to get cash, the customer needs to have a card called a Switch card or a similar debit card. Debit cards can be used as an alternative to paying by cheque. When the customer pays for their goods they will be asked if they want 'cashback'. The customer details are read off their card using a card reader and a voucher is produced that the customer then signs for the goods. For cashback the customer also signs for the amount of cash they have received. When a debit card is used, the money is transferred from the shopper's account to the store's bank account. This process takes place immediately.

Use the text and the image from Exercise 3 to experiment with different wrapping styles. Save each version under a different name and produce printouts of your results.

ACTIVITY

Mail merge

Mail **merging** involves combining a list of, say, names and addresses, with a standard letter, so that a series of similar letters is produced, each addressed to a different person. The list is created either by using the wordprocessor or by importing data from a database of names and addresses. The letter is typed, using the wordprocessor, with blanks where the data from the list will be inserted.

THE JARGON DRAGON

merge – to combine data from two different sources

NOW DO EXERCISE 4

Performing a mail merge

In this exercise you will learn how to:

- create a letter to be sent to different people
- create a name and address list for the recipients of the letter
- insert the variable fields into the letter
- merge the name and address details with the letter to produce the personalised letters.

1 Load Word and create a new document. Click on <u>T</u>ools and the following menu drops down. Move down to L<u>e</u>tters and Mailings.

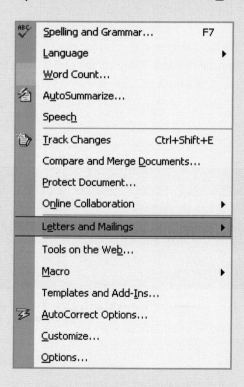

2 The following menu appears. You need to select <u>M</u>ail Merge Wizard... .

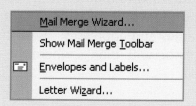

Click on <u>M</u>ail Merge Wizard.

3 The screen divides into two with the right-hand side containing instructions for you to follow.

Make sure that Letters is selected. You can then start typing.

4 Type in the following letter, making sure that you leave two lines blank at the top of the page:

> Dear
>
> As you know you will soon be taking your end of year examinations. For those of you in year 11, these will be your GCSE exams. We will be holding a revision club on Mondays and Wednesdays from 4 p.m. to 6 p.m. A variety of staff will be on hand to help you with your revision questions. You should take advantage of this as it is completely free.
>
> There will be a meeting on Wednesday 3rd May at 4 p.m. in the hall for any of you interested in taking up the offer.
>
> Happy revision and good luck.

Click on Next: Starting document.

5 Make sure that the option 'Use the current document' has been selected.

exercise 4

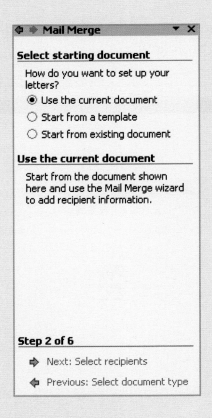

Click on Next: Select recipients.

6 In the following screen, select 'Type a new list'.

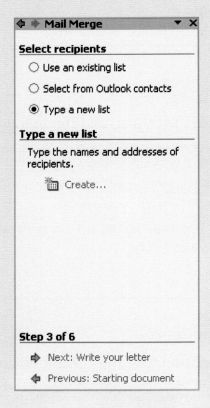

Click on Create... .

7 The following screen appears. Here you can select the name and address details.

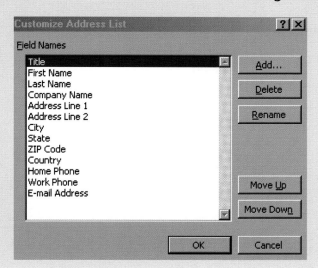

To send the letters to the pupils you need to have the following information for the names and addresses:

Surname
Forename
Street
Town
Postcode

8 Click on the Customize... button and the following screen will appear:

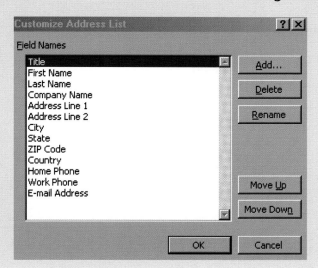

exercise 4

Make sure that Title is highlighted. Click on the <u>D</u>elete button to remove it from the list.

The following confirmation screen appears:

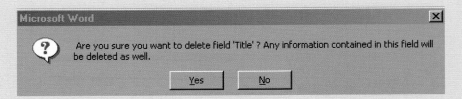

Click on the <u>Y</u>es button to confirm that you want it deleted.

9 Move the cursor to First Name.

Change this to Forename by clicking on Rename and then typing in **Forename**. Click on the OK button.

In a similar way change Last Name to Surname.

10 Now make the following changes by following Steps 7 and 8:

Delete Company Name.

Rename Address Line 1 to **Street.**

Rename Address Line 2 to **Town.**

Rename City to **Postcode.**

Delete the rest of the fields.

Your list will now look like the screen opposite:

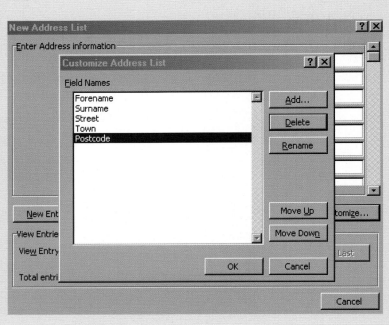

11 Click on the OK button. The following screen appears where you can type in your list of names and addresses:

New Address List

Enter Address information

Forename	
Surname	
Street	
Town	
Postcode	

[New Entry] [Delete Entry] [Find Entry ...] [Filter and Sort...] [Customize...]

View Entries

View Entry Number   [First] [Previous] 1 [Next] [Last]

Total entries in list   1

[Close]

12 We now enter the pupil data (i.e. the pupils' names and addresses) into our list.

Enter the details as shown below:

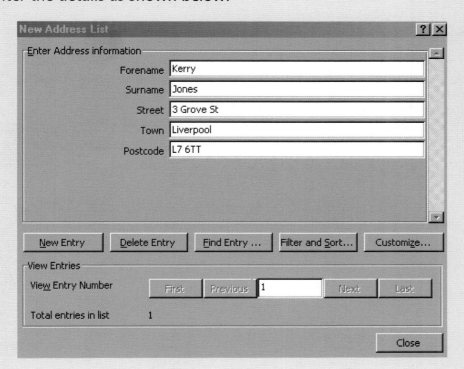

New Address List

Enter Address information

Forename	Kerry
Surname	Jones
Street	3 Grove St
Town	Liverpool
Postcode	L7 6TT

[New Entry] [Delete Entry] [Find Entry ...] [Filter and Sort...] [Customize...]

View Entries

View Entry Number   [First] [Previous] 1 [Next] [Last]

Total entries in list   1

[Close]

When you have typed in the details, click on <u>N</u>ew Entry.

Now repeat this by typing in the details for these two pupils:

Forename	Adam	Robin
Surname	Keel	Jackson
Street	12 Moor Grove	34 Fell St
Town	Liverpool	Warrington
Postcode	L13 7YH	WA 4ER

Now click on the Close button.

13 You will see a screen where you can name the file of names and addresses and also specify where it is to be stored. If you are storing your work on a floppy disk, make sure that Save <u>in</u> is altered to the floppy A drive.

Type in the filename **Pupil list** and then click on the <u>S</u>ave button.

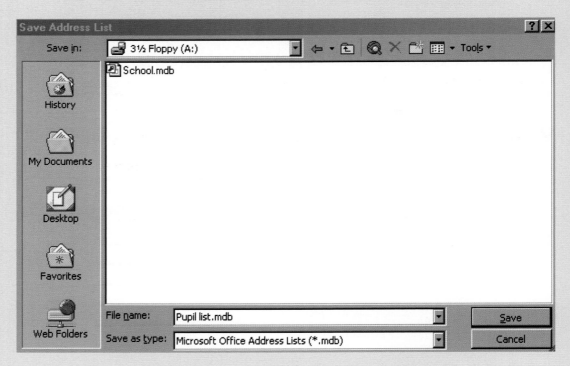

14 The following screen appears:

	Surname	Postcode	Forename	Street	T...
☑	Jones	L7 6TT	Kerry	3 Grove St	Liverpool
☑	Keel	L13 7YH	Adam	12 Moor G...	Liverpool
☑	Jackson	WA 4ER	Robin	34 Fell St	Warrin...

Mail Merge Recipients

To sort the list, click the appropriate column heading. To narrow down the recipients displayed by a specific criteria, such as by city, click the arrow next to the column heading. Use the check boxes or buttons to add or remove recipients from the mail merge.

List of recipients:

[Select All] [Clear All] [Refresh]
[Find...] [Edit...] [Validate] [OK]

Make sure that there are ticks by the three records. This means that you have selected them for the mail merge.

Now click on the OK button.

15 Near the bottom right of the screen click on Next: Write your letter.

Look at the right section of the screen. It should look like this:

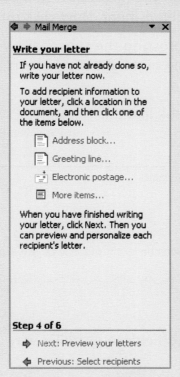

Mail Merge

Write your letter

If you have not already done so, write your letter now.

To add recipient information to your letter, click a location in the document, and then click one of the items below.

📄 Address block...
📄 Greeting line...
📧 Electronic postage...
📋 More items...

When you have finished writing your letter, click Next. Then you can preview and personalize each recipient's letter.

Step 4 of 6

➡ Next: Preview your letters
⬅ Previous: Select recipients

16 Click on More items… .

The following window will be opened:

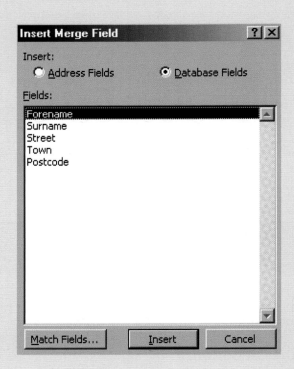

17 Move the cursor to a position in the original document above the word 'Dear' and then click on the Insert button on the above screen. This will insert the Forename details here. Now click on the Close button.

Leave two spaces by pressing the spacebar twice. Click on More items… again and then highlight Surname in the above screen and press the Insert button.

Your letter will now look like this:

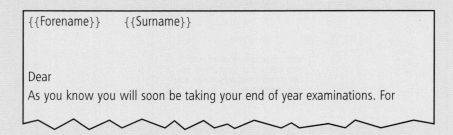

18 Now add the following fields in a similar way until your letter looks like this:

```
{{Forename}} {{Surname}}
{{Street}}
{{Town}}
{{Postcode}}


Dear
As you know you will soon be taking your end of year examinations.
```

19 Add the Forename field next to Dear like this:

```
{{Forename}} {{Surname}}
{{Street}}
{{Town}}
{{Postcode}}


Dear {{Forename}}
As you know you will soon be taking your end of year examinations.
```

20 You can now get the computer to insert the variable data into these fields to complete the mail merge.

Click on Next: Preview your letters.

The first name and address details will be inserted and your first letter will look like this:

```
Kerry Jones
3 Grove Street
Liverpool
L7 6TT

Dear Kerry

As you know you will soon be taking your end of year examinations. For those
of you in year 11, these will be your GCSE exams. We will be holding a
revision club on Mondays and Wednesdays from 4 p.m. to 6 p.m. A variety of
staff will be on hand to help you with your revision questions. You should take
advantage of this as it is completely free.

There will be a meeting on Wednesday 3$^{rd}$ May at 4 p.m. in the hall for any of
you interested in taking up the offer.

Happy revision and good luck
```

21 Click on Next: Complete the merge.

22 Click on Print... to print out the three letters.

23 On closing the windows down, you will come to the screen shown below. Here you can save the letter.

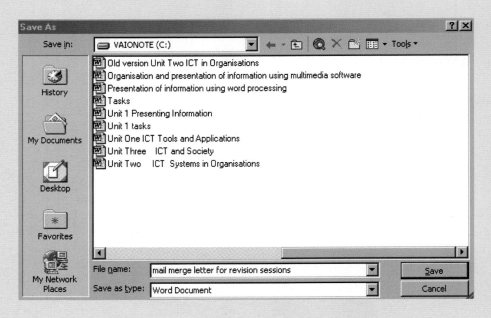

Publishing

Publishing involves producing professional documents. Usually, these documents consist of more than just simple text. For example, they can include diagrams, photographs, tables, worksheets, etc. Published documents may have special features such as text flowing around the artwork (diagrams, photographs, etc.) or the use of more than one column.

Publishing is done using specialist **desktop publishing** software (DTP for short). Most wordprocessing packages offer many of the features of DTP packages.

What equipment is needed for desktop publishing?

Computer

A very powerful computer is needed with lots of memory and a large hard drive. This is because manipulating pictures on the screen takes a lot of computing power.

THE JARGON DRAGON

desktop publishing – combining text and pictures on a screen to produce posters, newsletters, brochures, etc.

A large screen should be used because you often have to view two pages on the screen at the same time. If the screen is small, then the text on these pages will be very small and difficult to read.

Printer
Usually an ink-jet printer is used that is capable of printing in colour. Laser printers produce better quality, but colour laser printers are very expensive.

Scanner
A scanner is used to scan photographs and hand-drawn artwork into the document. If there is a large amount of text to input, this can also be scanned in, provided you have optical character recognition (OCR) software.

Digital camera
Digital cameras are able to take photographs that are digitised and stored inside the camera. There is no need for a film or the development process. Instead the images (i.e. digitised photos) are transferred to a computer. The images may then be altered, sized and incorporated into a DTP-prepared document.

THE JARGON DRAGON

thumbnails – rough designs drawn on paper

Publishing features

Planning your design: making use of thumbnails
It is a good idea to plan out a design for your document on paper first. **Thumbnails** are rough designs on paper. They are used to plan the layout of the page. You can try different layouts and then decide on the best one. Shaded boxes or a bunch of quick, parallel lines are used for columns of text. Darker boxes are used to show photos or artwork (diagrams, clip art, etc.). Lines and squiggles of varying thickness are used for headlines and subheadings.

Some tips for your design:

- Do not worry about details. Just get the main features in the best place.
- Try to get everything in proportion. If there is a picture that occupies one third of the page, then make it occupy a third on your thumbnail.
- Make lots of sketches. Put everything in different places and see what you think.
- Don't start using the software until you have picked a final design.

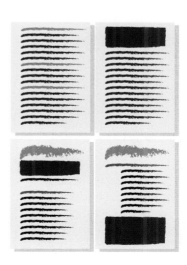

templates – electronic files which hold standardised document layouts

Using templates

Rather than create a design from scratch you can use a design that has already been created. These designs are called **templates**. Some templates allow you to alter them slightly. The template will often guide you through a series of choices that will tailor-make the design.

Some programs include their own set of designer templates for a variety of documents.

Templates determine the structure of the document. They set things like:

- **fonts**: the style of the letters and numbers used
- **page layout**: margins, justification (how the sentences are lined up), indents, line spacing (the spacing between lines of text), page numbering, etc.
- **special formatting**: bold, italics, etc.

Here are some advantages in using templates:

- Templates can save you time.
- The appearance of documents will be consistent if everyone in an organisation uses the same template.

There is an excellent website that contains advice about drawing pictures and cartoons. Take a look at it on:

http://desktoppub.miningco.com

Communication, searching and selection of information using the Internet

The importance of the Internet to businesses and organisations should not be underestimated. Communication between businesses or between a business and its customers is at the heart of any business. Using the Internet makes it easier for this communication to take place.

Using e-mail to communicate between individuals and groups

This section will cover the important aspects of e-mail.

Electronic mail (**e-mail** for short) has become an established communication method, just like the telephone.

E-mail is a method of sending messages from one terminal to another via a communications link. To communicate using e-mail you need the following:

- an e-mail address of your own
- the e-mail address of the receiver.

THE JARGON DRAGON

electronic mail (e-mail) – e-mail messages and documents can be created, sent and read without the need for them to be printed out

Sending an e-mail

You can write your message using e-mail software. Next you need to use your communications software and modem/terminal adapter to connect to a service provider's file server. Once you are connected, you can transfer your message.

E-mails are usually short, to-the-point messages. If you want to send a long letter you should use your wordprocessor to write it and once it has been checked you should save it. You can then write a short e-mail explaining to the person receiving the letter that the file is going to be attached to the e-mail. You will also need to mention what wordprocessing package and version you have used. If you know that the recipient has a different wordprocessing package, you can save the letter as a text file, as all wordprocessors can read these.

You then need to attach the document file to the e-mail. We will look at how file attachments are made later on. Pictures and photographs are often sent with e-mails as file attachments.

Replying to an e-mail

When you receive e-mail you will notice that there is a button to click for your reply. All you have to do is type in your reply, as the e-mail address you are sending it to is automatically included. You can also send the message that was sent to you so that your reply is set in context. It also means that the receiver does not have to refer to their original e-mail.

The screen on the next page shows the e-mail preparation screen from AOL. Notice that you can format the text (bold, italics, etc.). Notice also that there is an address book and you can attach files using the Attachments button.

Send To:		Copy To:		Send Now

Subject: [   ]

Arial [ ] 10 [ ] **B** *I* U | ☰ ☰ ☰ | A A | 🖼 ▼ ❤ ▼ | ABC✓ | ✏ ▼

Send Later

Address Book

Email Extras

Help

Attachments

☐ Request "Return Receipt" from AOL members

Address book

Internet Service Providers (ISPs) have a feature called an address book for managing your e-mail addresses. In the **address book** are the names and e-mail addresses of all the people to whom you are likely to send e-mail. Instead of having to type in the address when writing an e-mail, you just click on the e-mail address or addresses in the address book.

Mailing lists

Mailing lists are lists of people and their e-mail addresses. They are used when a copy of an e-mail needs to be distributed to all the people in a particular group. For example, if you were working as part of a team and you often needed to send each member of the team the same e-mail, then you would set up a mailing list. Every time you needed to send the members of the team e-mail, you could use the list to save time.

File attachments

You can attach files to e-mails as **file attachments.** For example, you could attach a file containing a photograph of yourself obtained from a digital camera, a piece of clip art, a picture that you have scanned in, a long document, etc. Basically, if you can store something as a file, then you can attach it to an e-mail.

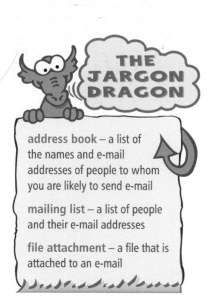

THE JARGON DRAGON

address book – a list of the names and e-mail addresses of people to whom you are likely to send e-mail

mailing list – a list of people and their e-mail addresses

file attachment – a file that is attached to an e-mail

You can attach more than one file to an e-mail, so if you had six photographs to send, you could attach each of them and send them together.

Before you attach a file you must first prepare an e-mail message to send, explaining the purpose of your e-mail and giving some information about the files that you are sending (what their purpose is, what file format they are in, etc.).

Once the e-mail message has been completed, click on the File Attachment button and select the file you want to send. A box will appear to allow you to select the drive, folder and eventually the file that you want to send.

If you want to send more than one file, repeat the file attachment process. Usually, if there is more than one file to send then the files will be compressed to reduce the time taken to send them.

Aspects of the Internet

In this section we will be looking at some **Internet** terms and other aspects of the Internet.

Web browser
A web browser is a program that allows access to the **World Wide Web** (WWW).

Web server
A web server is a computer that contains the information that users of the Internet can access using their web browser. A web server needs to be permanently connected to the Internet so that users are able to access the information all the time. Web servers for Internet Service Providers contain many websites. If you develop your own website, then the site will usually be stored on the web server of the Internet Service Provider that you use.

Features of communication software such as web browsers
No matter which web browser you use, there are some features that are common to them all. Here are some of the main ones.

Links (favourites, favourite places or bookmarks)
When you surf the World Wide Web you are quickly moving from one web page to another. On each of these web pages there are links to other web pages and when you click on one it

THE JARGON DRAGON

Internet – worldwide network of computer networks. The Internet forms the largest connected set of computers in the world

World Wide Web – a system of file servers on the Internet that supports special documents in a language called HTML. It also supports graphics, audio and video files

takes you to a different web page which may be on the same site or a different one. If you want to go back to a site, it is sometimes hard to remember the links you took to get there. By putting a web page in your 'favourites', you are storing its name and web address so that you can return to it at a later date. When you add a site to your favourites, you are creating a shortcut to the site.

History

A history list shows all the sites/pages that you have visited in the order in which you have visited them. This is useful if you want to go back to a previous site during a surfing session. History lists can also tell you the sites that other users have visited.

History allows you to view the sites that you have recently visited

Navigation

Browsers have a toolbar displaying the buttons that you use to move around the site and perform certain actions.

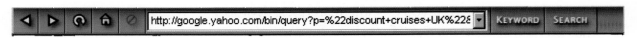

The Navigation button for the Internet Service Provider AOL

These buttons would typically include:

Back – go back to the previous page

Forward – jump forward to the next page

Refresh (also called **Reload**) – refresh the contents of the page

Home – return to the page that you use as your home page (i.e. your starting point) or the page that your Internet Service Provider uses as their home page

Stop – stop trying to load the page.

The buttons for Back, Forward, Refresh, Home and Stop (working from left to right)

Cache (sometimes referred to as temporary pages)

This is a storage area on your hard drive where some text and images from web pages are stored so that they load quickly when they are visited by the user more than once.

Finding your way around the Internet

There are three ways to find your way around the Internet:

1   By typing in a web address.

    If you know the web address of a website, then you simply type it in. Web addresses are everywhere; you can find them in magazines, advertisements and even on the side of planes. Web addresses look like this:

    www.nelsonthornes.com

2   By 'surfing' the Internet.

    Surfing the Internet means moving rapidly from one web page or website to another until you find something of interest. In doing this you are making use of the hypertext links. The hypertext links are in the form of either underlined text or text in a different colour. When you move your mouse pointer over a hypertext link it changes shape (usually to a hand). On double clicking the right mouse button, you will be taken to the new site.

3   By using a special program called a search engine.

    A search engine can be used to search for information on a certain subject. You simply enter key words or subject names, and the program will search for those sites with information containing your key words. As there is so much information on the Internet, finding what you want can be quite difficult. If you are careful and specific about stating what you want to find out about, then you have more chance of getting the information you need.

How can I find what I want on the Internet?

To find what you want on the Internet you need to perform a search. To do this you need a search engine. Your Internet service provider (the company you use to connect you to the Internet) will provide one, but there are others to choose from. These include:

Yahoo	www.yahoo.com
Lycos	www.lycos.com
WebCrawler	www.webcrawler.com
Excite	www.excite.com

If you get either a huge amount of information or no information at all, you are probably searching the wrong way.

Searching using a single word

The simplest search uses a single word.

Here is some useful advice when searching for a single word:

1 Start by entering something very specific.
2 If you don't find anything, then broaden your search.
3 If you still don't find anything, then broaden your search further.

Searching using a phrase

Searching using a phrase means searching using several words. If you type in 'computer laws', you will get a huge number of references because as well as those on computer laws, you will also get all the references to 'computer' and all those to 'laws'.

You need to tell the computer to group the words 'computer' and 'laws' together and this is done by placing them in inverted commas like this:

"computer laws"

In doing this you are telling the search engine to find the words 'computer' and 'laws' only when they are next to each other on the page.

Multiple search criteria (also called Boolean searches)

Multiple searches make use of simple logic when performing searches. Multiple search criteria use keywords in the following way:

AND   search on Term 1 AND Term 2

OR   search on Term 1 OR Term 2

NOT   search on Term 1 but NOT Term 2

Examples

Retail AND Computers will search for web pages containing both the words 'Retail' and 'Computers'.

Retail OR Computers will search for web pages that contain 'Retail' or 'Computers' or both terms.

> *By making use of search conditions, search the Internet for information on:*
>
> - *garden design software*
> - *image manipulation software*
> - *sensors*
> - *working safely with computers.*

Organisation and analysis of numerical information using spreadsheet software

Spreadsheets: the basics

You will probably have used spreadsheets before, so this is a reminder.

The grid into which you put your data is often referred to as a worksheet. The words 'spreadsheet' and 'worksheet' are often used interchangeably. The worksheet is the working area of the spreadsheet and is arranged as follows:

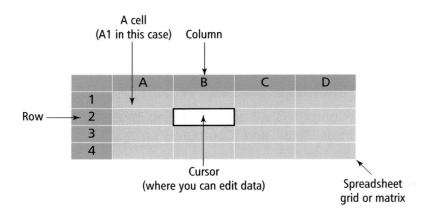

A cell
(A1 in this case) Column

Row → 2

Cursor
(where you can edit data)

Spreadsheet
grid or matrix

THE
JARGON
DRAGON

cell – an area on a
spreadsheet produced by
the intersection of a column
and a row in which data can be
placed

Cells

In the above diagram, the rectangles are called **cells**. If a particular cell needs to be referred to, you use the column letter followed by the row number. Cell C3 is the cell where column C intersects row 3. In other words, cells are referred to like this: COLUMN (letter) and then ROW (number). Hence S4 is a cell reference whereas 3E is not. It does not matter whether large (called upper case) or small (lower case) letters are used. This means that b3 is the same as B3.

What can be put into a cell?

You can put the following into a cell:

- words (titles, row headings, column headings, etc.)
- numbers (ordinary numbers, currency, dates, etc.)
- formulae (used to perform calculations with the numbers).

Excel

Excel is most popular spreadsheet software package in use and is provided either separately or as part of the integrated software package Microsoft Office. The version used in these sections are Excel XP and Office XP.

Excel is ideal if you want to produce tables (Microsoft Word can also be used for producing tables). Spreadsheets are especially useful for doing repetitive sums. Excel is also excellent for producing graphs and charts from a set of data.

The menu bar and toolbars

When you load Excel the screen on the next page appears.

There are many different toolbars and you can choose which are displayed by clicking on View and then Toolbars. A tick is shown beside the toolbars to be displayed.

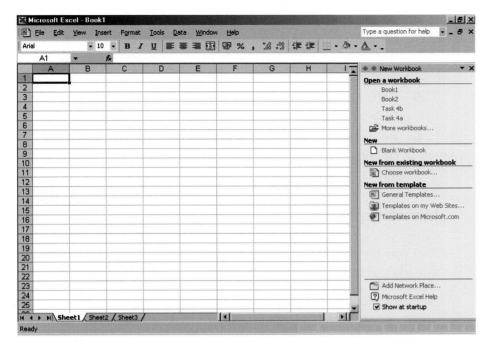

Using Undo

It is easy to issue the wrong command. The spreadsheet software may then do something you did not expect. As well as issuing the wrong commands, you can also press the wrong buttons by accident. Suddenly something happens or the screen goes blank. What can you do if this happens?

First thing is don't panic.

You can undo the last command in this way:

- In the menu bar click on Edit and then select Undo from the list.

If more than one wrong command has been issued, then you can use Step 1 several times.

Undo is very useful if you delete something by mistake.

Tips when using a spreadsheet for the first time

1 Do not work out any of the calculations using a calculator. The whole point of using the spreadsheet is to avoid having to do this yourself.
2 Use formulae wherever possible. This means that if you change the numbers in any of the cells then the spreadsheet will automatically recalculate to take account of the new values.
3 Make sure that any formulae you enter start with an equals (=) sign.

4   You may need to widen the columns. If the result of a calculation appears like this ###### it means that the number is too big to fit in the current width. By widening the column, you can correct this.

5   Plan the layout of the spreadsheet first on paper. It is easier to get it right at the start than to try to change it later.

6   Do not worry too much about the appearance of the spreadsheet. It is more important that it works. You will learn about improving the appearance of a spreadsheet later on.

Inserting rows and columns

When you are designing a spreadsheet of your own, you may find you need to insert a column between two columns that already contain data. You also might need to insert an extra row.

To insert a column, follow these steps:

1   Use the mouse to position the cursor on any cell in the column to the right of where you want the new column to be inserted.

2   Click on Insert in the main menu bar and select Columns from the list.

3   Check that the column has been inserted in the correct place. Notice that insertion of the column pushes all the data to the right of the cell the cursor is in, one column to the right. Any formulae in these cells will be adjusted automatically.

To insert a row, follow these steps:

1   Place the cursor on any of the cells in the row below where the new row needs to be placed.

2   Click on Insert in the main menu bar and select Rows from the list.

3   Check that the row has been inserted in the correct place.

Deleting a row or a column

1   Move the cursor to the row or column that you want to delete.

2   Select Edit from the menu bar and then choose Delete.

3   The box to the left will appear (this box is called a dialogue box).

4   Select either Entire row or Entire column and click on OK. If a column is being deleted, those cells in columns to the right of it will move and fill the gap.

If a row is being deleted, those cells in the rows below the one being deleted will move up to fill the gap.

Mathematical operators

You will not find the divide sign ÷ or the multiplication sign × on the computer keyboard. Instead, * is used for multiply and / is used for divide. Mathematical operators are summarised in the following table.

Operator	Use
+	Addition
−	Subtraction
*	Multiplication
/	Division
%	Percentage

Formulae

If you type in a formula to add two cells together like this: C3 + C4, then the spreadsheet will just enter 'C3 + C4' in the cell where the cursor is. 'C3 + C4' will therefore be treated as text. To distinguish between text and formulae, the equals symbol, =, needs to be typed in first.

Here are some calculations and what they do. Notice that you can use upper or lower case letters (i.e. capital or small letters).

=C3+C4 (adds together the numbers in cells C3 and C4)

=A1*B4 (multiplies the numbers in cells A1 and B4)

=3*G4 (multiplies the number in cell G4 by three)

=sum(b3:b10) (adds all the cells from b3 to b10 inclusive)

=C4/D1 (divides the number in cell C4 by the number in cell D1)

=30/100*A2 (finds 30% of the number in cell A2)

NOW DO EXERCISE 5

Producing graphs and charts

In this exercise you will learn how to:

- select data for charting
- select a chart type
- give the chart a title
- put the chart with the data
- size a chart.

Charts and graphs make it easier to understand numerical information. Take the following information for example. The table shows the temperatures and rainfall for a British seaside resort for the first eight months of 2001.

Month	Mean temperature (°C)	Mean rainfall (inches)
January	5.8	3.3
February	7.0	2.1
March	7.3	3.0
April	9.3	2.2
May	13.7	0.4
June	16.0	0.6
July	17.4	0.6
August	17.6	0.5

To see if there are patterns or trends in this data, you can draw a line graph using a spreadsheet package.

1 Type the data accurately into the worksheet like this:

	A	B	C
	Month	Mean Temperature (°C)	Mean Rainfall (inches)
1			
2	January	5.8	3.3
3	February	7	2.1
4	March	7.3	3
5	April	9.3	2.2
6	May	13.7	0.4
7	June	16	0.6
8	July	17.4	0.6
9	Aug	17.6	0.5

2 Highlight the area where all the cells contain data.

Month	Mean Temperature (°C)	Mean Rainfall (inches)
January	5.8	3.3
February	7	2.1
March	7.3	3
April	9.3	2.2
May	13.7	0.4
June	16	0.6
July	17.4	0.6
Aug	17.6	0.5

3 Click on Insert and then Chart... .

This menu pops up:

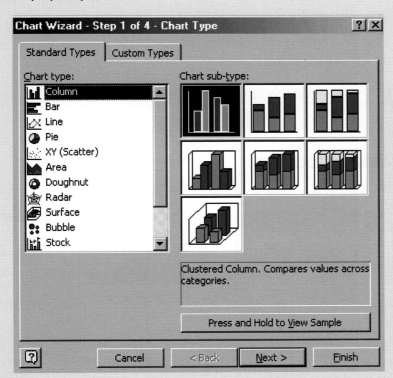

exercise 5

4 Choose Line as the chart type.

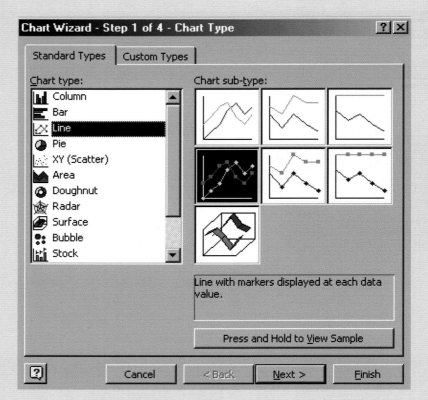

5 Click on <u>N</u>ext>. (For each step of the chart wizard just click on <u>N</u>ext>.)

6 For Step 3 of the chart wizard type the text **Temperature and rainfall for Weymouth** in the Chart <u>t</u>itle box.

Notice that the title is displayed. You can also add X- and Y- axis titles but none are needed here.

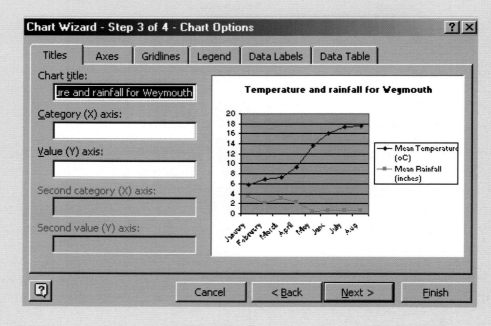

7 Click on Next> and the following screen is displayed:

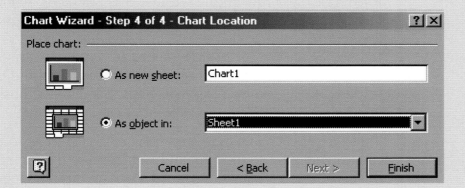

You can place the chart with the data in the worksheet. Make sure that As object in: is selected and then click on Finish.

8 The chart now appears next to the data in the worksheet like this:

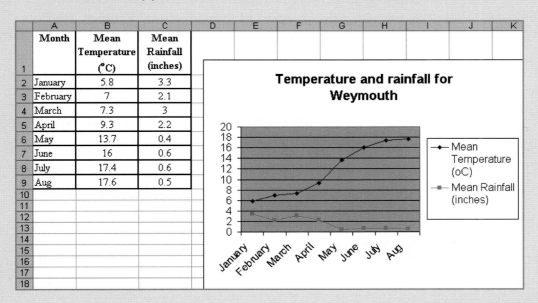

The size of the chart can be altered by clicking on the corners to get the handles. By dragging the handles you can alter the size.

Using graphs like this one you can see trends and make forecasts. You can see easily that the temperature increases from January to August. Notice that the increase is more rapid in May than in the other months. The rainfall in the months January, February, March and April is fairly constant. There is then quite a decrease in May. Notice that the rainfall during the summer stays steady.

It is much easier to make the above observations by looking at the graph rather than the numerical data in the table.

Cut and paste

To cut cells, select them (the selected cells will be highlighted) then click on Edit and then Cut. The cells will be placed in a temporary storage (called the clipboard) by the computer. You can now move the cursor to another part of your worksheet where you want the cell or cells to be placed and then click on Edit and then Paste. You can move cells to a different position in the same worksheet or a different one using this method.

If the worksheet contains cells with formulae that refer to the cells you are moving then do not worry because the formulae will be adjusted automatically to take into account the moved cells' new positions.

Copy and paste

When you cut cells, they are taken out of the worksheet. Suppose you wanted to use the same cells in a different worksheet without having to type them in. You can use Copy. Copy is similar to Cut, except that a *copy* of the cells is put onto the clipboard. The spreadsheet from which the cells are copied remains unaltered. Once copied, the cells can be pasted anywhere in the same worksheet, or a different one.

Printing formulae

When you print out a worksheet, it will always print out the results of any formulae along with any text or numbers. It can sometimes be useful to be able to see these formulae so that they can be checked. Here is a simple exercise to show how to display the formulae on the screen and then print them out.

NOW DO EXERCISES 6,7 & 8

Printing a selected area of a spreadsheet

In this exercise you will learn how to:

- use the AutoSum button
- copy formulae
- show the formulae in the worksheet.

1 Set up a worksheet and enter the following data:

	A	B	C	D	E	F
1	Item	June	July	August	September	Total
2	Swimwear	600	150	142	112	
3	Ski-Wear	50	35	60	98	
4	Shorts	85	87	82	50	
5	Golf Clubs	104	69	75	82	
6	Football	20	32	146	292	
7	T-Racquets	85	90	50	80	
8	Totals					
9						

2 Total column B and put the result in cell B8. The quick way to do this is to press the AutoSum button on the toolbar with the cursor on cell B8. The AutoSum button can be found on the standard toolbar, and it looks like this:

$$\Sigma$$

If the AutoSum button is not there, then you will need to display the standard toolbar. To do this click on <u>V</u>iew and then <u>T</u>oolbars, then select the standard toolbar.

Be careful how you use AutoSum. Check that the cell range indicated by the dotted rectangle is correct.

3 Total row 2 and put the result in cell F2. Again this can be done by positioning the cursor on cell F2 and then pressing the AutoSum button.

4 Copy the formula in cell F2 down the column to cell F7. You do this by moving the cursor to cell F2 containing the formula. Now click on the bottom right-hand corner of the cell and you should get a black cross shape. Hold the left mouse button down and move the mouse down the column until you reach cell F7. You will see a dotted rectangle

exercise 6

around the area where the copied formula is to be inserted. Now take your finger off the button and all the results of the calculation will appear. This is called relative copying because the formula is changed slightly to take account of the altered positions of the two numbers which are to be added together.

5 Copy the formula in cell B8 across the rows to cell F8.

Your worksheet will now look like this:

	A	B	C	D	E	F
1	Item	June	July	August	September	Total
2	Swimwear	600	150	142	112	1004
3	Ski-Wear	50	35	60	98	243
4	Shorts	85	87	82	50	304
5	Golf Clubs	104	69	75	82	330
6	Football	20	32	146	292	490
7	T-Racquets	85	90	50	80	305
8	Totals	944	463	555	714	2676

6 Let's insert the formulae wherever there are calculations.

Select the Tools menu and then click on Options.

The following screen will appear:

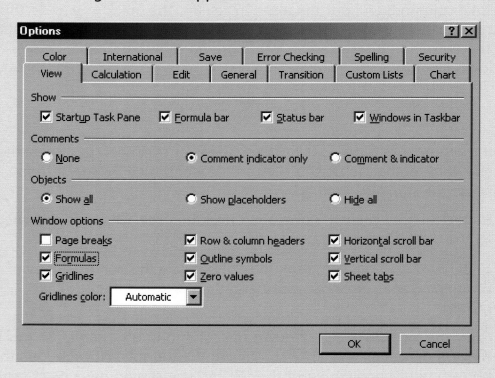

7 In the bottom part of the above screen you will see a box marked Formulas. Click on this box and a tick will appear indicating that the

formulae will be displayed. The following screen containing the formulae now appears:

	A	B	C	D	E	F
1	Item	June	July	August	September	Total
2	Swimwear	600	150	142	112	=SUM(B2:E2)
3	Ski-Wear	50	35	60	98	=SUM(B3:E3)
4	Shorts	85	87	82	50	=SUM(B4:E4)
5	Golf Clubs	104	69	75	82	=SUM(B5:E5)
6	Football	20	32	146	292	=SUM(B6:E6)
7	T-Racquets	85	90	50	80	=SUM(B7:E7)
8	Totals	=SUM(B2:B7)	=SUM(C2:C7)	=SUM(D2:D7)	=SUM(E2:E7)	=SUM(F2:F7)

8 When you try to display the formulae, they often require more space than the current column width so you may need to widen some of the columns. Do this and save, then print a copy of the worksheet containing the formulae on a single sheet. To do this click on File and then Page Setup... and make sure that the settings are the same as those shown on the following screen:

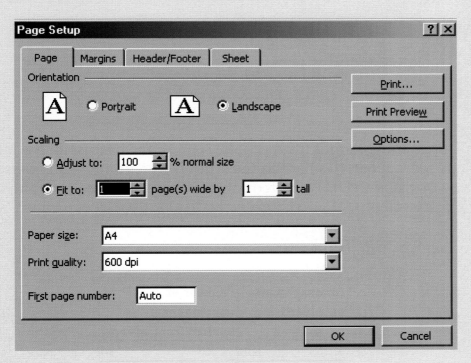

Notice that 'Landscape' has been selected and also 'Fit to 1 page'

Click on OK.

exercise 6

Producing a scattergraph

In this exercise you will learn how to:

- produce a scattergraph
- give a tile to a chart
- label axes
- print in landscape.

A mobile hairdresser advertises in the local paper. The hairdresser spends different amounts on advertising and she records the number of appointments booked from the different adverts. The details are shown in this table.

Amount spent on advertising	Number of appointments booked from adverts
£30	34
£65	28
£105	33
£145	39
£235	49
£250	54
£310	120

The hairdresser thinks that the more she spends on advertising, the more bookings she will get. It is hard to see if this is true from the numbers in the table. To see if there is a pattern, she decides to use the computer to draw a scattergraph.

1 First enter the data into the worksheet like this.

	A Amount spent on advertising	B Number of appointments booked from adverts
1		
2	£30	34
3	£65	28
4	£105	33
5	£145	39
6	£235	49
7	£250	54
8	£310	120

2 Select the data by clicking and dragging the mouse from cells A1 to B8. The selected area will be shaded like this:

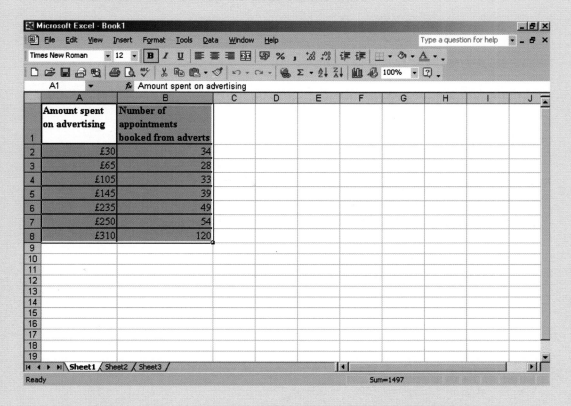

3 Click on the chart icon on the standard toolbar (it is the button with the picture of a bar graph on it).

4 Step 1 of the chart wizard appears. Select the Chart type XY (Scatter) and the Chart sub-type, as shown here:

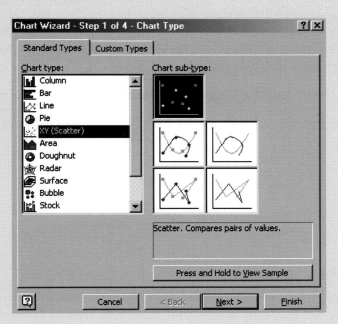

5 Click on <u>N</u>ext >. Step 2 of the chart wizard appears. Check that Series in: Col<u>u</u>mns is selected. The screen should be the same as this one:

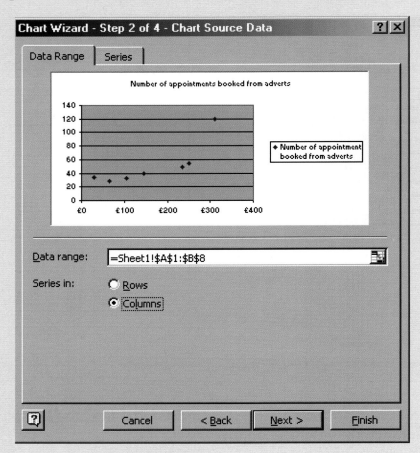

6 Click on <u>N</u>ext >. Step 3 of the chart wizard is shown.

In the Chart <u>t</u>itle box enter:

Graph to see any correlation between the amount spent on advertising and the appointments booked.

In the 'Va<u>l</u>ue (X) axis' box type in **Amount spent on advertising**.

In the '<u>V</u>alue (Y) axis' box type in **Appointments booked**.

The screen in Step 3 of the chart wizard should now look like the one at the top of the next page.

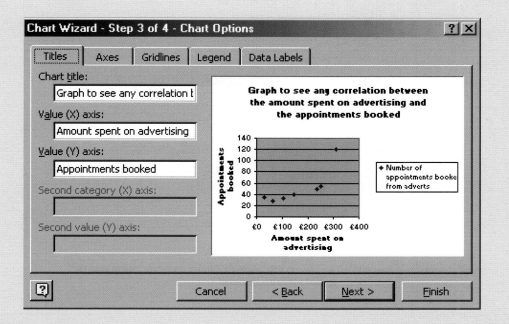

7 In Step 3 of the chart wizard click on the tab for Legend. The screen will change.

Now you can position the legend (this is the box next to the graph that explains the data). In this case, we will remove the legend. To do this, make sure that the box Show legend is left blank. The legend now disappears.

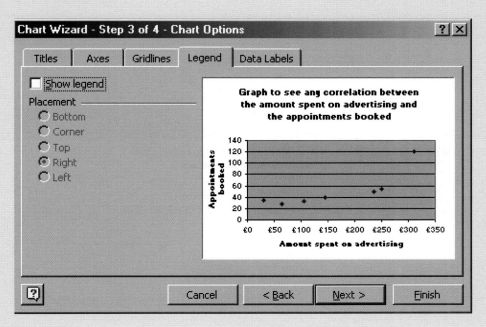

8 Click on Next > to go onto the next step of the chart wizard. Step 4 asks you if you want to put the chart with the data, or to put it into its own worksheet. Click on 'As new sheet' to put it into its own worksheet.

exercise 7

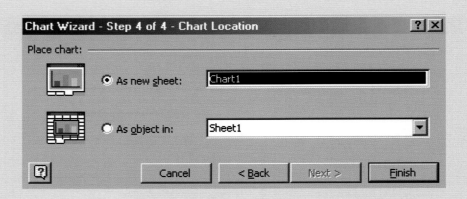

9 Click on <u>F</u>inish. The chart is now displayed.

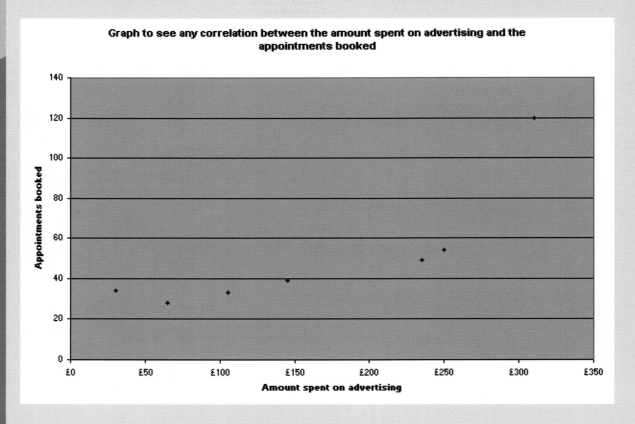

Boys versus girls

In this exercise you will learn how to:

- set numbers to a certain number of decimal places
- use a function to calculate averages
- test each mark using an IF function to print a message on who did best, boys or girls.

Here are some examination results. They show the percentage of girls and the percentage of boys who got 'A' grades in various subjects. We are going to find out from this data whether the boys or the girls did best.

1 Type in the data exactly as it is shown here. Check it to make sure your data is typed in accurately. You will need to widen column A to fit in the subject names. Make the text bold where it is shown in bold below. To do this, highlight the text and then click on the bold button on the toolbar.

	A	B	C
1	**Advanced Level exam results 2001**		
2	Percentage pass rate with 'A' grades		
3			
4	**Subject**	**Boys**	**Girls**
5	Art and design	23.5	28.4
6	Biology	16.8	20
7	Business Studies	10	11.3
8	Chemistry	25.6	27.7
9	Computing	8.9	7.5
10	Economics	22.7	22.6
11	English	17.3	16.2
12	French	26.4	23.9
13	Geography	15.8	23
14	German	32.9	26.8
15	History	17.9	19.1
16	Mathematics	28.9	30
17	Physics	24.1	27.4
18	Psychology	8.1	13.7

2 Notice that the numbers do not line up neatly. This is because whole numbers do not have a decimal point after them. For example, if you enter 30.0, just 30 appears. You can set the numbers to one decimal place.

Highlight all the numbers.

exercise 8

Click on <u>F</u>ormat and then C<u>e</u>lls... .

This screen appears:

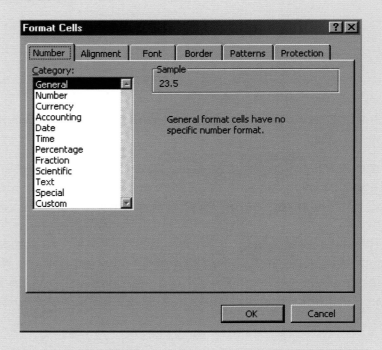

3 Set the <u>C</u>ategory to Number.

Then click on the down arrow of the <u>D</u>ecimal places box so that it is set to 1.

One decimal place will now be shown for all the numbers you selected.

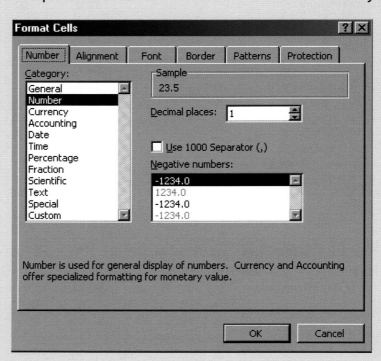

4 Click on the OK button.

Your worksheet will look like this:

	A	B	C
1	**Advanced Level exam results 2001**		
2	Percentage pass rate with 'A' grades		
3			
4	**Subject**	**Boys**	**Girls**
5	Art and design	23.5	28.4
6	Biology	16.8	20.0
7	Business Studies	10.0	11.3
8	Chemistry	25.6	27.7
9	Computing	8.9	7.5
10	Economics	22.7	22.6
11	English	17.3	16.2
12	French	26.4	23.9
13	Geography	15.8	23.0
14	German	32.9	26.8
15	History	17.9	19.1
16	Mathematics	28.9	30.0
17	Physics	24.1	27.4
18	Psychology	8.1	13.7

5 We will now find the average (or mean) mark for the boys and girls.

Put the following into cell A19: **Average percentage**.

To give the average of all the numbers in the cells from A5 to A18 and put the answer into cell B19, enter into cell B19 the formula **=AVERAGE(B5:B18)**.

Enter a similar formula into cell C19. This time it is **=AVERAGE(C5:C18)**.

Your worksheet will now look like this:

	A	B	C	D
1	**Advanced Level exam results 2001**			
2	Percentage pass rate with 'A' grades			
3				
4	**Subject**	**Boys**	**Girls**	
5	Art and design	23.5	28.4	
6	Biology	16.8	20.0	
7	Business Studies	10.0	11.3	
8	Chemistry	25.6	27.7	
9	Computing	8.9	7.5	
10	Economics	22.7	22.6	
11	English	17.3	16.2	
12	French	26.4	23.9	
13	Geography	15.8	23.0	
14	German	32.9	26.8	
15	History	17.9	19.1	
16	Mathematics	28.9	30.0	
17	Physics	24.1	27.4	
18	Psychology	8.1	13.7	
19	**Average percentage**	15.8	21.3	
20				

exercise 8

You can now see that the girls do better than the boys.

6 Type the text **Who did best at this subject?** into cell D4.

Now type the formula **=IF(B5>C5,"Boys","Girls")** into cell D5.

This basically says that if the number in cell B5 (i.e. the boys' mark) is greater than the number in cell C5 (i.e. the girls' mark), then the text 'Boys' will be placed in cell D5. If not, the text 'Girls' will be displayed in cell D5.

Your screen should now look like this:

	SUM ▾ ✗ ✓ *fx*	=IF(B5>C5,"Boys","Girls")		
	A	B	C	D
1	Advanced Level exam results 2001			
2	Percentage pass rate with 'A' grades			
3				
4	Subject	Boys	Girls	Who did best at this subject?
5	Art and design	23.5	28.4	=IF(B5>C5,"Boys","Girls")
6	Biology	16.8	20.0	
7	Business Studies	10.0	11.3	
8	Chemistry	25.6	27.7	
9	Computing	8.9	7.5	
10	Economics	22.7	22.6	
11	English	17.3	16.2	
12	French	26.4	23.9	
13	Geography	15.8	23.0	
14	German	32.9	26.8	
15	History	17.9	19.1	
16	Mathematics	28.9	30.0	
17	Physics	24.1	27.4	
18	Psychology	8.1	13.7	
19	Average percentage	15.8	21.3	

7 Now copy the formula down the column. This saves having to type it in for each row and altering it slightly each time. You do this by moving the cursor to the cell containing the formula. Now click the bottom right-hand corner of the cell and you should get a black cross shape. Hold the left mouse button down and move the mouse down the column until you reach cell D18. You will see a dotted rectangle around the area where the formula is to be copied. Now take your finger off the button and the results will be inserted. This is called relative copying because the formulae are changed slightly to take account of the altered positions of the marks for each subject.

The completed worksheet now looks like the one at the top of the next page.

exercise 8

	A	B	C	D
1	**Advanced Level exam results 2001**			
2	Percentage pass rate with 'A' grades			
3				
4	**Subject**	**Boys**	**Girls**	**Who did best at this subject?**
5	Art and design	23.5	28.4	Girls
6	Biology	16.8	20.0	Girls
7	Business Studies	10.0	11.3	Girls
8	Chemistry	25.6	27.7	Girls
9	Computing	8.9	7.5	Boys
10	Economics	22.7	22.6	Boys
11	English	17.3	16.2	Boys
12	French	26.4	23.9	Boys
13	Geography	15.8	23.0	Girls
14	German	32.9	26.8	Boys
15	History	17.9	19.1	Girls
16	Mathematics	28.9	30.0	Girls
17	Physics	24.1	27.4	Girls
18	Psychology	8.1	13.7	Girls
19	**Average percentage**	15.8	21.3	

Using simple functions

In the examination results spreadsheet in Exercise 8 a simple function (called AVERAGE) was used. We need not have used this because most people know the formula for working out the average of a set of numbers. Functions just save us time and brain-power, as the formula is already set up. Functions are therefore useful.

A function must start with an equals sign (=) and it must have the range of cells to which it applies in brackets after it.

For example, to find the average of the numbers in a range of cells from A3 to A10 you would use:

=AVERAGE(A3:A10)

Here are some other functions:

Maximum
=MAX(D3:J3) displays the largest number in all the cells from D3 to J3 inclusive.

Minimum
=MIN(D3:J3) displays the smallest number in all the cells from D3 to J3 inclusive.

Mode

=MODE(A3:A15) displays the mode (i.e. the most frequent number) in the cells from A3 to A15 inclusive.

Median

=MEDIAN(B2:W2) displays the median of the numbers in the cells from B2 to W2 inclusive.

Sum

=SUM(E3:P3) displays the total of the numbers in all the cells from E3 to P3 inclusive.

There are lots of other functions you can use, and for a list of them you can use the on-line help facility.

THE JARGON DRAGON

absolute referencing – when a particular cell is used in a formula and the formula is copied to a new address, the cell address does not change

relative referencing – when a particular cell is used in a formula and the formula is copied to a new address, the cell address changes to take account of the formula's new position

Using absolute and relative cell references

There are two ways in which you can make a reference to another cell. They are not the same, and it is important to know the difference if you want to copy or move cells.

An **absolute reference** refers to a particular cell. It therefore always refers to the same cell.

A **relative reference** refers to a cell that is a certain number of rows and columns away. When a cell containing a relative reference is copied or moved to a new position, any cell to which the reference is made will also change position so that it remains the same number of columns and rows away, i.e. it is in the same relative position.

To understand the difference let's look at two examples.

The first example shows relative referencing, with cell B4 containing a relative reference to cell A1. This reference tells the spreadsheet that the cell to which it refers is three cells up and one cell to the left of cell B4. If cell B4 is copied to another position, say E5, then the reference will still be to three cells up and one to the left, so the reference will now be to cell D2.

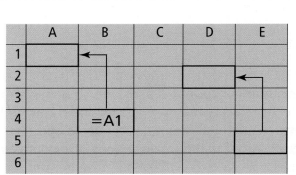

Example 1: relative cell referencing in a spreadsheet

With absolute cell referencing, if cell B4 contains a reference to cell A1, then if the contents of B4 are copied to a new position, the reference will not be adjusted and it will still refer to cell A1.

	A	B	C	D	E
1					
2					
3					
4		=A1			
5					
6					

Example 2: Absolute cell referencing in a spreadsheet

In most cases you will want to use relative cell references, and the spreadsheet will assume that all ordinary cell references are relative. Sometimes you may want to refer to the same cell even when the formula referring to the cell is copied to a new position.

In this case you must make sure the formula contains an absolute cell reference. To do this, a dollar sign is placed in front of the column and row number.

Cell B6 is a relative cell reference. To change it to an absolute cell reference you need to add dollar signs, like this: B6.

Formatting cells to match data types

There are many different types of data and some of these are shown in the following table:

Type of data	Example of data
Date	12/12/02
Integer number (a whole number)	34
Decimal number	3.14
Percentage	4%
Currency	£3.45
Text	John Smith

If the general number format is used (which it will be, unless you tell Excel otherwise) the numbers will be shown with up to eleven digits (including all the numbers up to and after the decimal point). A cell that contains a formula will show the results of the formula rather than the formula itself.

Cells need to be able to hold the type of data you want to put into them. The spreadsheet will interpret the data you put into the cell. What is displayed in a cell depends on the cell format.

Although each cell is set to the general number format, it can change automatically depending on the data you type in. If you type in a pound sign followed by a number, the spreadsheet will assume you are dealing with currency and will format the cell to currency automatically. It will only show the currency to two decimal places, so if you typed in £1.349, '£1.35' would be shown.

For large numbers you often use commas to make them easier to read (e.g. 3,000,000). When a number is entered with commas, the spreadsheet will apply the number format with the thousands separator, and use a maximum of two decimal places.

If a number is entered ending in a % sign (e.g. 4%), then the spreadsheet will set the cell automatically to the percent format with two decimal places.

When does 3 + 3 = 7?
Three plus three can equal seven if you have failed to consider the cell formats.

Suppose you have 3.51 in cell A1 and 2.86 in cell B1 and both cells have been set to integers. If the formula =A1+B1 to add these two cells together is placed in cell C1, and this cell is set to integer, then the result of the calculation will be 7. This is because 3.51 had been set to 4 and 2.86 to 3.

You can see that you have to be careful with cell formats. Make sure that you match the cell format to the number of decimal places of the numbers being entered. In this example, all the cells should have been set to two decimal places.

Cell presentation formats
Data can be presented in cells in a variety of different ways. We will look at these in this section.

Aligning cells
When you enter data into a cell, the spreadsheet automatically aligns (i.e. positions) the cells according to the following:

- Numbers are aligned to the right.
- Text is aligned to the left.

Do not put any spaces in front of numbers in order to align them as this will make it impossible for the spreadsheet to use the numbers in calculations.

If you want to align the data differently, you can use the special buttons for alignment on the formatting toolbar. Using this method, you can align them to the left, right or centre.

Using cell presentation formats

You can pre-set cells to a certain presentation format using the Format Cells screen.

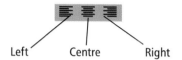

Left   Centre   Right

NOW DO EXERCISE 9

Organisation and analysis of structured information using database software

All organisations need to hold a store of data. In a school the data could be about pupils or staff. In a company, it could be about customers or stock. These stores of data need to be organised in some way so that items of data can be found easily. When these organised stores of data are computerised, the result is a called a database.

This section explains what a database is and how to create one. First we need an application to computerise the database. The example we will use is a pupil database for a school. First, though, it is important to understand some key terms which are used when talking about databases.

Fields, records and files: what do they all mean?

Here are some database terms you will need to familiarise yourself with:

Setting up a database in Excel and printing a selected area

In this exercise you will learn how to:

- set up data so that the spreadsheet package can recognise it as a database
- enter data into a database
- sort data into order
- print a selected area of the database.

You have been asked to set up a database for a job agency. The database will contain information on all the jobs held by the agency.

1 Enter the data into the database exactly as shown below. The first row contains the field names and subsequent rows contain the job records. **Important note**: Do not leave any blank rows between the data. When setting up a database in Excel, always make sure that the field names are in neighbouring cells along the first row.

	A	B	C	D	E
1	Job Number	Job Type	Area	Employer	Pay
2	1010	Systems Analyst	London	Am Bank	£35,000
3	1023	Programmer	Blackburn	Minstral Finance	£28,000
4	1012	Accountant	Liverpool	Mutual Insurance	£42,000
5	1034	Sales Clerk	Liverpool	Mututal Insuranc	£18,000
6	1011	Sales Manager	Birmingham	DC Switches Ltd	£28,000
7	1045	Sales Manager	Lancaster	Air Products LTd	£31,500
8	1024	Electrical Engineer	Bristol	Manners Ltd	£27,800
9	1021	Network Manger	Warrington	D&Q Ltd	£19,800
10	1000	Trainee Programmer	Cardiff	PCSoft	£7,500
11	1002	Systems Analyst	Liverpool	AmSoft	£24,000
12	1013	Junior Accountant	Liverpool	AmSoft	£17,000
13	1018	Accountant	Manchester	DC Switches Ltd	£45,000
14	1035	Sales Clerk	Preston	FR Venn & Co	£16,900
15	1078	Shipping Clerk	London	P&R	£21,800
16	1080	Trainee Programmer	London	Arc Systems	£19,300
17	1079	Programmer	London	Arc Systems	£35,600

2 We want to sort the database into order according to salary, with the highest paid jobs first. To do this move the cursor to cell E2 (where the first salary figure is).

Click on <u>D</u>ata and then on <u>S</u>ort... . The following screen appears:

Sort dialog box:

Sort [?] [X]

Sort by
[Pay ▼] ⦿ Ascending ○ Descending

Then by
[▼] ⦿ Ascending ○ Descending

Then by
[▼] ⦿ Ascending ○ Descending

My list has
⦿ Header row   ○ No header row

[Options...]   [OK]   [Cancel]

3 Select <u>D</u>escending and then click on the OK button. The pay will now be sorted with the highest pay first.

	A	B	C	D	E
1	Job Number	Job Type	Area	Employer	Pay
2	1018	Accountant	Manchester	DC Switches Ltd	£45,000
3	1012	Accountant	Liverpool	Mutual Insurance	£42,000
4	1079	Programmer	London	Arc Systems	£35,600
5	1010	Systems Analyst	London	Am Bank	£35,000
6	1045	Sales Manager	Lancaster	Air Products LTd	£31,500
7	1023	Programmer	Blackburn	Minstral Finance	£28,000
8	1011	Sales Manager	Birmingham	DC Switches Ltd	£28,000
9	1024	Electrical Engineer	Bristol	Manners Ltd	£27,800
10	1002	Systems Analyst	Liverpool	AmSoft	£24,000
11	1078	Shipping Clerk	London	P&R	£21,800
12	1021	Network Manger	Warrington	D&Q Ltd	£19,800
13	1080	Trainee Programmer	London	Arc Systems	£19,300
14	1034	Sales Clerk	Liverpool	Mututal Insuranc	£18,000
15	1013	Junior Accountant	Liverpool	AmSoft	£17,000
16	1035	Sales Clerk	Preston	FR Venn & Co	£16,900
17	1000	Trainee Programmer	Cardiff	PCSoft	£7,500

4 A client comes into the job agency and only wants jobs that pay a minimum of £20,000. She would like a list of these jobs. We therefore need to select only part of this spreadsheet for printing. To do this click on <u>V</u>iew.

Now click on <u>P</u>age Break Preview.

5 This box appears, explaining what you do. Click on the OK button.

exercise 9

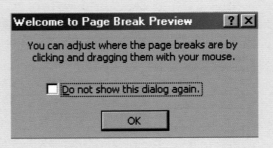

6 The cross can now be used to mark out the area on the spreadsheet that needs printing. Highlight the area from cells A1 to E11. Your spreadsheet will look like this:

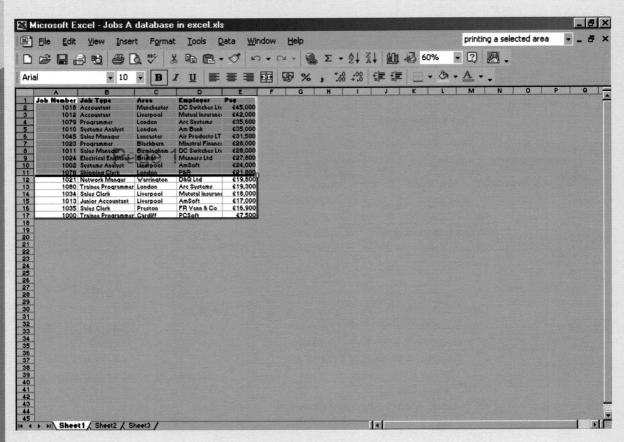

7 Click on the Printer button to print the selected area.

Data
These are details of a specific person, place or thing.

Information
Information is data that has been rearranged into a form that is useful to the user.

Fields
A field is a single item of data. In other words, it is a fact about a person, place or thing. A surname would be an example of a field.

Records
Information about a particular person, place or thing is called a record. A record consists of fields. All the information about a particular pupil (e.g. pupil number, surname, forename, etc.) is contained in a record.

Files
A collection of related records is called a file. The group of records for all the pupils in the school is called the pupil file.

Tables
In one type of database, called a relational database, we do not store all the data in a single file. Instead the data is stored in several tables, although the data in the separate tables can be combined together if needed.

Why use a computerised database?

Using a computerised database to hold data has many advantages, which include:

- It is easy to alter the structure of the database for example if you miss a field out and need to add it later. Suppose you left out a pupil's telephone number from your database design. As soon as you realise it is missing, you can add it to the database.
- Keeping the database up-to-date is easy. You can modify, delete or add details.
- You can process the data in many different ways. You can summarise, calculate, select or sort the data.
- Reports (another name for printouts) of the results can be produced, such as a list of all the pupils who are in a certain form.

Preparing the database structure

A school keeps details on all its pupils in a database. As well as personal details (name, address, etc.), the school also holds details of the forms and form teachers.

The person who is developing the database asks the headteacher for a sample of the data.

This sample of the data is shown below:

Description of data stored	Sample data
Pupil number	1029
Surname	Jones
Forename	Luke
Date of birth	15/03/87
Street	1 Queens Road
Town	Wavertree
Postcode	L15 3PQ
Contact phone number	0151-202-1414
Home phone number	0151-305-1010
Form	5A
Teacher number	112
Form teacher title	Dr
Form teacher surname	Hughes
Form teacher initial	J

The database developer looks at this sample and decides to use three tables to hold the data rather than one.

The three tables are called Pupils, Forms and Teachers. The fields in each table are as follows:

Pupils
Pupil number
Surname
Forename
Date of birth
Street
Town
Postcode
Contact phone number
Home phone number
Form

Forms
Form
Teacher number

Teachers
Teacher number
Teacher title
Teacher surname
Teacher initial

The data is put into three tables rather than one because it saves time – you do not have to type the same details about the teacher over and over again, once for each pupil. If there are 25 pupils in each form, the teacher's details (e.g. Teacher number, Teacher title, Teacher surname, etc.) would need to be entered 25 times. If, instead, we put these details in their own table, we can access them from the Forms field and we only need to type them in once.

Data types
Once you have given a field a name you have to specify the type of data that is allowed in the field. This means you restrict the type of data which can be entered into a certain field.

The possible data types available in Access (and most other databases) are shown in the table below:

Data type	Description
Text	Used for storing names, words and numbers not used in calculations (e.g. telephone numbers, code numbers, bank account numbers)
Number	Used for storing numbers that can be used in calculations
Date/Time	Used for storing dates and times
Currency	Used for storing monetary values to two decimal places
AutoNumber	These are numbers given in sequence allocated by the computer. Each record is given a different number. If you use AutoNumber the number given will always be unique
Yes/No	Used for storing data such as Yes/No, True/False, etc.
OLE Object	Used for storing data from other programs. You could, for example, put a picture in the database
Memo	Used for storing long notes which are not suitable for putting in a field

Picking a primary key
When a table is created a **primary key** needs to be chosen. The primary key is one or more fields that uniquely define a particular record (i.e. a row) in the table.

In the case of the Pupils table, we could use Surname, but it is quite common to have pupils with the same surname in the same school. How many Smiths or Jones are there in your school? Date of birth might be chosen, but what if you had twins in the same class? It is hard to think of a field that would be unique for the pupils' personal details.

primary key – a field that uniquely defines a row in a table in a relational database

Instead, we can create a field called Pupil number that would give each pupil a unique number that is used to identify them. If you look at the table above, there is a data type called AutoNumber which is a number that is automatically allocated to each pupil. The computer remembers the last number it has given so when a new pupil joins, they will be given the next number in the sequence.

In the Forms table, there is already a unique field. There are no two forms with the same name so Form can be used as the primary key.

The Teacher number is the unique field in the Teachers table, so Teacher number is chosen as the primary key.

Deciding on the fields to go into each table

If there is someone who will be the main user of the database, then they will know better than you what fields should be included in each table.

Here are lists of the fields we would need in each table:

Pupils table	Forms table	Teachers table
Pupil number	Form	Teacher number
Surname	Teacher number	Teacher title
Forename	Teacher surname	
Date of birth	Teacher initial	
Street		
Town		
Postcode		
Contact phone number		
Home phone number		
Form		

The primary keys in each of the tables are underlined.

Notice that the Form field appears in two tables: the Pupils table and the Forms table. This is the common field (i.e. it is the one that appears in both tables) and it forms a link between the two tables. If we wanted to know form details for a particular pupil, then these can be obtained via this link.

The links between tables are called the **relationships** and these make relational databases very powerful tools.

THE JARGON DRAGON

relationships – the ways in which tables are related to each other in a relational database

Determining the types of relationships

After the fields have been placed into different tables, we need to think about the relationships between the tables.

Relationships between tables can be one-to-one, one-to-many or many-to-many. Many-to-many relationships can cause problems, but we need not concern ourselves with these here.

One-to-many relationships

If we look at the relationship between the Pupils table and the Forms table we can see that:

One Form in the Forms table can appear many times in the Pupils table.

We also need to look at the relationship from the other end (i.e. from the Pupils table to the Forms table). Each Form in the Pupils table corresponds to a single occurrence of the Form field in the Forms table.

The relationship between the Forms table and the Pupils table is a one-to-many relationship.

One-to-one relationships

With a one-to-one relationship, one record in one table has only one matching record in one of the other tables.

Many-to-many relationships

Here one record in a table matches many records in another table. When the tables are looked at from the other end, then one record again matches many.

This type of relationship is called a many-to-many relationship. If you think you have a many-to-many relationship, then you will need to see your teacher since you cannot link tables with this kind of relationship.

NOW DO EXERCISES 10, 11, 12 & 13

Creating the Pupils table

In this exercise you will learn how to:

- load the database software
- set where to save the database
- set up the structure of a table
- save the table.

1 Load the database software (i.e. Access). Get your teacher to explain how this is done.

You will get a screen like this:

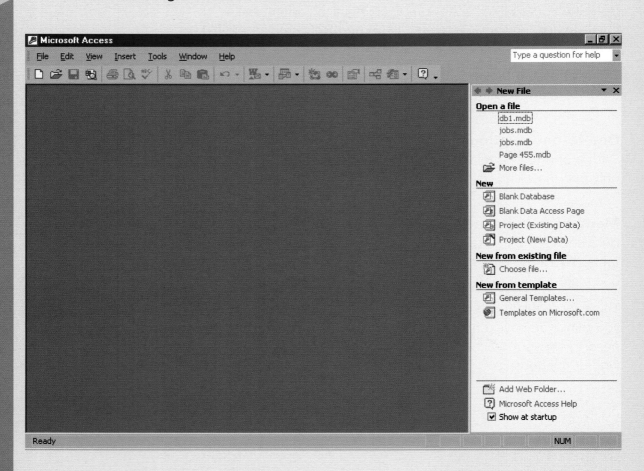

Click on 'New Blank Database'.

2 You should now decide where you want to save the database that you are creating.

Your teacher will tell you where to save your database. We will change the drive so that it is saved on the floppy disk (i.e. the A drive).

Also, type in the filename **School**.

Click on the Create button.

3 The following screen appears:

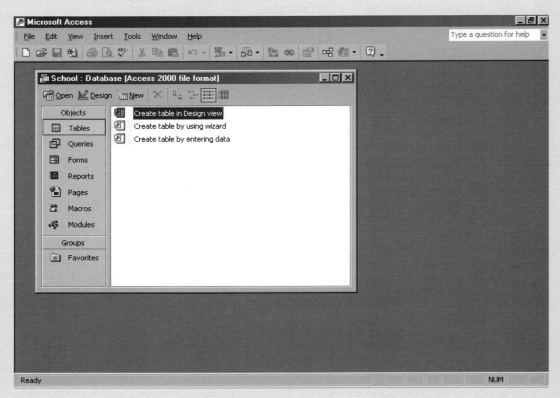

Click on 'Create table in Design view'.

4 The following screen appears, where you can specify the Field Name, Data Type and Description. It is on this screen that you set out the structure for the table.

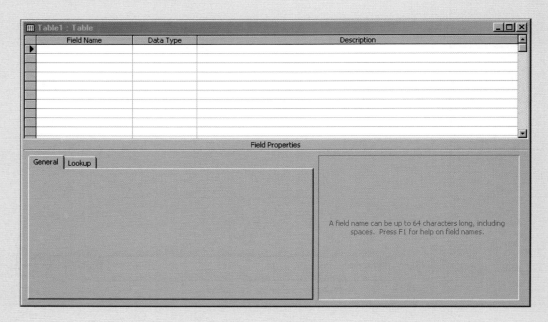

Where the cursor is positioned (i.e. on the first line of the table and in the column below Field Name) enter the name of the first field: **Pupil number**. Press Enter.

The cursor now moves onto the Data Type column. Double click on this and a list of data types will appear. Select AutoNumber from this list. This tells the computer to allocate a unique number to each pupil. The first Pupil number will be 1, the second Pupil number will be 2 and so on. Because the computer does this automatically you do not have to remember what the next number should be.

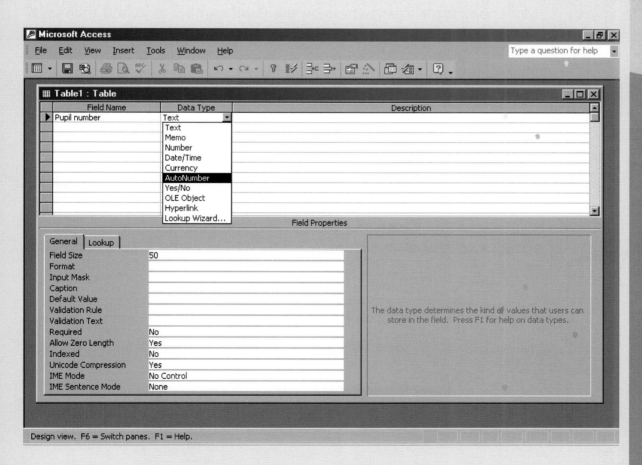

In the Description column, type in the description for the field: **A unique number allocated by the computer to each pupil**. Press Enter and the cursor moves to the next line.

In a similar way, complete the structure of the database as shown below.

exercise 10

	Field Name	Data Type	Description
🔑	Pupil number	AutoNumber	A unique number allocated by the computer.
▶	Surname	Text	The surname of the pupil.
	Forename	Text	The forname of the pupil.
	Date of birth	Date/Time	The date of birth of the pupil.
	Street	Text	The first line of the pupil's address.
	Town	Text	The name of the town in which the pupil lives.
	Postcode	Text	The postcode of the pupil's residence.
	Contact phone number	Text	The phone number where a parent or guardian can be contacted during the day.
	Home phone number	Text	The home phone number of the pupil.
	Form	Text	The form that the pupil is in at school.

5 A primary key now has to be set for this table. Pupil number is a unique field for this table, and is therefore chosen as the primary key.

Move the cursor to anywhere on the Pupil number field and then click on the button with the key on it on the toolbar to set this as the primary key.

Set primary key

6 Make sure that a picture of a key is shown next to the Pupil number field like this:

	Field Name	Data Type	Description
🔑▶	Pupil number	Text	A unique number allocated by the computer.

7 Now save the table by clicking on the Save button 🖫 on the toolbar.

You will be asked for a Table Name. Type in the table name **Pupils**.

Click on OK. The table is now saved.

8 Click on the Datasheet button on the toolbar. ▦

A blank datasheet appears into which you can enter data.

9 Enter the following data into the datasheet:

	Pupil number	Surname	Forename	Date of birth	Street	Town	Postcode	Contact phone	Home phone	Form
	1	Jones	Kerry	01/12/1989	3 Grove St	Liverpool	L7 6TT	234-0121	221-1098	7A
	2	Keel	Adam	23/07/1986	12 Moor Grove	Liverpool	L13 7YH	254-0911	230-0343	11B
	3	Jackson	Robin	12/01/1990	34 Fell St	Warrington	WA 4ER	01925-19191	230-0098	7B
	4	Green	Amy	01/01/1989	121 Pat St	Liverpool	L13 6RT	254-0087	254-0087	8C
	5	Black	John	08/09/1990	12 Pine Grove	Liverpool	L7 9YT	927-3856	221-2312	7A
	6	Hughes	Jane	03/09/1990	15 Lire St	Liverpool	L8 6GH	232-9540	230-3422	7B
	7	Green	Emma	01/09/1986	10 Moor Lane	Warrington	WA 5FT	01925-12000	01925-20202	11A
	8	Keel	John	01/02/1988	12 Moor Grove	Liverpool	L13 7YH	254-0911	230-0343	10C
	9	Black	Jenny	30/12/1986	34 High St	Liverpool	L7 6GF	927-8999	221-9034	11B
	10	Hughes	James	17/12/1986	5 Bankfield Rd	Liverpool	L12 7TY	945-3493	230-0921	11A
	11	Adams	Tracy	02/09/1990	12 Manor Rd	Liverpool	L23 5TG	927-2929	432-8929	7B
	12	Jackson	Jordan	04/01/1989	15 Beech St	Liverpool	L7 6RF	487-0387	221-0098	8C
	13	Green	Sarah	25/12/1989	45 Teck St	Liverpool	L9 6ED	487-6398	234-9273	7A
	14	Crowley	John	30/09/1990	12 Green Lane	Liverpool	L3 6FD	487-0293	235-8193	7B
	15	Turton	Brian	12/09/1990	1 Beech Rd	Liverpool	L6 6YH	254-0111	323-3030	7C
	16	Forton	Julie	09/09/1990	34 Cedar Drive	Liverpool	L9 6DC	320-3423	324-0101	7B

When all the data has been entered, click on close (the cross at the top right of the window).

You will now see the name of the table listed like this:

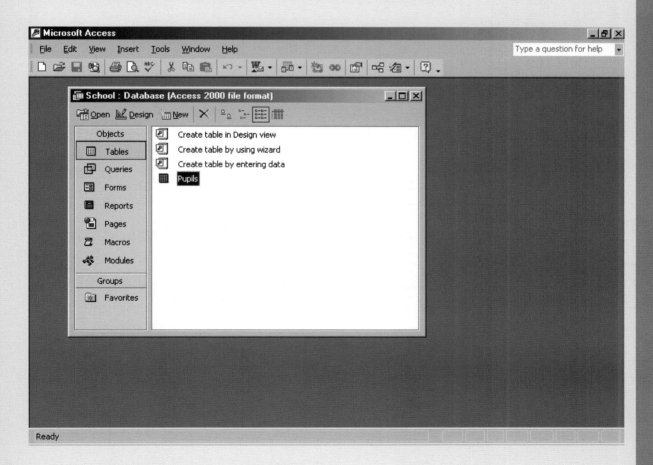

exercise 11

Opening the Pupils table

In this exercise you will learn how to:

• open a previously saved database.

1 Load Access. The following screen will appear when you have changed the drive to the A drive (i.e. the floppy drive).

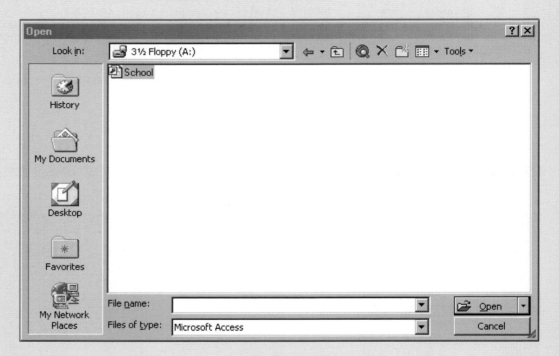

2 Either double click on the file School or move the cursor to School and then click on the Open button.

You will now be shown a list of the tables.

Double click on the table Pupils.

3 The table is now opened in the datasheet view as shown below.

Pupil number	Surname	Forename	Date of birth	Street	Town	Postcode	Contact phone	Home phone	F
1	Jones	Kerry	01/12/1989	3 Grove St	Liverpool	L7 6TT	234-0121	221-1098	7A
2	Keel	Adam	23/07/1986	12 Moor Grove	Liverpool	L13 7YH	254-0911	230-0343	11
3	Jackson	Robin	12/01/1990	34 Fell St	Warrington	WA 4ER	01925-19191	230-0098	7B
4	Green	Amy	01/01/1989	121 Pat St	Liverpool	L13 6RT	254-0087	254-0087	8C
5	Black	John	08/09/1990	12 Pine Grove	Liverpool	L7 9YT	927-3856	221-2312	7A
6	Hughes	Jane	03/09/1990	15 Lire St	Liverpool	L8 6GH	232-9540	230-3422	7B
7	Green	Emma	01/09/1986	10 Moor Lane	Warrington	WA 5FT	01925-12000	01925-20202	11
8	Keel	John	01/02/1988	12 Moor Grove	Liverpool	L13 7YH	254-0911	230-0343	10
9	Black	Jenny	30/12/1986	34 High St	Liverpool	L7 6GF	927-8999	221-9034	11
10	Hughes	James	17/12/1986	5 Bankfield Rd	Liverpool	L12 7TY	945-3493	230-0921	11
11	Adams	Tracy	02/09/1990	12 Manor Rd	Liverpool	L23 5TG	927-2929	432-8929	7B
12	Jackson	Jordan	04/01/1989	15 Beech St	Liverpool	L7 6RF	487-0387	221-0098	8C
13	Green	Sarah	25/12/1989	45 Teck St	Liverpool	L9 6ED	487-6398	234-9273	7A
14	Crowley	John	30/09/1990	12 Green Lane	Liverpool	L3 6FD	487-0293	235-8193	7B
15	Turton	Brian	12/09/1990	1 Beech Rd	Liverpool	L6 6YH	254-0111	323-3030	7C
16	Forton	Julie	09/09/1990	34 Cedar Drive	Liverpool	L9 6DC	320-3423	324-0101	7B

Record: 1 of 16

Creating the Forms table

In this exercise you will learn how to:

- set up a table.

The Forms table needs to be created in a similar way to the Pupils table.

1 You need to make sure that the Forms table has the following structure:

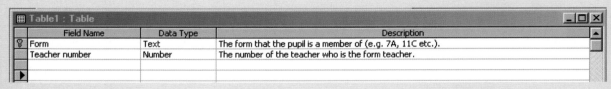

Field Name	Data Type	Description
Form	Text	The form that the pupil is a member of (e.g. 7A, 11C etc.).
Teacher number	Number	The number of the teacher who is the form teacher.

Make Form the primary key.

2 Close this window. You will now be asked to give the table a name. Give it the name Forms by typing **Forms** in the following window:

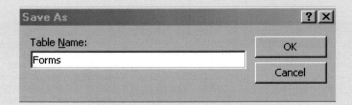

3 Click on OK.

You will now see the Forms table listed like this

exercise 12

4 Enter the following data into the Forms table:

Form	Teacher number
7A	3
7B	1
7C	2
8A	5
8B	4
8C	10
9A	8
9B	9
9C	13
10A	12
10B	15
10C	6
11A	11
11B	17
11C	7
	0

5 Save the data in your table.

Validation checks

When data is being entered into a database it is important that certain types of error can be spotted by the program. The user can then be alerted to check and if necessary re-enter the data.

When the structure of the database is being designed, a series of validation rules can be devised to govern what can and cannot be entered into each field. It is impossible to trap every type of error; if someone's address is 4 Bankfield Drive and the user incorrectly types in 40 Bankfield Drive, then no simple **validation check** would be able to detect this.

THE JARGON DRAGON

validation check – a check performed by a computer program to make sure that the data is allowable

Data type check

Databases automatically check to make sure the data being entered into a field is of the type allowed for that field, so text, for example, cannot be entered into a field that has a numeric data type. This type of check is called a data type check.

If a field is given the data type 'text', you can enter any characters from the keyboard into this field. You can, therefore, enter numbers into a text field, but you cannot perform any calculations on them.

exercise 13

Creating the Teachers table

In a similar way, create the Teachers table. Make sure that you make Teacher number the primary key.

1 The structure of this table should be as follows:

Field Name	Data Type	Description
Teacher number	AutoNumber	A unique number allocated to each teacher when they join the course.
Teacher title	Text	The title of the teacher (e.g. Ms, Miss, Mrs, Dr or Mr)
Teacher surname	Text	The surname of the teacher.
Teacher initial	Text	One initial for the teacher.

Save this structure and give the table the name **Teachers**.

Open the Teachers table and enter the following details:

Teacher number	Teacher title	Teacher surname	Teacher initial
1	Mr	Hughes	H
2	Ms	Frampton	G
3	Dr	Chan	H
4	Miss	Hughes	J
5	Mr	Hughes	W
6	Mrs	Jackson	Y
7	Mrs	Green	D
8	Miss	Jones	G
9	Mr	Doyle	R
10	Mr	Poole	G
11	Mrs	Hopper	C
12	Mr	Kendrick	A
13	Miss	Adams	N
14	Miss	Stringer	P
15	Mr	Tarrant	H
16	Ms	Green	E
17	Miss	Ellen	S
18	Dr	Dolby	T
19	Miss	Harrington	G

Always try to specify the most appropriate data type when setting up the structure of a database.

Range checks

As well as checks on data type, you can devise other kinds of checks. Range checks are performed on numbers to make sure that they lie within a specified range. Range checks will only pick up absurd values. For example, if you typed in the number of children in a household as '50' rather than '5' then a range check will spot the error; if you typed in '7' then the range check would not pick up the error.

Presence checks

You can specify that some fields must always have data entered into them. For example, every pupil must have a pupil number, since it is allocated to them automatically when they join the school. Some fields, such as Telephone number, can be left blank since not everyone has a telephone. Checks such as this are called **presence checks**. Presence checks make sure that data has been entered into a field.

In Microsoft Access we have to decide on two things when we want to validate data: the validation rule and the validation text.

Validation rule

The **validation rule** decides whether a piece of data is valid or not.

The easiest validation checks are on numbers and dates. For example, the database can check that a number being entered is above a certain value, below a certain value or within a range of values.

Validation text

The **validation text** is a message that appears if the data breaks the validation rule. Here is an example:

THE JARGON DRAGON

presence check – a check to make sure that a field in a database has data in it

validation rule – the rule governing a validation check

validation text – the message displayed if the validation rule is breached

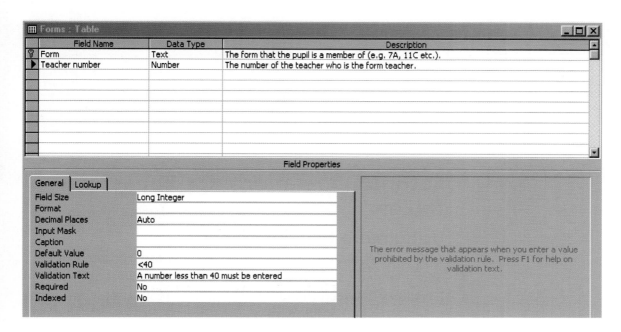

This screen shows the table structure being set up for the Forms table. The cursor is on the field 'Teacher number'. Because there are less than 40 teachers in the whole school we do not want the user to be able to type in a number 40 or more.

Notice in the diagram that the validation rule is given in the Field Properties box. The validation rule is as follows:

<40

We also need to enter the validation text, i.e. a message that will appear should the user enter any value that is 40 or more. Rather than just tell the user that they are wrong, it is better to tell them what values they *can* enter.

A suitable message for the validation text would be as follows:

A number less than 40 must be entered.

The validation rule should be tested by entering some data into the table. Data that passes the validation rule should be entered along with some data that will fail the test. The screen below shows the message appearing when the Teacher number for Form 9C is changed to 40.

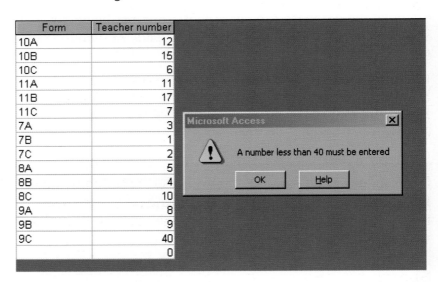

Setting up relationships between tables

Using more than one table

Single tables are not strictly speaking databases, and they have only a limited use. If you put more than one table together and have links between the tables, you have a really useful database called a relational database.

We have already looked at the reasons for using three tables rather than one; in the previous section they were called Pupils, Forms and Teachers.

The Pupils table
The Pupils table contains all the pupil details. Each pupil on joining the school is given a unique Pupil number. This prevents confusion with other pupils.

The Forms table
The Forms table combines teacher and form information so that we can identify the teacher of each form.

The Teachers table
This table contains the details of all the teachers in the school.

Forming relationships between tables in Access
In order to form a link (called a relationship) between two tables, the same field must appear in both tables, but they do not both need to be primary key fields.

It is important that you make sure these common fields have exactly the same name and the same data type.

If AutoNumber has been used as a field in one table, then you can use a different number field in the other table and still be able to link them because they are both numbers. However, you cannot link a text field in one table with a number field in the other.

Make sure that the name of the field is spelt the same in both fields and check that the use of upper case and lower case letters are the same. You can create a link between two fields that have identical field names.

Searching and sorting using related tables
Because the three tables are related you can extract and combine data from any of the tables. This is done using a **query**. A query is used to extract specific information from a database. Queries are used to ask questions of databases.

THE JARGON DRAGON

Query – extracting specific information from a database

NOW DO EXERCISES 14 & 15

exercise 14

Creating relationships between tables

In this exercise you will learn how to:

- create relationships between the tables.

1 Load Access and open the Schools database. You will see a screen like this. Notice the three names of the tables listed.

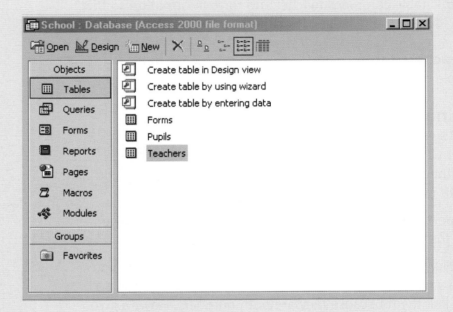

2 Click on the Relationships button on the toolbar.

3 The following screen appears. This is where we tell the computer what tables we want to use.

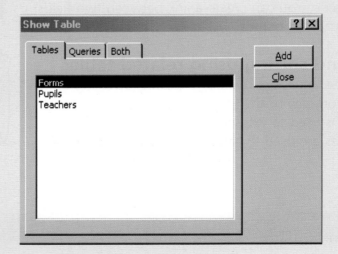

Make sure that Forms is highlighted and then press the Add button.

Click on Pupils and then press Add.

Click on Teachers and then press Add.

Then click on the Close button.

4 The three tables are shown below. Notice the names of the tables at the top and also the names of the primary keys in bold.

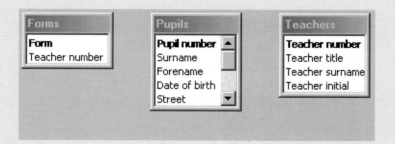

Notice that not all the fields are shown. This is because some of the boxes are too small. To make them bigger move the cursor to the bottom corner of the box. You will see the cursor change to a double-headed arrow. Drag this to enlarge the box. Your boxes will now look like this:

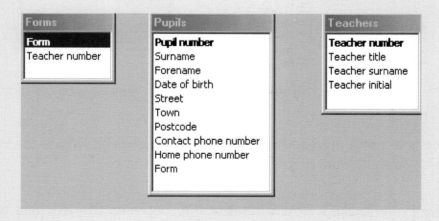

5 Click on the Form field in the Forms table and hold down the mouse button. Now drag the small rectangle to the Form field in the Pupils table.

Release the mouse button.

The following window will now appear:

exercise 14

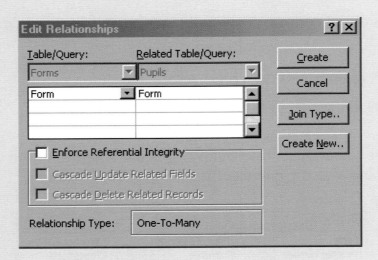

Notice that the Relationship Type is One-To-Many.

Click on the box marked Enforce Referential Integrity.

Click on the Create button.

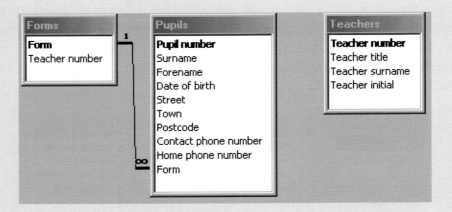

A line is drawn between the two tables (see above). Notice the way the one-to-many relationship is indicated on this line.

6 We will now make a similar relationship between the Teachers table and the Forms table. Now, this would have been a one-to-one relationship but due to staff absences a teacher sometimes looks after two forms, so the Teacher number can appear more than once in the Forms table. This means that the relationship is one-to-many.

In a similar way to that described for Step 5, click on Teacher number in the Teachers table and drag it across to Teacher number in the Forms table. Enforce the referential integrity by putting a tick in the box.

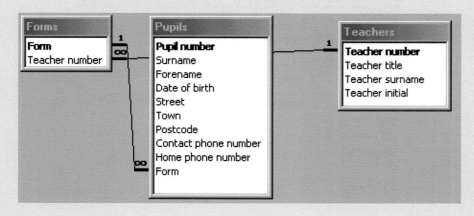

Click on Create.

Your screen showing the relationships will now look like this:

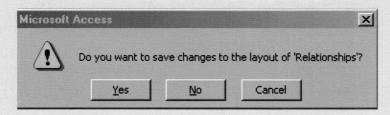

You have now created a relational database.

7 Close the window and you will be asked if you want to save the changes.

Click on the Yes button.

Extracting data from the database

In this exercise you will learn how to:

- create a query using a wizard
- run a query.

Once there are relationships between the tables, you can extract and combine the data from more than one table. This is done using a query. Queries are used to ask questions of databases.

1 Load Access and then select the Schools database. This screen will appear:

2 Click on the Queries button In the screen above. The queries screen will now appear:

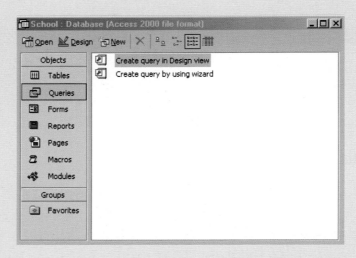

exercise 15

Click on 'Create query by using wizard'.

3 The following screen appears, to guide you through the process of producing a query:

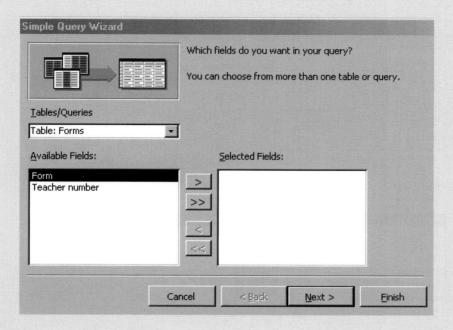

Make sure that 'Table: Forms' appears in the Tables/Queries box.

Click on Form so that it is highlighted in the Available Fields: box.

Form will now appear in the Selected Fields: box. Your screen will look like this:

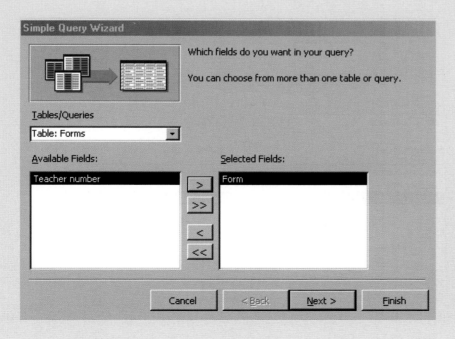

4 Click on the drop-down arrow in the Tables/Queries box and select Table: Pupils. Add Surname to the selected fields in a similar way to that in Step 3.

After doing this you will see the following screen:

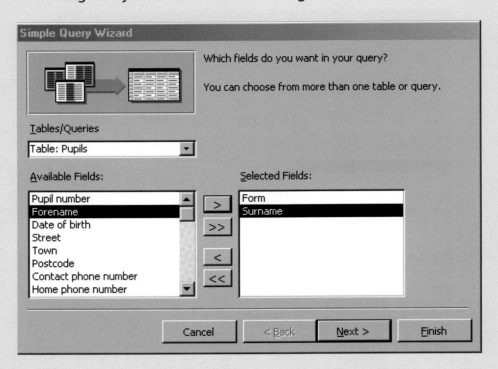

5 Now add the field Surname in the Teachers table in a similar way. Your screen will now look like this:

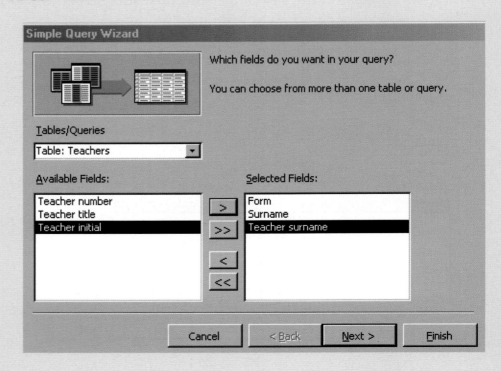

Click on the <u>N</u>ext> button.

6 The screen below now appears. Make sure that <u>D</u>etail has been selected and then click on the <u>N</u>ext> button.

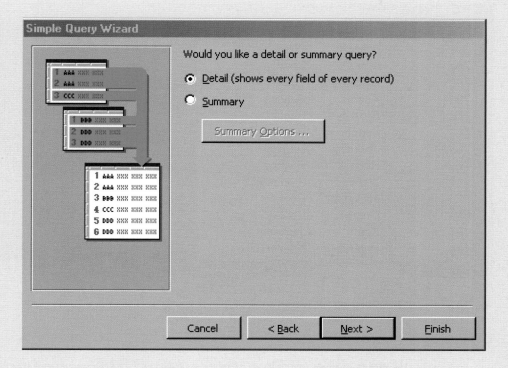

7 Change the name of the query to **List of forms, pupils and form teachers**.

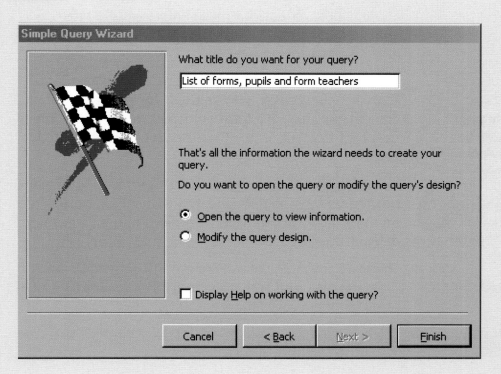

Click on Finish.

The query will now run and the results are shown below.

	Form	Surname	Teacher surname
▶	7A	Green	Chan
	7A	Jones	Chan
	7A	Black	Chan
	7B	Adams	Hughes
	7B	Crowley	Hughes
	7B	Forton	Hughes
	7B	Jackson	Hughes
	7B	Hughes	Hughes
	7C	Turton	Frampton
	8C	Jackson	Poole
	8C	Green	Poole
	10C	Keel	Jackson
	11A	Hughes	Hopper

List of forms, pupils and form teachers : Select Query

Record: 1 of 16

Entering data: the use of data entry forms

So far, whenever data has been entered into a table it has been entered directly using the datasheet view. The datasheet looks a little bit like a spreadsheet and may be intimidating for an inexperienced user.

To make things easier, we can use a **form**. A form on the computer is just like a form on paper. You have the title of each field next to a box, into which the user types the data for that field.

As well as being used to enter data into tables, forms can also be used for viewing data one record at a time. While a record is on the screen you can make alterations to the data. You can also delete the record.

The main advantage of using a form to enter data rather than the datasheet view, is that the form allows you to see all of the fields for one record, at once.

THE JARGON DRAGON

form – a screen used to enter data into a database. It can also be a document that is used to collect data

NOW DO EXERCISE 16

Creating a data entry form

In this exercise you will learn how to:

• create a data entry form for putting data into a table.

Here we will create a form for entering the pupil details into the Pupil table.

1 Load Access and the School database. Click on Forms and the following screen will appear:

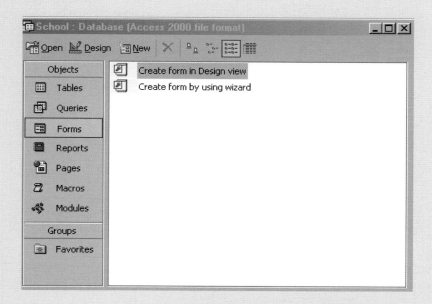

2 Click on 'Create form by using wizard'. This screen will appear:

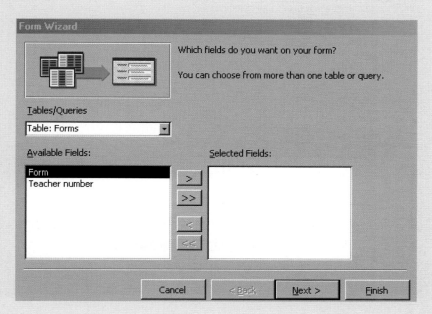

You can see the name of the table in the top-left box, and a list of all the fields that are available in this table in the box underneath. You can add these fields to the form one by one, by clicking on the button with the single arrow on it.

3 Change the table to Pupils.

The following screen will appear:

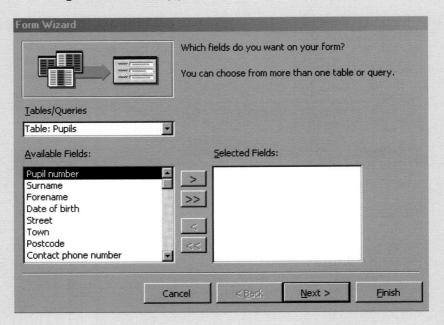

As we want to add all of these fields to our form, we can just click on the button with the double arrows on. This will add them all in one go.

Your screen will now look like this:

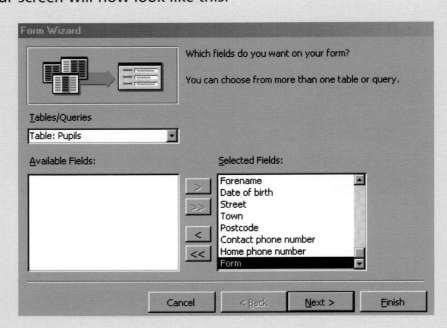

4 Click on the <u>N</u>ext> button. The Form Wizard screen appears.

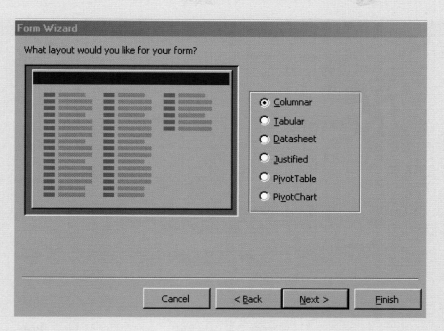

Select <u>C</u>olumnar as the layout and then click on <u>N</u>ext>. This will arrange the field names and boxes for the data in columns on the form.

5 The screen below appears, in which you select the style of the form you want to use.

Notice that when you move through the list of styles on the right a picture of the style appears on the left.

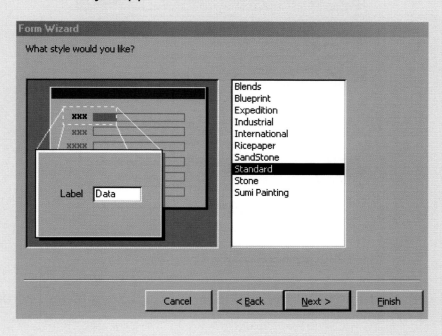

exercise 16

Select Standard as the style and then click on <u>N</u>ext>.

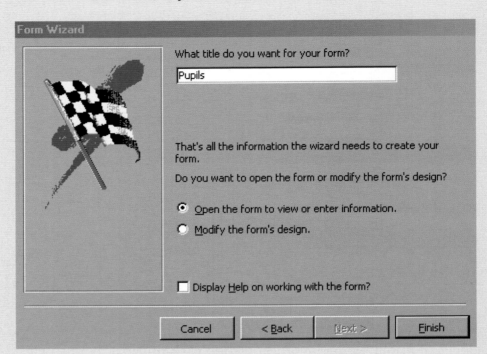

The form has been given the name Pupils. We will keep this as the name.

Click on the <u>F</u>inish button.

After a brief wait, the form below appears:

You can use the toolbar at the bottom of the screen to move from one record to another.

Producing reports showing the results of searches and sorts

A **report** is a printout of the results from a database. In most cases a report is produced on paper by printing the results on a printer. A report can also be produced on the screen but if there is a lot of detail in a report then it may be better to print it out so that it can be studied more closely.

Reports give the user control over what information is printed and how it is laid out on the paper (or screen).

In the School database, a report could be produced to show which pupils are in each form.

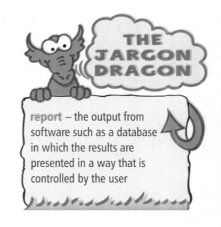

THE JARGON DRAGON

report – the output from software such as a database in which the results are presented in a way that is controlled by the user

NOW DO EXERCISE 17

Organisation and presentation of information using multimedia software

Presentation software

Presentation software can be used when you have to give a talk. The purpose of the talk could be to inform, or to sell a product or service.

Presentation software takes the place of an overhead projector that uses slides. Presentations can be done on the computer screen if the audience is small. If there is a large audience, the computer can be connected to a special projector that projects the image onto a large white screen.

The presentation software we will use here is Microsoft PowerPoint which is included with the Microsoft Office set of programs.

Establishing the structure of the presentation

Before starting work on the computer, you need to think about the purpose of the presentation and the type of audience. This will determine the language level and tone of your presentation.

Producing a report

In this exercise you will learn how to:

- select tables and fields to be used for a report

- structure a report

- view and print a report.

1 Load Access and the Schools database. Click on Report, when the following screen will appear:

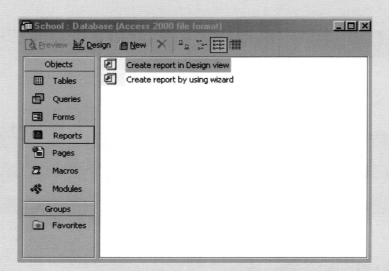

2 Double click on 'Create report by using wizard'. You will now see the following screen:

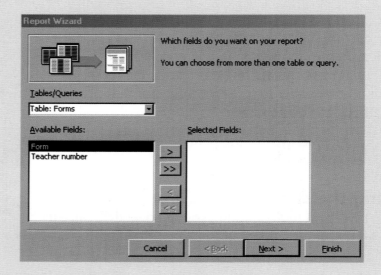

3 Using this screen you can select the table and the fields from each table that you want to include in the report.

Add the following to the Selected Fields: Form (from the Forms table) and Teacher surname from the Teachers table.

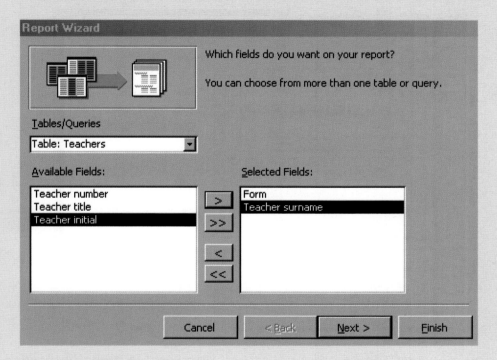

Click on the Next> button.

4 The following screen appears:

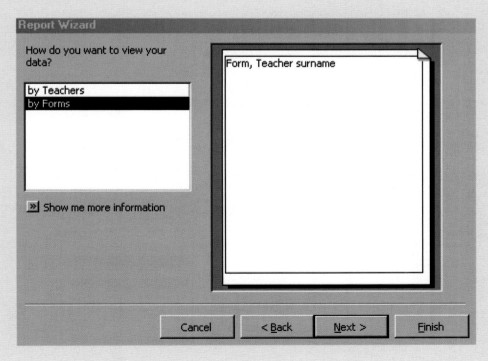

exercise 17

Ensure that 'by Forms' is selected. Click on the Next> button.

5 The grouping levels form is shown:

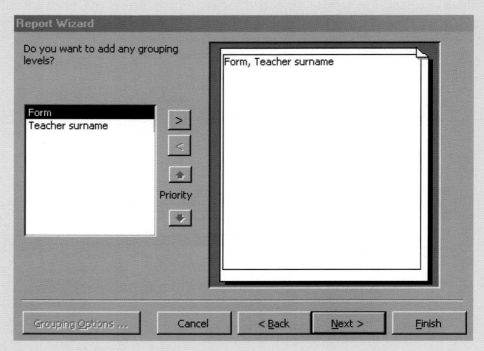

Click on the Next> button.

6 The report should be ordered according to Form in ascending order. Click on the arrow to select Form. Make sure that the button is set to Ascending (if you click on it you can change it to Descending).

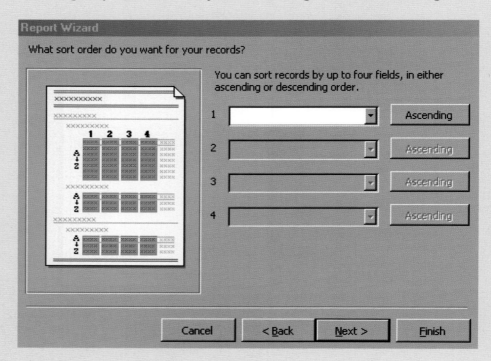

Click on the <u>N</u>ext> button.

7 The following screen appears:

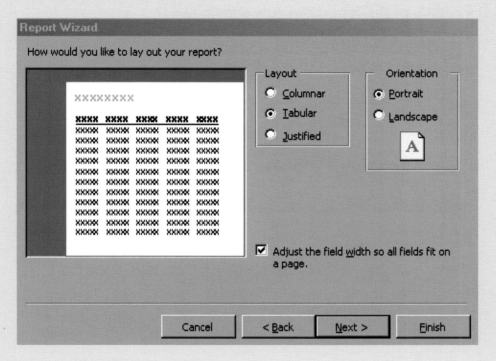

Make sure that <u>T</u>abular and <u>P</u>ortrait are selected.

Click on the <u>N</u>ext> button.

8 The following screen appears:

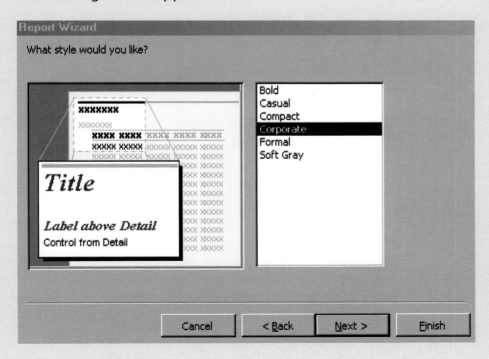

If you highlight other styles you can see what they look like. Select Corporate and then click on the <u>F</u>inish button.

The results of the report are now shown like this:

Forms			
Form		*Teacher surname*	
7A		Chan	
7B		Hughes	
7C		Frampton	
8A		Hughes	
8B		Hughes	
8C		Poole	
9A		Jones	
9B		Doyle	
9C		Adams	
10A		Kendrick	
10B		Tarrant	
10C		Jackson	

Page: 1

The report can be printed out by clicking on the printer icon .

If the presentation is extremely important, say as part of a job application, or if it is to be used over and over again, then it is worth spending a lot of time thinking about and producing it. You should consider:

- number of slides
- the design (it is best to use a design that is set up already, called a design template)
- colour scheme (you can choose a number of colours that work well with the chosen design template)
- a title for the presentation
- a subtitle if needed
- animation effects
- * whether other objects such as tables, clip art, drawings, etc. are to be included.

Using templates

<u>Templates</u> determine the overall structure of a document and they can be used to make your presentation look professional. A good thing about templates is that specialists have decided on the colours that look right together. You are then left to think about what to put on your slides.

THE JARGON DRAGON

templates – electronic files which hold standardised document layouts

Presentations

In this exercise you will learn how to:

- pick a design template
- pick a colour scheme
- prepare slides
- animate text
- run a presentation
- save a presentation.

1 Load the PowerPoint software. The opening screen will appear.

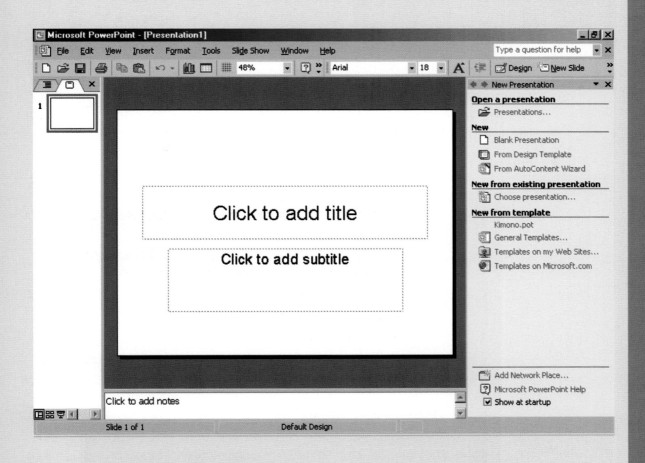

2 Click on From Design Template in the New section of the screen.

exercise 18

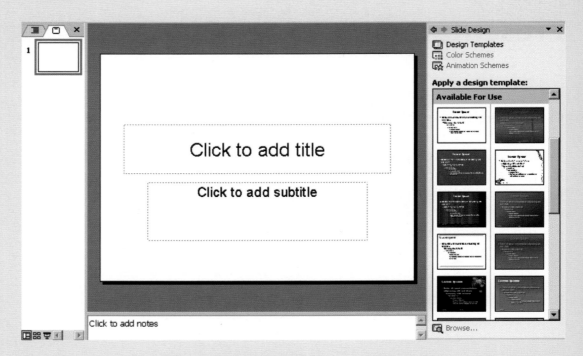

You will see a selection of templates shown as small screenshots. To choose one of them, double click on the picture. You will now see the main screen area change.

As you can now see a large version of your chosen template, you may change your mind about using it. To do this you simply double click on the template you prefer.

3 You will now be guided through setting up your slides.

exercise 18

Click on the top box and enter the following title: **Computer Graphics**.

Click on the bottom box and enter: **Advantages of using CAD**.

Your first slide will now look like this:

4 To make the title more eye-catching, we can get the text to move. This is called adding animation effects.

Click on Animation Schemes in the Slide Design section of the screen.

5 There are different levels of animation. Move to the Exciting section.

Now click on Neutron.

Try some of the other animation effects by clicking on them to see what happens.

6 You can change the background colour of the slide by clicking on Color Schemes in the Slide Design section. Again if you click on each one in turn you can select a colour that you feel is right.

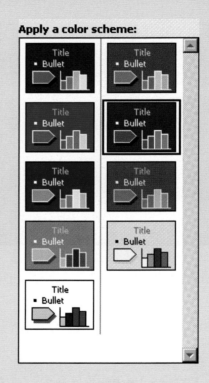

7 To save the slide click on <u>F</u>ile and Save As.

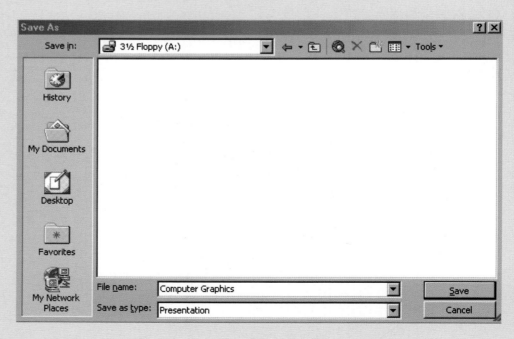

Your teacher will tell you where to save your work. Check that the filename **Computer Graphics** is in the File <u>n</u>ame: box. Now click on the <u>S</u>ave button.

8 To create the next slide click on the following button on the toolbar :

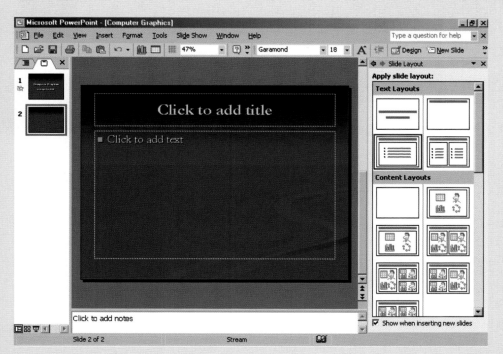

Notice that this slide is different. This is because the first slide is used to introduce the presentation.

9 Click on the 'Click to add title' section and type in the title: **Advantages of using CAD**.

Move to and click on the 'Click to add text' section.

Key in the text as shown on the following slide:

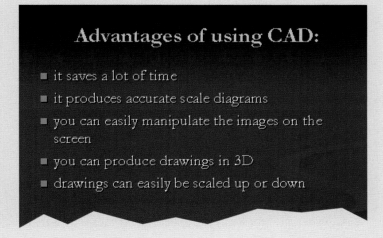

exercise 18

10 Notice that as the presentation is built up, small versions of the slides are displayed to show the sequence of the slides.

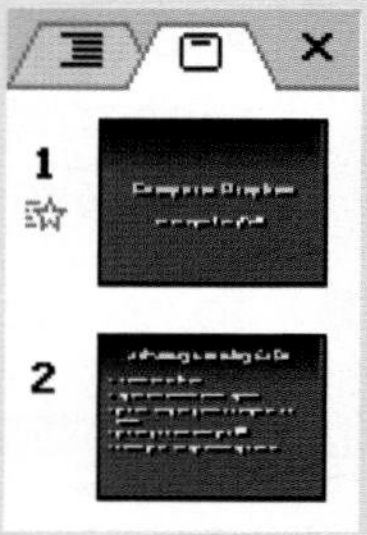

11 Click once on Slide 1 in the above list. To play the presentation, click on situated at the bottom left-hand side of the screen. This starts the slide show from the current slide.

12 Save your presentation using the same filename as before.

Tips

Here are some tips to help you make a good slide:

- Keep a constant colour scheme and design throughout the presentation.
- Only have between five and seven words per line.
- Only have five to seven bullet points per page.
- Do not write in complete sentences (only give the main points).
- Don't overdo the animation and other special effects.
- Put only one concept on each slide.

Above all, use the KISS principle (Keep It Simple and Straightforward).

ACTIVITY

The best way to learn PowerPoint is to experiment. Trying things for yourself is the best way to learn about any software. Don't be worried about making mistakes.

If you want to find out how to do something, then use the Help.

Use the Help in PowerPoint to write instructions on how to do each of the following:

- *change the colour of the text*
- *change the font*
- *increase the size of the font*
- *delete a slide from a presentation.*

Getting the message across – developing your business documents

The whole purpose of a document is to communicate something to the reader. If you are producing an advertisement or a poster then you need to attract the attention of the viewer. Someone walking past should notice it and read what you have to say. For posters and adverts, good design is essential, and the success of an advert can easily be gauged by the response that it produces.

Adverts and posters are just two types of document. All documents should be produced to a high standard and need to be designed carefully. Websites, documents and reports are all improved if you think about the design as well as the content.

When a document is designed it is important to consider:

- the page layout
- the use of type
- the use of graphics.

Using ICT tools

ICT tools are the software and hardware that allow you to do useful things using ICT. Each piece of software can be used for a different purpose, so it is important to choose the right tool for the job. In order to use the software successfully, you will need to learn some of the techniques.

There are many types of software designed for different applications. Here are some of the most popular types of applications software:

- publishing
- spreadsheets
- databases
- multimedia
- image creation
- control technology
- monitoring data.

Later on in this section you will learn how to make use of these types of applications software.

Before designing a document or a web page it is important to think about the following:

What is the objective of the document or web page?

Documents and web pages communicate information to the reader. You need to consider the type of message that you are trying to communicate (i.e. get across).

Thinking about the purpose of a document

Here is a list of different types of document, and their purposes:

Type of document	Purpose of the document
Poster	To inform
Flyer	To advertise/sell
Advertisement	To advertise/sell
Form	To collect information
Leaflet	To advertise or inform
Invitation	To inform
Letter	To Inform
Memo	For reference

Some documents have more than one purpose. For example, it is possible for a letter to both inform and sell.

Thinking about the target audience

The target audience is the people your document is aimed at. You need to make sure that the design of the document is appropriate for the people who will be reading it. For example, a poster advertising a school disco for 14–16-year-olds would need a different design from a poster advertising a drink-driving campaign. If you are talking about ICT to people who also know about ICT, then you can use technical terms without having to explain them. Non-specialists, on the other hand, need to be told what terms mean.

Thinking about the tone and writing style of a document

The way you communicate depends on who you are communicating with. For example, a letter to a friend or someone you know well may be very informal and contain jokes. In a letter applying for a job, a formal approach is appropriate. Invitations to a party can be colourful and jolly, and special printed paper, may be appropriate. Invitations can use unusual fonts that stand out.

In some forms of communication, you can add pictures, photographs and even cartoons to brighten up the document. For example, an invitation to an eighteenth birthday party might contain a photograph of the person concerned in an embarrassing situation.

Some documents need to be more complex than others. For these documents, the style is important. For example, some documents are simply text, with all the letters in the same font and size. Other documents contain text in different sizes and types of font. They may contain diagrams, photographs or even cartoons and you would need to consider the size and position of these on the page.

Presentation style

With a letter applying for a job, your presentation style needs to be appropriate. Fancy fonts, coloured text, etc. would not be right. With an invitation to a party, on the other hand, you would expect to see colour and eye-catching images.

Layout

Paper comes in a variety of sizes, although A4 is the most popular. The size of the paper is important, as is the way the text, diagrams, etc. appear on the page. You need to ask yourself whether the document is going to be a booklet, folder, bulletin, brochure, pamphlet or an entire book.

The approximate size of the finished product is important since this determines the size of the paper that it can be printed on. Paper does not come in all sizes. There are set paper sizes so you have to choose the one that is best for your product. If you were producing a poster, you might want to print on paper larger than A4. This would cause problems unless you had a printer or plotter capable of printing on larger paper. One alternative would be to print it on A4 and then enlarge it to A3.

With some documents there may be a limit on the number of pages, so you would need to keep inside this limit. It is also important to ask whether each sheet is printed on one or both sides.

How many copies?

If you were just producing a few copies of a document, then you could easily do this on your computer. All you need to do is alter the number of copies in the print menu. If you require more copies then you should probably print out one copy and photocopy it. During the photocopying you can go from single-sided text to text on both sides of the paper. If you require very large numbers of copies to be printed to a high standard, then it would be better to use a professional printer.

Accuracy, clarity and consistency

If you are producing a document or a website with more than one page, then make sure that all the pages follow a consistent design. This means that they should have the same:

- fonts and text sizes for headings, sub-headings and the main text
- page layout
- text features
- number of columns (if they are used).

Any documents you produce should be accurate. This means that they should not contain any spelling mistakes or incorrect grammar. To help you with both of these, most wordprocessing packages come equipped with spelling and grammar checkers.

Spellcheckers

Spellcheckers are often provided as part of wordprocessing, desktop publishing and graphics packages. The spellchecker checks to see if each word in the document is in the spellchecker's dictionary. If a word is not, the spellchecker alerts the user who can then check the word and correct it if necessary. If you used the word 'care' instead of 'core' then as both are spelt correctly, the spellchecker will be unable to spot

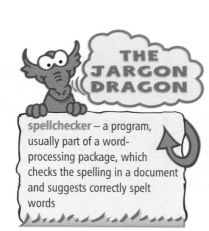

THE JARGON DRAGON

spellchecker – a program, usually part of a word-processing package, which checks the spelling in a document and suggests correctly spelt words

the mistake. Spellcheckers are able to spot if the same word has been typed in twice, one after the other.

Grammar checkers

Grammar checkers can be used to check that:

- sentences end with only one full stop
- there is a capital letter at the beginning of each sentence.

Here is some text that someone has typed in. Can you spot what is wrong with it?

```
I no their are mistakes in my spelling but I
will use the spell cheque to cheque them.
```

If you look at this sentence you will see that the words are all spelt correctly. You will also notice that some of the words are the wrong ones. The spellchecker will not pick this up because there are no spelling mistakes. Using the grammar checker may pick up some mistakes such as the word 'their'. This should read 'there'.

Type this sentence in, then use the spellchecker and then the grammar checker:

Spellchecking and grammar checking will not ensure that your document makes sense. It is therefore important to proof-read your document. It is a good idea to get someone else to read through your work as they might spot mistakes that you have missed.

Proof-reading your material

Proof-reading means checking that the content of your material is:

- accurate
- relevant
- clear.

THE JARGON DRAGON

grammar checker – a program (usually part of a wordprocessing package) that checks a document for grammatical errors and suggests corrections

RESEARCH TASK

Report reviewing documents
In this section you have learnt about some of the documents that are used to convey information in organisations. There are many types of document and your task is to find out about them.

Task one
Here are the names of some documents:

Business letters
Personal letters
Memos
Agendas
Flyers
Posters
Adverts
Price lists
Catalogues
Web pages
CD sleeves (to fit inside a CD)
Invoices (an invoice is a request for payment)
E-mail

There are many other kinds of documents that you could find out about.

You are required to produce a report reviewing a minimum of ten different types of document that can be produced using software. For each of the documents that you mention you should explain clearly the purpose of the document and how it would normally be used.

Task two
Here are some applications packages that can be used to produce documents. Some of the documents may be printed out while others may simply be viewed on screen.

Wordprocessing
Publication and presentation software
Spreadsheets
Databases
Multimedia
E-mail

For each of the software applications in the list above, explain how it can be used to produce business documents such as the ones described in Task one.

Task three
When developing business documents, you need to consider the following:

- *content*
- *layout*
- *purpose.*

Collect a variety of documents, or obtain screenshots of those available only on the computer, and describe for each document its:

- content
- layout
- purpose.

You should then evaluate each document for suitability of purpose. Does it do what it is supposed to do? What, if any, are the problems with the document and what can be done to improve it? You could also collect various documents which perform a similar purpose and compare them.

To find out more about business documents you could:

- Ask a friend or a relative to get some examples of documents that they use at work.
- Look up 'business documents' in business studies textbooks in your school or local library.
- Look up 'business documents', 'writing business documents', etc. on the Internet using simple searches.
- Use the Help facility of Word to look up some of the documents that are already stored as templates. This will give you a good idea of the sorts of information that would normally be held on each document.

FIND IT OUT

RESEARCH TASK

Producing documents

For this task you should use appropriate applications software to produce some of the documents that you have described in Tasks one to three (pages 118–19).

Investigating how ICT is used in organisations

You need to understand how and why different applications are used in organisations. Most organisations use generic software (database, wordprocessing, spreadsheet, presentation, etc.). Some organisations have more specific requirements that cannot be met with generic software. In this section we will be looking at these more specialist applications.

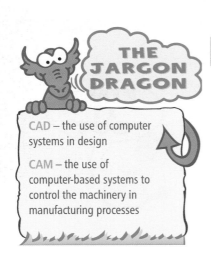

THE JARGON DRAGON

CAD – the use of computer systems in design

CAM – the use of computer-based systems to control the machinery in manufacturing processes

Automating and controlling processes

CAD and CAM

CAD is the use of computer systems in engineering, architecture, kitchen design, etc. to support the design of products, buildings or the placement of objects (kitchen units, bathroom furniture, etc.) CAD can also cover desktop publishing where a product such as packaging is to be designed.

CAM is the use of computer-based systems to control the machinery in manufacturing processes.

RESEARCH TASK

Finding out about CAD/CAM
You are required to research an organisation's use of CAD/CAM.

First of all you are required to use research material to find the answers to the following questions:

1 *What do the abbreviations CAD and CAM stand for?*
2 *Describe features that you would expect to find in*
   a *CAD software*
   b *CAM software*
3 *Explain two uses of CAD/CAM.*
4 *Briefly explain the difference between sensing software and control software.*
5 *Some organisations make use of image manipulation software. Explain what is meant by image manipulation software.*

CAD/CAM in the fashion industry

When you think of CAD/CAM you are most likely to think of engine parts being designed on the computer and then made using a computer-controlled lathe or milling machine.

But CAD is also used in other industries, such as the fashion industry where it is used to design items of clothing. The designer used to use a sketchpad to draw the designs. They worked in pencil so that if they made a mistake or something needed to be altered, then they could just rub it out. With CAD it is much easier. They can make adjustments easily and keep saving the previous designs so that they can go back to them if they need to.

Once a design has been finalised, the CAM (computer-aided manufacture) machine can be programmed to cut out the fashion designs that were produced using the computer. The main advantage of using ICT in this way is that fewer people are needed. You no longer need a person to cut the cloth to produce the pieces to be stitched together.

FIND IT OUT

You are now required to find information about the way organisations use the following types of software:

- CAD/CAM
- sensing
- control
- image manipulation.

Your main information source will be the Internet.

You may find some material in books. CAD/CAM is used in engineering so you should look at engineering books as well as ICT books.

You may also find material in magazines, many of which are available on the Internet.

Some useful advice:

- Make sure that all your work is wordprocessed, spellchecked and grammar checked.

- *Use pictures to help you explain things (line diagrams, photographs, clip art, etc.).*
- *Do not simply cut and paste large chunks of text from the Internet. You need to put material into your own words. Your work should be original.*
- *Include a list of the places where you have found your information, e.g. website addresses, book titles, etc.*

Capturing, manipulating and enhancing graphics images

Graphics images need to be put into many documents and websites. Obtaining an image in the first place is called capturing the image. Capturing an image can be done in the following ways:

- by using a digital camera (for a photographic image)
- by using clip art from a disk or CD/DVD (clip art includes drawings and photographs); there are also plenty of sites on the Internet where you can download free clip art
- by obtaining an image from a website or web page on the Internet (be aware of the copyright restrictions when doing this)
- by scanning an image in (this could be a picture, diagram or photograph).

Manipulating or enhancing the image

Once the image has been captured, it may need adjusting in some way. Graphics software is available that allows you to alter (i.e. manipulate) images. Here are some of the ways that an image can be manipulated or enhanced:

- It can be sized (i.e. made bigger or smaller).
- The contrast can be altered.
- The brightness can be altered.
- Part of the image can be cropped (this is just like cutting the part you want out of the picture).
- Individual colours in the image can be adjusted.
- It can be saved in a different file format.

Monitoring and recording physical and environmental data

There are some organisations that have to use sensors to continually monitor and record data. This data can be physical such as pressure, flow rate, temperature, etc. It may relate to the environment in some way. Environmental data includes measurements of temperature, atmospheric pressure, wind speed, quantities of pollutants in the air and so on.

Here are some situations that involve the monitoring and recording of data:

- process control in a factory
- remote weather stations
- roadside pollution monitoring stations.

In the next unit there is an example of a traffic control system and also a pollution monitoring system.

File management and standard ways of working

In order to work effectively and prevent problems it is useful to have some standard ways of working. This means that you work so as to minimise the problems that you could have with hardware, software and data. Information in ICT systems can easily be lost or misused. If you do not have standard ways of working you may lose data, software or hardware.

Here are some things you need to do when producing work for this unit and the other two units.

Learn how to spellcheck and grammar check your work. After these checks, proof-read your work to make sure that there are no mistakes.

Keeping back-up copies

Keep **back-up** copies of files. If you are using a network then you should check that the files are continually backed up. To be safe, it is best if you can also store a copy of your data on your own disk.

THE JARGON DRAGON

back-up file – a copy of a file which is used in the event of the original file being corrupted (damaged)

THE JARGON DRAGON

virus – a program that has been designed to do damage to a computer system

Virus checking

The more different computers you use, the greater the chance of getting a computer **virus**. You should make sure that the computers you use have a current copy of a virus checker on them. Any disks should be scanned for viruses. Only files from known and trusted sources should be downloaded from the Internet.

Respect copyright: don't copy work and present it as your own

Do not put any work which is copyright protected into your assignments. This includes material off the Internet and photographs scanned in from books and magazines. Remember that the people who supply this material may do it for a living. Copying the material deprives them of some income. Unauthorised copying is theft. The law takes this very seriously – it is a criminal offence.

Managing your work

You will be required to produce an assignment by a certain date. This date is called the deadline. Deadlines are important and must be adhered to. Do not sit back when you are given an assignment thinking that you have plenty of time. You need to leave plenty of time for unexpected things to happen such as your printer breaking down, etc.

Planning your work to meet deadlines
Here is some advice that will help you meet deadlines:

- When you are given an assignment, make sure you know when the deadline is.
- Ensure that you understand what you are required to do.
- Check to see if you have to do some research.
- Check to see if there are any skills you need to learn to complete the work.
- Make a plan of what you have to do and when.
- Do not waste time. If you are allowed to do some of the work in class, plan your work so that you have something to do in the lesson.
- Try to complete the assignment a few days early.
- Remember that assignments are like buses – you wait a while for them to come and then they all come together.

Use filenames that are sensible and remind you of your files' contents

If your name is Jack do not be tempted to call your files Jack1, Jack2, Jack3, etc. If you want to go back to one of these files in the future you won't remember the name. You need to choose a name that says a little about the contents of the file. In Word you can have a filename with up to 255 characters. This means that you could have a file called

Unit one assignment for hand in date 12/12/02

This takes a long time to type in so you could abbreviate it like this:

Unit1ass12/12/02

Most computer packages give a file extension to your filename. For example, a document in Word has the file extension .doc after the filename. A document on computer crime might be called Computer crime.doc

You do not need to type in the file extension as the wordprocessor adds this automatically. Other packages use different file extensions. Excel, the spreadsheet package, uses the file extension .xls.

Store files so that they are easy to find

If you had lots of separate bits of paper to store then you would try to store similar bits of paper together in a folder. If you had gas bills then you would store these together in one folder. Electricity bills would be stored in another folder.

Computer files can also be stored in folders. You could keep all the files for a certain assignment together in the same folder. If you do not use separate folders then finding the files becomes a lot more difficult.

Taking account of relevant legislation (i.e. laws) and codes of practice

There are various laws which state what you can and can't do when using computer equipment or data. These laws are dealt with in detail in Unit 3. You may have been given a code of practice when you started your course which tells you what you can and cannot do with the computer equipment in your school/college.

The laws applicable to computing that you should know about include:

- The Data Protection Act 1998
- The Copyright, Designs and Patents Act 1988
- The Computer Misuse Act 1990

You will also need to know about the health and safety regulation surrounding the use of display screen equipment.

Working safely

Working with ICT equipment is not dangerous compared to some occupations, such as working on building sites. Nevertheless, there are some things you can do to prevent accidents and health problems. To make sure that your body is not damaged over time you need to make sure that:

- you are seated comfortably
- your desk and monitor are at the correct height
- your keyboard and mouse are suitably positioned
- you have brief rest periods away from the computer
- there are near and distant objects on which you can re-focus your eyes.

You should:

- avoid working for long periods on the computer
- avoid bad posture (i.e. do not slouch in your chair)
- avoid eye strain.

Here are some health and safety rules that you should follow:

- The monitor should be at a comfortable distance from your eyes. It should also not be placed at an awkward angle to your eyes.
- The keyboard should move separately and its angle of use should be adjustable.
- A wrist rest should be available.
- Chairs should have an adjustable back rest to support your lower back. To aid arm movement there should be no or very low arm rests.

- The base of the chair should be height adjustable.
- The chair should swivel so that the body can move easily between activities.
- A foot rest should be available, especially for short people.
- There should be enough clearance for your knees between the seat and the table.
- Adjustable blinds should be used on the windows to avoid glare on the screens.
- Copy-holders should be used to hold documents so that head movement is minimised.
- Do not ignore aches and pains, particularly in your mouse hand and wrist, after prolonged computer use. This could be the start of a medical condition called **RSI**.

THE JARGON DRAGON

RSI (repetitive strain injury) – a muscular condition caused by repeatedly using certain muscles in the same way. It builds up slowly until every muscle movement can be agony

'What do you mean, "where was I last week?". You said to get a wrist rest and the firm would pay for it. That's where I was last week. I took my wrists for a week in Benidorm for a rest!'

This unit will help you to:

- understand how real organisations use ICT
- give you practice at looking at ICT uses.

You will also learn about:

- how and why organisations use ICT
- the main components used to design an ICT system
- how ICT systems are designed.

Most organisations use ICT in their work. Some organisations have all aspects of their operation computerised, while others still use a mixture of manual and computerised systems. In this unit you will look at how businesses and other organisations use ICT.

As well as understanding how organisations use ICT, it is important to be able to develop an ICT system yourself. In this unit you will also learn how to design, implement and test a system and represent it graphically (using flowcharts or data flow diagrams).

You will learn about flowcharts and data flow diagrams later on.

In this unit you will learn about:

How and why organisations use ICT   130

Main components   177

Graphical representation of systems   192

How ICT systems are designed and
implemented   201

How and why organisations use ICT

The unit will look at the hardware and software organisations use, and the ways in which data flows within organisations and between different organisations. Communication systems are very important to organisations and these will be emphasised in this unit.

At the start of the unit the areas of an organisation will be outlined. A range of different types of organisation will be looked at to see how they use ICT.

ICT systems are developed to meet the needs of the organisation. A self-employed painter and decorator would have very limited uses for an ICT system. These uses might include using a wordprocessor to type up quotes for jobs or using simple accounts software to make up end-of-year accounts. Such a user has needs that are met by a limited use of ICT. When more people are involved in an organisation, the needs of the organisation are split into areas called functional areas. Large organisations have lots of needs and these are usually met using ICT systems.

The use of ICT has had a huge impact on organisations. Nowadays it is almost impossible to find any organisation that does not use ICT. No matter how small an organisation, there is always a way that it could be run more efficiently by the use of ICT.

Before a system can be used it needs to be designed and developed. Usually the process starts with a manager identifying a problem with the existing system (a system is a way of doing things). For example, a college may have problems with teaching staff being able to contact other teaching staff, especially if the staff work on different sites. Such a problem could be solved by the use of e-mail with a terminal located in each staffroom.

Once a system has been designed and developed, it then needs to be implemented. This means that the old system (if there was one) will need to be replaced by the new system.

In order to understand the benefits of ICT it is necessary to understand a little about organisations in general. Although organisations differ a lot in what they do (for example, compare an airline with a hospital), they still have some common areas. For example, a hospital and an airline both have to keep records about the personnel they employ, they have to have a way of paying these people, and they also need to hold information about their suppliers. Suppliers are the companies that supply organisations with goods and services.

Not all organisations use ICT to its full extent. Some businesses are only partly computerised and will be looking to introduce new systems in the future. Other organisations use the latest ICT equipment to help them keep ahead of their competitors. Some organisations are completely reliant on ICT and could not exist without it, such as Internet book and CD stores.

Dividing large organisations up into departments

Large organisations are often divided up into departments that carry out the main functions of a business. These functions are those areas of activity that must be carried out in order for a business to achieve its objectives. It is hard to talk about a typical organisation because they are all very different.

The four main functions carried out by an organisation are as follows:

Sales
This is an important part of a business because it brings money into the business. The sales function aims to persuade customers to buy products or services. It also deals with customer orders. This may involve telephone sales, dealing with order forms, and dealing with orders made over the Internet (called e-commerce). It usually also involves the marketing of goods and services by preparing catalogues, mail shots, sales presentations, etc.

Purchasing
Manufacturing companies make products from components. For example, a car manufacturer such as Ford buys parts from other companies and assembles them to produce cars. The lack of one component could hold up the whole production line, so it is important that all the components are immediately available when needed. Purchasing involves placing orders with suppliers (i.e. the firms who supply the components). It also involves tracking orders and chasing up parts that should have been delivered.

case study

Amazon: an Internet bookstore

Amazon is an Internet bookshop and all its business is conducted over the Internet. There are no shops and as few staff as possible, yet it still sells huge quantities of goods. ICT equipment is used extensively. Amazon is the largest bookshop in the world.

Amazon has websites where customers can browse and buy a wide range of goods, including not only books but also DVDs, videos, software, music CDs, mobile phones and even wine!. You should take a look at the UK site for Amazon at: www.amazon.co.uk

The Amazon website. Take a look for yourselves at what it offers (©2001 Amazon.com, Inc.)

To set up a good website you need to pay programmers and website designers. This money is paid out at the start of the project. Websites need to be constantly maintained and this again costs money. The reasons for this maintenance are:

- new books that have just been published need to be included on the site
- books that are no longer available need to be removed
- the prices of books can change.

Payments for books are made using a **credit card** or a **debit card**.

How does Amazon choose to communicate with customers, suppliers and staff?

Electronic communication is used. Customers come to the Amazon website and then make their purchases electronically. Some customers who are worried about keying in their credit card numbers are offered the

THE JARGON DRAGON

credit card – a plastic card containing a magnetic stripe that is used to make purchases. You are given a limit, called a credit limit, and you are not allowed to go above this.

debit card – a plastic card with a magnetic stripe on it. It is a form of payment and can be used to make purchases. The money is instantly transferred from your account to the store's account.

alternative method of phoning up with the details. All dealings with suppliers are done electronically.

Security issues
All personal information, including credit card numbers, is encrypted before sending it over the Internet.

Privacy issues
Amazon needs to collect personal information about their customers. They need the following information in order to process a customer order:

- The customer's name, e-mail address, delivery address, credit or debit card number and the card's expiry date.
- Their telephone number, which enables Amazon to contact a customer urgently if there is a problem with an order.
- Amazon asks customers to give reviews of books. When a customer gives a review they may ask for the customer's e-mail address.
- Amazon uses the information about what books a customer has bought to make suggestions about others they might like.

How does Amazon.co.uk protect customer information?
The Amazon website operates from a network of servers (powerful computers). When you place an order a secure server is used. This makes use of special software that encrypts all the information you send to it. This means it is impossible for someone to hack into or obtain your details as they travel along the telephone cable.

Data protection
The UK part of Amazon, called Amazon.co.uk, has to abide by the **Data Protection Act 1998**. Since the company stores personal information about its customers, it has to register under the Act. It has to say how it intends to use the personal data and also say who it sends the details to.

One of the requirements of the Data Protection Act is to make sure that personal details are safe from unauthorised access.

THE JARGON DRAGON

Data Protection Act 1998 – a law that restricts the way personal information is stored and processed on a computer

case study

Amazon: an Internet bookstore

Drawbacks of being an Internet business

There are a number of drawbacks of being an Internet business. These include:

- many people cannot use the Internet
- people are frightened of giving out credit card details over the Internet
- bogus companies exist and people are not sure if the Amazon site is one of them
- many people do not have a credit or debit card
- it is easier to take goods back to a shop.

Advantages of being an Internet business

- Advertising is easy. You can have banner adverts on other people's sites so that if someone clicks on them they go to the Amazon site. They get a commission each time a person goes from their site to Amazon and makes an order.
- Customers type in their own details. There is no need to employ staff to do this.
- Customers are less likely to make a mistake with their own details. Information typed in may be more accurate.
- There are no expensive high street premises to pay for.
- All goods can be sent out from a central warehouse.
- As more and more customers place orders, huge amount of information about them, including their likes and dislikes, are recorded. This information can be used to market other products.

Questions

To answer the following questions, you will need to access the Amazon UK website at: www.amazon.co.uk

1 *What items other than books does Amazon sell?*
2 *Give two reasons why you feel that Amazon has risen to being the largest bookshop in the world.*
3 *Explain how Amazon has used the Internet to communicate with its customers.*
4 *Explain how Amazon has used the Internet to market and sell its goods.*
5 *Why is Amazon able to sell goods cheaper than in a traditional shop?*

Even if an organisation is not involved in manufacturing, it will still need to make purchases of services (gas, electricity, telephone, water, etc.), cleaning, office equipment, stationery, car rental, etc. There needs to be a way of placing orders for these items.

Purchasing involves:

- finding a suitable supplier
- establishing payment and discounts and discussing delivery schedules
- placing an order
- taking delivery of the order or chasing up delivery
- checking that the goods received are the same as those ordered
- paying the invoice (i.e. the bill) when it arrives.

Operations

Some organisations do not produce an end product but instead provide a service. The day-to-day tasks of providing the service may be considered to be the 'production' part of the business, and this part is sometimes referred to as the operations function. Types of businesses with large operations departments include building societies and travel agents.

Finance

The finance department, sometimes called the accounts department, is responsible for all financial record keeping. Basically this involves keeping manual or computer records of all the money coming into and going out of the business. The finance function also covers the payment of wages and the collection of tax and National Insurance contributions, and making sure that the legal requirements for their collection have been adhered to. Finance also sets up department budgets and makes sure that department managers do not overspend.

Managing stock control

Most organisations require some stock to be kept, even if it's only supplies of office stationery. It is important to keep track of the amount of stock so that items are re-ordered when stocks are getting low.

The four main areas in a business are:

* sales
* purchasing
* finance
* operations.

By referring to a holiday company (e.g. First Choice, Airtours, Thomsons, etc.), explain briefly, for each functional area, the sorts of jobs that would be carried out.

Many companies make goods from raw materials or components and the lack of a single item can stop a whole production line and cause a company to lose large amounts of money. Accurate stock-taking is an important part of a business. Stock-taking involves checking to see how many of each product you have in stock. One way of avoiding running out of stock is for a company to buy so much stock that it is unlikely ever to run out. The problem with this approach is that stock costs money, so it means tying money up in stock rather than using it more profitably. Also, the more stock that is held the more difficult it is to find a particular stock item. Storage space costs money and you also need staff to move and store stock. The more stock you have the greater these costs.

Keeping too much stock creates some problems, for example:
* you need somewhere to store it
* it is hard to find an item amongst so much stock
* money is tied up in stock.

With a computerised stock control system, a balance is maintained between keeping the amount of stock held at any one time to a minimum while at the same time making sure that the demand for stock can be satisfied. Food retailers such as Tesco have very efficient stock control systems since many of the items (such as fruit and vegetables) have a shelf-life of only a couple of days. If they buy too much they may have to sell it at a reduced price or even throw it away. There is a case study on Tesco later in this unit which looks at how it deals with stock control.

RESEARCH TASK

Supermarkets have very efficient stock control systems. This prevents them from running out of items and also from having to reduce goods in price because they are near their 'best before' date.

The aim of this research task is to enable you to understand what stock control is all about.

Use a variety of information sources (books, the Internet, magazines, etc.) to find out the answers to the following questions.

1 *Why is it so important for organisations that buy and sell goods to have a stock control system?*
2 *Find out about how supermarkets use a system whereby goods are automatically deducted from stock when they are bought by customers. Write a brief summary of your findings.*
3 *The deduction of goods from stock may not always give the right number of goods in stock. Explain the reasons why this can happen.*
4 *Explain the term 're-order quantity' with reference to a stock control system.*
5 *Someone says 'why not simply order lots of a certain product so that you will never run out?'. What is the problem in doing this?*
6 *Use the Internet to find out about stock control packages. Write a list of the main features of this type of software.*

FIND IT OUT

Details about stock control are best found in a business studies textbook. A visit to your school/college library or your local library is worthwhile. Try to look for books aimed at GCSE or VGCSE level and then books aimed at A, AS or Vocational A level standard.
Use the Internet to find out information about specific stock control software. You may even find a demo or some screenshots of the software.

Think
IT THROUGH

Type the keywords 'Stock Control' into a search engine such as Yahoo: www.yahoo.com

You will get some information from companies who supply software as well as some notes about stock control in general. As well as looking at the websites, you should also look at the web pages as you will find a lot of useful material here.

Day-to-day processing tasks

There are some tasks in an organisation that need to be done every day. These tasks are called day-to-day processing tasks. Since these tasks take up a large amount of time and require large numbers of staff, it is important that ICT is used. This section looks at some types of day-to-day processing task.

Order processing

Any organisation involved in the supply of goods or services has to have a way of dealing with customers' orders. Order processing systems record the details of each order as it comes in. They then check to see if the goods are in stock and then organise payment. Sometimes a customer account is created and the customer is given credit. The customer only has to pay for the goods after they have arrived. Before the customer's order is processed, the system checks to see if the customer owes the organisation any money or if the value of the order will bring the customer's account above their credit limit. Once the order has been placed the system arranges for the order to be made up and delivered and for the customer to be invoiced for the price of the goods.

Payroll processing

All employees expect to be paid the correct amount and on time, so payroll processing is crucial to any organisation. Employees can be paid in different ways, for example salaried employees have their annual salary divided by twelve to be paid monthly, whereas other staff have an hourly rate of pay and are paid weekly according to the number of hours they have worked. These hours may be at a basic rate or at an enhanced overtime rate for working weekends, bank holidays, etc. In addition to their basic pay, some employees may receive bonuses, commission and so on.

Not all employees get the same pay, even if they are doing identical jobs. Some may be given more pay because they have worked in the organisation longer. Some people's pay may differ because the amounts deducted vary, for example the amount of tax. This depends on a person's tax code which in turn is determined by an individual's circumstances. Each employee is supplied with a detailed breakdown of the amount they are paid, including deductions, in the form of a payslip.

In addition to the money paid to employees, an organisation has to send money to many other organisations such as the Inland Revenue for income tax and National Insurance contributions, pension agencies for the payment of pension contributions, trade unions for the payment of subscriptions, and so on.

Because of the security and cost problems of dealing with the transfer of large amounts of money, many organisations use **electronic funds transfer (EFT)**, using **BACS (Bankers' Automated Clearing Service)** to transfer the money between the organisation's bank account and the employee's account. They can also use the system to make payments to the Inland Revenue.

THE JARGON DRAGON

electronic funds transfer (EFT) – the process of transferring money electronically without the need for paperwork or the delay that using paperwork brings.

BACS (Bankers' Automated Clearing Service) – an organisation set up by all the main banks to deal with standing orders and direct debits. Both of these involve making payments direct into bank accounts.

ACTIVITY

Answer the following questions:

1. *A mail-order company receives orders from its customers. Describe three ways that a company could supply an order.*

2. *Some systems require a customer to pay for their order as they make it. Give three ways that a customer could pay for an order.*

3. *Most companies will check their stock to see if the product is in stock. This is done using a terminal. Explain why they do this.*

4. *Explain briefly the steps involved in order processing.*

Forecasting

Forecasting means looking to the future and trying to predict it. A weather forecast tries to predict what the weather will be like later today, tomorrow or some other time in the future.

Spreadsheets are more useful to companies for predicting the future than a crystal ball

Weather forecasts may be wrong but the more information they are based on, then the more accurate they are likely to be. Forecasts are used in business to try to predict future sales and cash balances.

Predicting future sales

Predicting future sales is important in a manufacturing company because managers can use the information to determine how many of each product to make. If they make too many then they will not be sold. If they make too few, then they will have disappointed customers. Many companies use the previous year's sales to predict future sales.

Cash flow forecasts

Cash flow forecasts show the managers of a business when they expect to receive cash and when they expect to pay it out. Some businesses are seasonal which means that they sell more goods in certain months. The money they get in these months will need to be enough to pay bills in the months when the money coming in is low.

It is useful when you first start work and live on your own to be able to produce a cash flow forecast for your income and expenses (i.e. money you have to pay out).Using the cash flow forecast you could see if you were able to afford a holiday or to run a car. Cash flow forecasts are usually produced using spreadsheet software.

Marketing products and services effectively

The marketing function is responsible for identifying, anticipating and satisfying customer requirements profitably. Marketing does not just apply to goods; it can also apply to services. For instance, your school or college will need to do a certain amount of marketing to convince pupils/students to go there. Large companies have a separate marketing function but in smaller ones its role tends to get merged in with the sales function.

The following case studies will show you how and why different organisations use ICT.

This case study outlines a system that is used to monitor and control a process.

All busy towns and cities use a traffic control system to keep the traffic flowing freely. These systems are important during the rush hours (morning and evening). In the morning rush hour the lights on the main routes into the town are kept on green longer than usual. During the evening rush hour the lights on routes out of the city are kept on green longer. If the lights were on a set sequence at all times, there would be long delays during the rush hours.

Traffic control systems are computer controlled and they use **sensors** set into the road to detect the amount of traffic.

The aims of the traffic control system are:

- to improve the traffic flow
- to improve driver and pedestrian safety by reducing frustration
- to make sure that any delays in a journey are kept to a minimum
- to reduce damage to the environment caused by fumes from waiting traffic
- to reduce the use of fossil fuels.

In the early days of traffic control the traffic lights would be switched off at busy junctions and a policeman would take over. The policeman could take account of the increased traffic flow in a certain direction and allow this traffic a longer time period to go through the junction. A great deal of concentration was needed and it took up a great deal of valuable police time. The next stage was to keep the lights switched on but this time vary the sequencing manually by cabling the traffic lights to a control room and having a camera above the junction to allow the operator to see the effects of their sequencing. Since an operator was needed for each junction, this limited the system to only the busiest of junctions and did not solve the problem elsewhere.

The next stage was the development of a computer-controlled system. In this system the traffic flow is assessed on the basis of the quantity of vehicles around

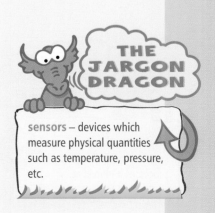

THE
JARGON
DRAGON

sensors – devices which measure physical quantities such as temperature, pressure, etc.

case study

The Metropolitan Borough of Sefton's Traffic Control Centre

the whole area, and using this information the system can detect in which direction the majority of the traffic is flowing. It can then make sure that in the morning, cars on main routes into a town are given more green lights than usual so that the traffic in this direction runs more smoothly. In the evening the situation can be reversed.

The system is a **real-time** system, and the data concerning the number of cars passing is determined by underground detector cables that are set into the road surface before a junction. This is an example of automatic sensing.

Remote control systems
Remote control systems rely on communication lines being set up between the traffic signals and the central computer situated in the traffic control centre. One such system is as follows.

SCOOT (Split Cycle and Offset Optimisation Technique)
The SCOOT traffic control system is used by most local authorities. Where the traffic signals are fairly close together, it is important to coordinate adjacent signals. It is quite easy to set up the system so a green signal is obtained at each signal (traffic light or pedestrian light) at the same time. The real problems are encountered when you need to coordinate the signals over a series of conflicting routes.

The SCOOT system uses a computerised simulation, and the inputs to the system are the details about the traffic obtained from sensors situated near junctions and crossings throughout the area. These sensors are operated in real time, so the computer is always kept up to date with the latest traffic information. The data is sent using either wire-based cables or fibre optic links (i.e. the existing telecommunications cables). Once the computer has analysed the data, it can then amend the traffic signal timings and the offset between the signals. The offset is the phasing between each traffic signal and the next along a road.

THE JARGON DRAGON

real time – a real-time system accepts data and processes it immediately

SCOOT optimises traffic control in three ways:

1   Split optimiser

During any particular cycle, the time at which each stage receives a green signal at a junction and the length of time that it is green, is a proportion of the total cycle time. The length of the green period given to each approach, called the green split, is constantly varied by SCOOT depending on the current demand on each approach.

2   Cycle optimiser

The cycle time of each junction is also continually adjusted. At low flow periods, SCOOT reduces the cycle time to around 28–48 seconds depending on the number of stages, while during the peak periods the cycle time may rise to 120 seconds to cope with the high traffic volume. Additionally, a small junction located between two large junctions may not require a cycle time as high as the other two, so in this case the junction will be made to double cycle, i.e. while the two large junctions are cycling at 120s the small junction may cycle at 60s.

3   Offset optimiser

The third optimiser attempts to link each set of signals along a particular route to provide a progression – or 'green wave' – for traffic heading in the direction of the major flow.

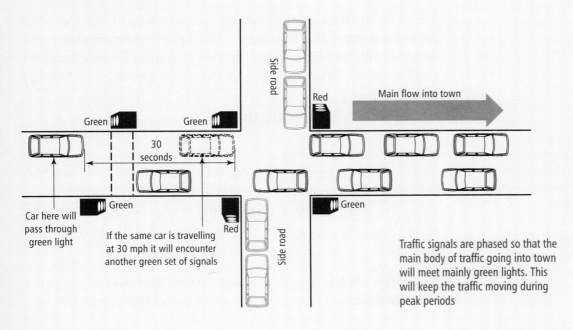

Side road

Red

Main flow into town

Green

Green

30 seconds

Green

Car here will pass through green light

If the same car is travelling at 30 mph it will encounter another green set of signals

Red

Green

Side road

Traffic signals are phased so that the main body of traffic going into town will meet mainly green lights. This will keep the traffic moving during peak periods

case study

The Metropolitan Borough of Sefton's Traffic Control Centre

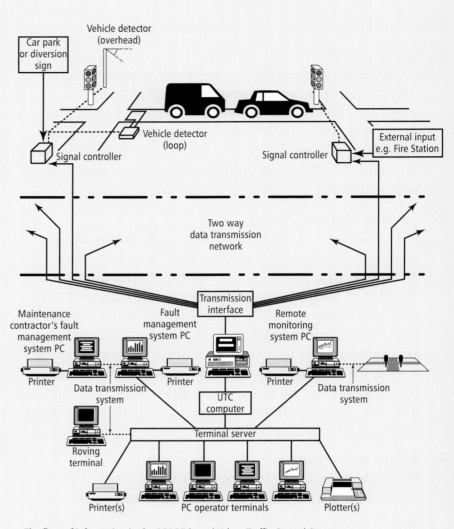

The flow of information in the SCOOT-based Urban Traffic Control System

There is another system which can be used in the event of an emergency. The Emergency Vehicle Priority System enables fire engines, ambulances and police vehicles to obtain an uninterrupted path through a system of linked traffic lights by giving a green signal to the vehicle as it reaches each light along the route.

Weather forecasting
The traffic control centre also has several remote weather stations which collect data about the weather and then relay the data to the centre using modems and telephone lines. The physical quantities measured by the system include:

- wind speed
- humidity
- air temperature
- ground temperature

Although the data from the weather station is also passed to the meteorological office for the production of weather forecasts, the data can be used to predict the likelihood of black ice on the road surface. When it looks as though there could be black ice forming overnight, an ice alert goes out which means that the gritting teams that put salt and grit on the road can be sent out.

There is another important sensor which picks up the amount of salt on the road surface. For instance, if a road had been gritted the previous night, and it had not rained or snowed, then there may well be enough salt left on the road to prevent the need for further gritting. This system saves on both the overtime money paid to the gritting teams and the cost of the grit and salt used.

Pollution monitoring

The Metropolitan Borough of Sefton has three remote air pollution monitoring devices which monitor two polluting gases (NO and SO_2) and these are situated at the busiest junctions in the Borough. The data from these devices is used to monitor the air quality and it is also used by the meteorological office to record air quality information for the region as a whole. Again, modems and telephone cables are used to transfer the data to the Borough's technical services department.

A remote air pollution monitoring system

The Metropolitan Borough of Sefton's Traffic Control Centre

Car speeding systems

These systems are used for sections of road where speeding is a problem. The system is fixed in position (unlike the police's radar traps). If a car passes through the next radar detector and is still travelling over the speed limit, a camera is activated and a photograph is taken of the vehicle which has the speed superimposed on it. The police develop the film and then use the PNC (Police National Computer) to search for the registered owner of the vehicle using the registration number as the search criterion. They can then establish, from the registered owner, who was driving the vehicle at the time and the appropriate action can then be taken against them.

A speed camera. Some of these now take digital photographs so that the film no longer needs to be developed

Car park management systems

These systems provide a means of directing vehicles around a network to car parks with available spaces.

The system makes use of special signs indicating how many spaces are left, and these are operated by a central computer which uses data from how many cars have entered each car park and how many have left. The figure shows the car park management system which can be used to direct vehicles into city centre car parks where there are spaces available. The signs, which operate in real time, are linked to the SCOOT system.

Car park management systems can be used to direct vehicles to car parks with spaces

Remote monitoring

All traffic control systems use remote monitoring, which means that there is a link, using cable or telephone wires between the controllers for the lights, pelican crossing, etc. and the control centre. All the equipment used checks itself to see if it is working correctly, and if there is a fault it automatically reports the fault back to the control centre. In this way, the system does not need to rely on members of the public reporting faults and you do not need to employ staff to go round checking that everything is working properly. If a fault occurs on a main road, it can be seen on a large map in the control room. Green lights show that the signals are working correctly, and if a particular signal is faulty the light turns red.

Questions

1   *Explain why it is so important for traffic to be controlled in and around city centres.*

2   *The traffic control system makes use of a network. Briefly explain what a network is and why one is needed for this system.*

3   *Describe the sensors that are used to input the data into the traffic control system.*

4   *Describe three advantages to a motorist in the use of the traffic control system.*

Theatres need to keep track of the tickets that they sell for the concerts and plays they put on. Each ticket is for a particular seat and concert. The system used is called a booking system. Booking systems are found in football stadiums, concert venues, sports stadiums, etc. Such systems need to make sure that double bookings cannot occur and that the correct tickets are printed after payment has been made. Because tickets can be booked from a large number of places, it is necessary to use networks in which terminals (usually just a monitor and keyboard) situated anywhere in the country (or even the world) can access a central computer which holds all the booking details.

As you can book tickets for concerts months before they take place, theatres use ICT to help them.

The information needed before a ticket can be booked is:

- name
- address
- telephone number
- performance time
- number of seats required
- seats numbers to be booked
- method of payment.

The name and address is needed because the theatre wants to know who attends its concerts regularly. It can use this information to send out details of forthcoming concerts and any special offers. Tickets may also be sent through the post.

As soon as the seats are booked, the computer system locks the seats and this prevents anyone else from booking the same seats. If the person has to cancel their seats they can be unlocked and re-sold.

To save time typing in the address, the person booking the tickets is asked for their postcode and house number. The rest of the address is then looked up and filled in automatically.

Once the payment for the tickets has been made, the tickets are printed using a special printer. The diagram shows the printer used.

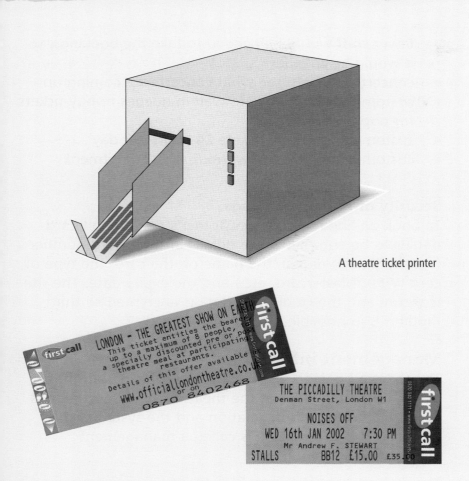

A theatre ticket printer

Keeping only the names and addresses of customers would not cause the theatre to have to register its use of the data with the Data Protection Commissioner. However, if the concerts that they attend are also stored then the data becomes more personal and has to be registered. Any customer is allowed to see the data stored about them if they ask, and the customer must be given the opportunity to be removed from any future mailing list.

As well as visiting the theatre in person to book tickets, people can also book over the phone. One of the problems with this is that booking clerks are needed to take the customers' details.

Booking over the Internet

The theatre staff carried out some market research and found that many concert-goers are on the Internet. A large number of people expressed an interest in booking tickets on-line. The advantages of booking tickets on-line are:

ICT in the theatre

- fewer staff would be needed to take the bookings, so it would be cheaper
- concert-goers can see what concerts are coming up
- customers do not have to wait in queues to buy tickets for popular concerts
- customers can book tickets 24 hours per day
- customers can browse without any commitment.

Security of on-line bookings

To book on-line requires a customer's credit/debit card details to be entered. These details include: card number (usually sixteen digits), the name on the card, the type of card (VISA, Mastercard, etc.) and the expiry date. The site is secure and the credit card data is encrypted so that tapping is impossible.

Management information

The theatre booking system provides information that is useful to the manager of the theatre. This information is called management information and the system that produces the information is called a management information system (MIS).

Screen from a theatre booking system. Notice that the management of the theatre can see how many seats out of the total number have been sold for a particular concert

The figure below shows some of the management information. Notice that you can find out how many seats have been sold for each concert. It is therefore possible for the manager to use this system to show the total value of all the tickets sold for a particular concert.

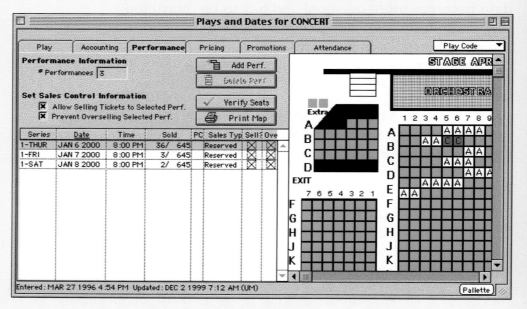

If you want to know more about theatre systems, then the manufacturer of the system described here has a website at: http://www.artsman.com

Questions

1 *The theatre sells seats to the public, so the ICT system is able to process these transactions. The theatre also needs to have a purchasing system. Explain the reasons why it needs a purchasing system.*

2 *Weekly reports are produced by the system and are discussed by the management at their weekly meetings. What details are likely to be included in these reports?*

3 *The theatre has a finance department. Describe some of the tasks that you would expect the finance department to perform using ICT.*

4 *Customer details are stored in a database. Give three reasons why these details are kept.*

5 *The theatre booking system is a real-time system. Explain what is meant by the term 'real time' and explain why booking systems are always real-time systems.*

easyJet: using the Internet to market a service

EasyJet will be familiar to you. It is the low-cost airline that featured in the TV programme called *Airline*. Its distinctive orange and white aircraft, with the web address on the side, can be seen at airports in many European cities.

The Internet is clearly important to easyJet, since it puts its web address rather than a telephone number (or even no details) on the side of its planes.

easyJet has its web address on the side of its aircraft

Using the Internet is at the heart of easyJet's business. You cannot book an easyJet flight through a travel agent, as that would make the flight more expensive. Instead you book direct by making a phone call or by using the Internet. To encourage customers, Internet bookings attract a discount.

At the moment 82 per cent of easyJet's sales are through the website. This is remarkable, considering many people are still unsure about entering their credit card details on-line. The booking system allows the user to exit at any time during the booking if they change their mind. Once a user has registered with the system, the system will remember the user's details so that they do not have to re-enter the information when they book again.

Take a look at the easyJet website at www.easyJet.com.

Questions

1 *Why is easyJet able to offer customers a discount if they book seats over the Internet?*

2 *The easyJet booking system has to operate in real time. Explain what the term 'real time' means and explain why it is essential for a booking system.*

3 *You have seen in the case study how easyJet uses ICT for marketing and selling seats. Describe two other ways easyJet could use ICT in other functional areas such as purchasing, finance or operations (i.e. all the activities required to run an airline).*

4 *easyJet uses a customer database containing details of all the customers who have flown with them before. List the information you would expect this database to hold.*

case study

ICT and the National Health Service (NHS)

The National Health Service (NHS) is responsible for state healthcare in Britain. It uses ICT equipment to help run the service.

Electronic records

If you have visited a hospital lately you will have noticed that there is still a lot of paperwork being used. An example of this is the handwritten patient notes on a clipboard at the bottom of the patient's bed. In the next few years all records kept will be in electronic format. This will make it easy for the records to be accessed by anyone who is authorised to view the records no matter where they are.

Each patient's details will be kept on a huge **database**.

There are many advantages in storing the data electronically rather than manually, and these include:

- patient details are available wherever there is a terminal (e.g. in the GP's surgery, in the consultant's consulting room, on the ward, etc.)
- patient information is available 24 hours per day
- there is only one lot of patient information so this makes updating easier
- mistakes are corrected easily
- using a **network**, more than one person can access a particular patient's record at the same time.

Hospital appointments can be booked at the GP's surgery

In the past, if a patient needed to attend hospital, the GP would have to write a letter to the consultant's secretary who would then write to the patient with an appointment. If the patient could not attend, then the appointment would be re-scheduled. All this takes time and wastes effort. If the GP could access the consultant's computer system while the patient was with the GP, an appointment could be made there and then that was suitable for the patient.

THE JARGON DRAGON

database – a series of files stored in a computer that can be accessed in a variety of different ways

network – a group of computers which are able to communicate with each other

Security problems

Patient medical records contain extremely sensitive information. This information must be kept confidential. Only the medical staff should be allowed access to this information. With electronic records, the records could be accessed from any terminal. To make sure that patient information is only accessed by authorised staff, **passwords** are used.

Medical advice can be obtained over the Internet

NHS Direct Online is a website where members of the public can gain access to lots of information about health, including:

- health features (monthly topics on popular health issues)
- healthy living (suggestions on changes to your lifestyle to improve your health)
- healthcare guide
- NHS A–Z (a guide to the NHS and the services it provides)
- conditions and treatments (a database of information about medical conditions).

The NHS **on-line** site is a very popular site, with over a million hits per week.

The opening screenshot from NHS Direct Online

THE JARGON DRAGON

password – a string of characters (letters and/or numbers) that the user (or the person who looks after the network) can select. It is used to authenticate the user to the system. Only if you type in the correct password will you be allowed access.

on-line – when a device is under the control of the computer it is said to be on-line

You can click on any part of the body for information about medical conditions

E-commerce

Hospitals have lots of suppliers of all sorts of materials and services. E-commerce involves dealing with these suppliers electronically rather than by using traditional invoices, orders, etc. Using e-commerce, goods and services can be found from on-line catalogues. Orders can then be placed on-line, and all the invoices are dealt with on-line. Payments for these orders are also made on-line.

Virtually all GPs now have a computer on their desk so that they can retrieve patients' files and print out prescriptions

These are some of the main advantages to the NHS of using e-commerce:

- orders from lots of hospitals can be joined together to take advantage of the discounts for big orders
- processing orders electronically involves fewer staff, thus saving money
- e-commerce is cheaper for the supplier so some of these savings may be passed to the hospitals.

Questions

1 *Explain briefly how e-commerce saves a hospital time and money.*

2 *Networks are used throughout hospitals. Explain how access to patients' records by medical staff (doctors, nurses, etc.) is improved by the use of networks.*

3 *It is important that hospitals do not run out of drugs, disposable equipment, etc. Explain how ICT can be used to assist in stock control.*

4 *NHS Direct Online is a website that has been set up to help people with medical problems. Describe briefly the advantages of this site and how it helps doctors reduce their workload.*

case study

ICT in a dentist's practice

Newcastle Dental School uses computer-aided learning (called CAL for short) to teach the dental students.

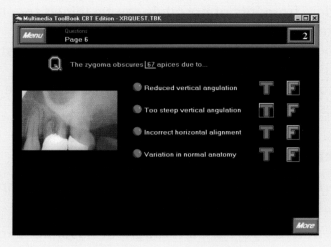

Using computer-aided learning to teach the dentists of tomorrow

Dentists are just like other businesses and they are able to advertise for new patients. Many of them now have websites like the practice below.

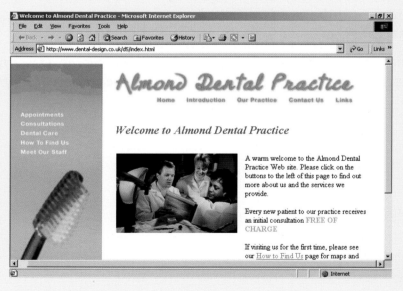

Many dentists use the Internet to advertise their services

A dental practice is a business. It will therefore have many of the administration problems that other businesses have.

Here are just some of the many things dentists have to do besides the obvious ones of filling teeth, making crowns and dentures, extracting teeth, etc:

- book appointments for patients
- re-schedule appointments for patients
- keep a diary for each dentist at the practice
- access treatment notes for each patient
- store up-to-date treatment details for each patient
- store photographs of patients and their teeth
- store X-rays with the patient notes
- hold details of payments made by patients (many patients have to pay for some or all of their treatment)
- order equipment from suppliers such as tools, materials for fillings, drugs, etc.
- submit claims for payment to the National Health Service for the work that they have done
- perform a payroll for the staff that they employ (e.g. receptionists, dental nurses, dental hygienists, etc.)
- keep details of staff rotas, contracts of employment, etc.
- store details of all payments made to do with the premises (heating, lighting, maintenance, etc.).

As you can see from the list, there is a lot of information that needs to be accurate and up to date. It is no wonder that all dentists use computer systems to help them.

There are other devices that can be connected to the system:

- There is a digital camera that can be used to take photos of a patient's teeth.
- There is a digital X-ray camera to take X-ray pictures that can be stored on the system.

Dentists use personal digital assistants (PDAs) to keep track of patients, appointments, etc.

Electronic data interchange (EDI)

A dentist usually has both private and NHS patients. With NHS patients, the dentist has to claim money from the NHS for the work they have done each month. In the past, they had to fill in forms to claim the money and then post them. There were a number of problems with this:

- staff made errors filling in forms and some forms had to be sent back to the surgery
- the claim forms had to be copied and stored somewhere at the surgery
- having to search for information on old claim forms took time.

THE JARGON DRAGON

EDI – electronic data interchange. A network link that allows companies to make payments electronically

ICT in a dentist's practice

Many dentists now use electronic data interchange (**EDI**). EDI works as follows. The dentist has a computer that is connected to the Internet. The forms are filled in on the computer and are then transferred electronically to the NHS computer system. The NHS then processes the forms using its computer system and authorises the payments to be made to the dentist. The computer then sends details of the payments to be made to the bank's computer which then makes the payment electronically to the dentist. The main advantages of the system are that it cuts down on paperwork and problems resulting from late payment due to the post.

Keeping a patient's data secure

When you next go to the dentist, have a look around and you will probably see a computer workstation near the dentist's chair. This workstation will provide the dentist with:

- appointment details
- clinical/treatment notes
- digitised X-ray and ordinary photographs the dentist has taken of your teeth.
- details of costs of treatments
- statistics such as how many patients the dentist has treated in the last week, for instance.

These kinds of dental records, along with medical records, contain sensitive information. For example, if you had dentures then you might not want anyone to know. Because a dentist holds personal details, they need to register under the Data Protection Act. This places certain obligations on the dentist to look after the details carefully and not to disclose them to others without permission. One person is normally given the job of registering the data with the Data Protection Commissioner and this person is called the data controller.

Because so much personal data is kept it would be hard to re-create it if it were lost. This means that backup copies need to be kept. These are usually stored in a secure, fireproof safe. In some cases the files containing the data are stored off-site, perhaps in the dentist's home.

Stock control

Dentists need to hold stocks of materials such as anaesthetics, filling materials, X-ray film and so on. They must make sure that they do not run out of these. As part of the dentist's management software, there is a stock control section. In this section the dentist can get feedback on items that they are running low on. Once the stock of these items drops below a certain amount, called the re-order level, then more stock is automatically ordered from the suppliers.

Questions

1   The patient database holds details about patients and their treatments. This information is confidential and needs to be kept secure. What steps can be taken to ensure:

    (a) that only authorised staff are able to view the patient information

    (b) that the data in the database is kept secure?

2   EDI enables dentists to claim money for treating NHS patients using the Internet. Explain how this system is an improvement over the old system in which paper and the ordinary mail were used.

3   The date when a patient finished a course of treatment or last came for a check-up is recorded in the patient database. This is so that a mail merge can be set up using wordprocessing software to send reminders after six months that patients are due for a check-up. Explain in general terms how this could be done using the database and the wordprocessing software.

4   Many staff are employed at a dentist's surgery (e.g. receptionists, dental nurses and dental hygienists). A payroll package is used to calculate their wages. Explain the types of things that the payroll package would normally do.

5   Many dental surgeries make use of wordprocessing software. Some surgeries make use of the mail-merge facility. Explain how mail merge can be used to remind patients about their six-monthly check-ups.

Britannia Airways

If you have ever taken a holiday abroad with Thomson Holidays, then you will have probably flown on a plane owned by Britannia Airways. Britannia Airways is owned by Thomson Holidays. It is a charter airline as opposed to a scheduled airline, which means that it usually books whole planes full of passengers through a holiday company rather than individual seats on planes. You can still book flights direct with Britannia, and there is a website where this can be done.

Britannia Airways aircraft can be seen at most UK airports

The cost of travelling to and from the holiday destination is only part of the total price of a holiday. Costs therefore need to be kept low for the airline to be profitable, though it still needs to provide a high level of customer service. ICT is therefore used throughout Britannia to reduce costs, maximise efficiency and customer satisfaction and increase profits.

Using ICT to communicate with customers, suppliers and staff

Before ICT systems were introduced, the only way that information could be passed from one part of the business to the other was by paper (memos, letters, etc.). As ICT developed, it was important that a system in one area was able to communicate with the systems in other areas. Now e-mail is the standard form of communication.

Improving business efficiency

The main part of Britannia's business is the planning and managing of flights. Flights are organised well in advance of the holidays and it is important to maximise the time the aircraft spend in the air and minimise the time they spend on the ground. It is only when the aircraft are flying that they make money for the business. Britannia also has to organise rotas for the flying staff (pilots and air stewards/stewardesses). It must also organise the purchase of in-flight meals, duty-free goods, fuel, cleaning services and so on.

Britannia's first step when arranging flights is to attend the annual International Air Transport Association (IATA) conference where all the airlines agree on take-off and landing slots. Once they know where and when these are, they can start planning the flights. A schedule is produced and all the departments in Britannia can start making their plans.

When Britannia decided to invest in a new ICT system, it had to be able to deal with all the parts of the business. Because there are many airlines similar to Britannia around the world, Britannia decided to see if there was a standard software package available to buy. This would be cheaper than paying a company to develop the software from scratch. The software would also be tried and tested. They looked at 45 packages and chose one. Together with the hardware (i.e. the computer equipment) needed to run the package, the system cost £6.5 million.

The main benefit of the new system was that it reduced the number of staff needed to deal with scheduling and running the flying programme. The best way to see this is by looking at the savings made. Comparing the year the new system was introduced with the previous year shows that the new system contributed an extra 1–2 per cent to the profit of the airline.

Strategic planning and forecasting

The on-the-day decision-making tools are a very important part of the software. These are used for deciding what to do if aircraft have to be diverted, are delayed on take-off

case study

Britannia Airways

or are affected by an air traffic control problem. The task performed by the software is to make the best decision, taking all the factors into consideration, to maximise profit and to minimise customer inconvenience.

Finance

Britannia's financial system was developed in-house. This means that the airline did not buy a package. This part of the ICT system is a 'direct operating cost' system. It is based on a large database with information about the charges at all the airports Britannia uses. This charge information includes everything from parking an aircraft overnight to loading it with breakfasts for passengers. The system checks the invoices which arrive from the airports used against the main database and makes sure that the costs are correct. Invoice errors are picked up which might previously have gone undetected. This saves Britannia a lot of money and adds an extra one per cent to the airline's profit. Electronic data interchange (EDI) is also used to exchange information with the suppliers.

The new management information system

The new system supplies important management information. It can be used to divide the business into different areas and look at their contributions to costs and overall profit. It can also be used to determine the holiday routes that are the most profitable. Using this kind of information, managers can make decisions about the running of the business.

The engineering system

Using the engineering system, aircraft maintenance work is carefully scheduled so that there is minimal time wasted between the completion of one task and the start of the next.

Questions

1 Britannia uses a large database for checking costs against invoices. Explain what is meant by:

(a) an invoice
(b) a database.

2 Businesses are usually divided into functional areas. Write down a list of the functional areas that you would expect Britannia to have.

3 For each of the functional areas mentioned in question 2, suggest three tasks that would be performed using ICT.

4 Britannia uses a computer network. Briefly explain why it is necessary for the airline to use a network.

case study

Tesco

Tesco is the largest food retailer in the world. Like many other large supermarkets, Tesco has concentrated on building large out-of-town stores with petrol stations, cafés and large car parks.

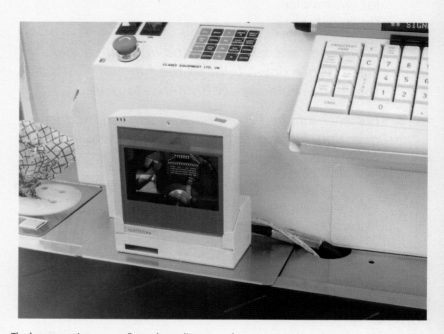

The laser scanning system (barcode reading system)

Tesco was one of the first high-street stores to use a barcode reader, which is now called a laser scanner. The objectives of the scanning system were to improve the service to customers and to increase company productivity and profits.

The scanning system uses a barcode reader to read the barcodes on the goods. What it is actually doing is reading the numeric code at the bottom of the barcode without needing the number to be typed in. As the barcode is passed across the scanner this number is read, the price and description of the goods are then obtained from the computer, the sale is registered and an itemised receipt is produced.

Benefits of the barcoding system to the customers

There are numerous benefits to customers, including the following:

- With the old system, prices were entered into the cash register manually. With the scanning system this is done automatically, which eliminates typing errors.
- The scanning system is much faster than the manual system, so customers spend less time waiting to be served.
- Produce such as loose tomatoes are weighed at the checkout so the customers no longer have to queue twice – once at the pricing point and again at the checkout.
- Customers can have their cheques and credit card vouchers printed automatically.
- Customers using a debit card such as Switch can withdraw cash from any checkout.
- More promotions can be offered, such as 'buy two and get one free' ('multisaver').
- An itemised receipt is produced like that shown opposite. Notice the information it contains.

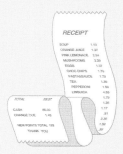

An itemised receipt from Tesco

Benefits of the barcoding system to the company

- Improved checkout accuracy: it is no longer possible for the till operator to key in the wrong price, so there are fewer errors and less fraud.
- Faster and more efficient throughput: there is, on average, a 15 per cent saving in time to register the goods in a shopping trolley compared with the manual system.
- Improved customer service: new services such as loyalty cards, multisavers, etc. mean that customers enjoy a better service.
- Improved productivity: there is no longer a need to price each item individually. Prices are provided on the front of the shelves on which the items are displayed. Weighing and pricing at the checkouts eliminates the need for separate price points.
- Sales-based ordering: sales information from the checkout is used to create the orders for stock replacement.
- Reduced stock levels: more efficient stock control means lower stock levels are needed, so less money is tied up in stock and there is less likelihood of running out of certain items on the sales floor.

Tesco

- Reduced wastage: perishable goods such as fresh meat and salads can be ordered accurately using the sales information obtained from the checkout.
- Promotional and sales analysis: scanned data can be used to assess the effectiveness of special promotions and can provide information about the sales of certain goods.

Disadvantages of the barcoding system to the company

- The stores become totally reliant on their computerised systems, and loss of the use of a system, even for a short time, can result in chaos.
- Shelf prices need to be checked carefully to ensure that the prices on the shelves match those on the computer.

The barcoding system

A barcode from a tin of Heinz baked beans

The diagram above shows a barcode from a tin of Heinz baked beans. The number at the bottom is called the European Article Number (EAN) and this number is allocated to all product manufacturers by the Article Number Association (ANA).

- The first two digits represent the country where the goods are produced.
- The next five digits identify the suppliers of the goods.
- The following five digits identify the product.
- The final number is a check digit and is used to check that the other 12 have been entered correctly.

EFTPOS and the use of debit cards

EFTPOS (electronic funds transfer at point of sale) is the method used by Tesco to transfer money from customers' credit card companies or debit cards directly to the Tesco bank account. A debit card is rather like a cheque since

THE JARGON DRAGON

EFTPOS – electronic funds transfer at point of sale. Where funds are transferred electronically at a point-of-sale terminal

the money comes straight out of a person's bank account, except there is no limit to the amount a person can spend – provided that the money is available in the account. With cheques there is a limit, usually £50 or £100, to the amount a customer can write.

Using checkout information for planning bakery production
Sales information from the checkout is used by the in-store bakeries to plan the production for the same day of the following week. This reduces waste and means stores are less likely to run out of bread.

Sales-based ordering
Sales-based ordering is the automatic re-ordering of goods from the warehouse using the sales information from the checkouts. If, for example, 200 tins of baked beans were sold from a certain store in one day, then 200 tins would be automatically re-ordered and delivered to the store the following day from one of the Tesco distribution centres.

Stock control
All ordering is performed by computer and there are fast electronic communication lines between the shops, the distribution centres and head office. There are also direct links to the major suppliers which means that the orders can go straight through to production lines. The advantage of this is that the stock arrives just when it is needed, so it is always fresh. Another advantage of this system is that money does not need to be tied up in stock and can be used for more productive purposes.

Electronic shelf labelling
Tesco is developing a system using liquid-crystal shelf labels containing the price, description and ordering information of goods. The label is operated from a computer using radio signals, which means that if a price is changed on the computer database, the price displayed on the shelf is changed automatically at the same time. This avoids human errors such as a price change on the computer not being transferred to the shelf.

case study

Tesco

Electronic data interchange

EDI is a method of speeding up the transfer of orders to suppliers. Using EDI eliminates the need for paperwork since the ordering is carried out between the supplier's computer and Tesco's computer. This system is less expensive and quicker than sending the orders by phone, post or fax and cuts out errors such as lost or wrongly printed orders. Tesco can send information to suppliers regarding sales forecasts and information about stock levels so that the suppliers can plan their production appropriately.

Once an electronic order has been placed, the invoice is generated automatically by the supplier's computer. This is sent back and checked by the Tesco computer before payment is made.

The hardware

We have looked at the systems in use by Tesco, and as you can imagine the computers used to run them need to be extremely sophisticated and powerful. The mainframe computers are situated in two computer centres and each one is capable of running all of the company's systems on its own. They are among the fastest commercial computers in the world.

Since computers are so vital to Tesco's operations, there are back-up procedures in place so that, if one of the computer centres were completely destroyed, the other would be able to re-establish the vital systems within 48 hours. The back-up procedures are tested each year so that staff know exactly what to do if a disaster were to occur.

Designing store layout using CAD

It is no longer necessary to use drawing boards for planning new stores and redesigning existing ones. Instead, computer-aided design (**CAD**) is used. This has reduced the time taken to plan new stores: a data bank holds designs and plans from existing stores which can be adapted, rather than new ones having to be generated each time. CAD is also able to show three-dimensional views of the stores, and colours, lighting and different finishes on materials can be altered simply by moving the mouse.

THE JARGON DRAGON

CAD – computer-aided design. Using a computer to design products, buildings etc. and to produce technical drawings

When a new store is planned, photographs of the proposed site can be used in conjunction with CAD to see what the area will look like with the Tesco store in place.

CAD is also used to design the warehouse layouts, and the roads and areas surrounding the distribution centres. This is important since the access roads need to be suitable for large articulated vehicles, and there must be ample room around the distribution centres for them to turn round.

Warehouse systems

Computers are used in the warehouse to monitor complex stock control procedures and make the best use of space, time and labour. Like all areas of retailing, better operating methods need to be found to ensure Tesco's continued success. As with all the other systems Tesco has in place, paperwork has been eliminated wherever possible, so the thick binders containing lists of stock items are replaced by computer terminals.

These terminals are mounted on fork-lift trucks and give the operators information regarding the movement of the pallets so that stock items can be moved quickly and efficiently. If some stock goes out of the warehouse, for example, then a slot is available for the new stock arriving and notification of this is obtained from the terminal. Efficient use of the available space means the trucks have to travel shorter distances and the whole process is therefore faster. The computer system also monitors where each fork-lift truck is situated in the warehouse so that a particular job can be given to the one best able to complete it in the least amount of time.

Electronic mail

Tesco, like most other large companies, has realised the benefits of using electronic mail. Conventional methods of communication can have a variety of problems such as lost post, unanswered telephones, engaged fax machines, people not at their desks, etc. Electronic mail eliminates many of these problems.

Some of the advantages to Tesco of using electronic mail are as follows:

case study

Tesco

- Unlike with a telephone call, the recipient does not need to be there when the message is sent. People can receive their mail at any terminal connected to the system.
- The sender can be sure that the messages are received.
- It is possible to send mail to a whole department or a group of people without knowing anyone by name.
- The electronic mail system can be used as a company information and noticeboard. You can, for example, find out about the latest job vacancies and appointments and look at the latest share prices.
- It is possible to send electronic mail to the major suppliers, thus speeding up orders etc.

Tesco and the Internet

Tesco is the first UK supermarket to offer a shopping and delivery service on the Internet for all the items it sells. The service is available at most stores and customers are able to register with the system and then browse through and select items from a range of 20,000 product lines. Each customer then selects their method of payment and a suitable time for the goods to be delivered to their home. For the delivery, there is a fixed charge of £5 and this is added to the customer's bill. At present the delivery service is available over quite a large area within the vicinity of the store. To pay by credit/debit card, the customer keys in his or her details which are then sent over the Internet. The customer then signs an authorisation slip when the goods are delivered.

The Internet business consultant for Tesco hopes that the Internet shopping service will attract working people who dislike spending the little free time they have in the supermarket. Customers can also shop 'off-line' using software and a product list available on CD-ROM, and send in the order using the Internet. You can take a look at this service yourself at the Internet address
`http//www.Tesco.co.uk`.

Communicating with customers

To be able to communicate with customers you need their addresses. In the past, if a customer bought goods and paid with cash, the store did not know who they were or where they lived.

Tesco

case study

Tesco, like many other stores, has a loyalty card (they call it a Clubcard). Each time the card is used, points are added. When the number of points earned reaches a certain value customers are given vouchers that can be used in the store instead of cash.

The scheme works like this:

- The customer fills in an application form to join the scheme.
- The customer is given a Clubcard that contains a magnetic stripe.
- Each time the customer goes to the store they take the card with them.
- When making purchases either by cash, debit card or credit card, the loyalty card links the customer to their purchases. This provides Tesco with valuable information on what goods are being bought by which customers.
- The card adds a certain number of points, based on the bill and the items bought, to the total.

Questions

1 Tesco now collects a lot of information about its customers. Having a loyalty card system enables the company to do this. Explain why Tesco's loyalty card scheme (called a Clubcard) enables it to collect customer details.

2 A reward card uses a magnetic stripe to contain details. Name the hardware devices used to read the data in the magnetic stripe.

3 Barcode readers are used to scan barcodes. Explain why the price of an item is not encoded in the barcode.

4 Explain what is meant by the term 'sales-based ordering'.

5 Give three advantages to Tesco of using electronic mail to communicate with its staff.

Running a school creates a lot of paperwork. Here is a list of just some of it:

- timetables
- reports
- examination entries
- attendance marks
- marks for classwork/homework
- staff absence details
- staff personnel details
- orders to suppliers
- invoices from suppliers of goods and services.

The government wants schools to be more accountable and to raise the standards of education. To this end, schools have to produce lots of facts and figures (called statistics) about such things as attendance and the pupils' results. This creates a lot of work for schools, so ICT systems have been designed to help them.

The old paper-based registers

Your school may still use paper-based registers, or you may have seen them used in the past. Your form teacher would have a list of the pupils' names in rows and columns for each day a.m. and p.m. At the start of each day, the form teacher would mark the a.m. column and in the afternoon they would mark the p.m. column. At intervals, the marks for each pupil would be counted and then worked out as a percentage of the total possible attendance marks. This took time and sometimes mistakes were made. Also, if a pupil got their mark and then decided to go home, this would not be noticed.

The new electronic registers

The new electronic registers are able to transmit the data recorded by the teacher from a terminal directly to the main computer system in the school office. Some systems do this without the need for any wires because the terminals use wireless communication.

The hand-held terminals can be used by the teachers, to retrieve facts and figures from the main computer system.

Advantages of the electronic system

- It is always up to date. As soon as the register is marked, the marks are immediately sent to the main computer.
- There are fewer errors. Marks do not need to be re-entered by copying them (i.e. typing them into the system). Also totals and percentages are calculated by the system rather than the teacher.
- It improves attendance. In some schools where attendance is a problem, the electronic register can be marked during each lesson. This makes it a lot harder for pupils to miss lessons without being noticed.
- The terminals can also be used by teachers to enter pupils' marks and grades into the main system. The teachers can also see how pupils are doing in other subjects.
- It saves time. The system bridges the gap between the teachers' records and the school's administration system, so it saves both the teaching and administration staff's time.
- It improves discipline. Teachers are able to record details about pupils' bad behaviour. The pupils know this, so they are less likely to misbehave.
- There is an e-mail facility and this can be used to send e-mails to anyone with a terminal. It is useful to be able to give messages direct to teachers rather than sending notes with pupils, particularly where the school occupies a split site.

An electronic register

case study

The electronic school

Parents can check up on their children's progress

There is a new website that parents/carers can access to find out information about their child's performance and attendance at school. The system uses the Internet and allows parents to access parts of the school's administrative computer where the grades/marks and attendance records are kept. To access the system the parents are required to enter a unique password and PIN (personal identification number) that they get from the school.

Future developments might include e-mail between teachers and parents, and the possibility of paying for school trips on-line.

This site can be found at: `www.MyChildAtSchool.com`

Electronic data interchange (EDI)

Examination entries can be made electronically using EDI. Rather than send a list of entries on paper, the school types the list into the system. It then sends this to the examination board which uses it directly without re-typing.

Examination results can be sent directly from the examination board to the school's main computer system. This means that the results do not need to be re-input and therefore that errors are not introduced during re-typing.

Questions

1　*Why do you think wireless communication is normally chosen for this system?*

2　*The system can be used for sending e-mails to other teachers. Explain why this e-mail facility is useful.*

3　*Explain what is meant by the term 'electronic data interchange'.*

4　*Explain how the following items of applications software would be of use in the school office:*

　(a) wordprocessor
　(b) spreadsheet
　(c) database.

5　*Give three advantages that this system has compared with the old system of paper-based registers.*

Main components

The main components of an ICT system can be divided into two parts: **hardware** and **software**.

Hardware

The main components of an ICT system include the following:

- Input devices – these enable the data to enter the system.
- Central processing unit – the brain of the computer.
- Backing storage – consists of the disk drives, tape drives, RW-CD, RW-DVD, etc. used to store data when the power is switched off.
- Output devices – these are used to produce the results of the processing. Output devices include such units as printers and monitors, used to provide output in the form of printouts, screen displays, etc.

THE JARGON DRAGON

hardware – the parts of a computer that you can touch and handle

software – the actual programs that allow the hardware to do a useful job

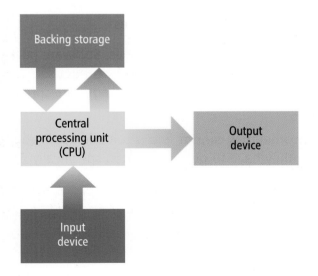

Backing storage

Central processing unit (CPU)

Output device

Input device

The main hardware components of a computer system

Software

Software is the general name for programs that can be run on computer hardware. There are two main categories of software: operating system software and applications software.

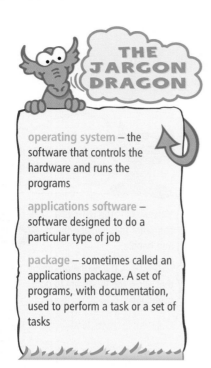

THE JARGON DRAGON

operating system – the software that controls the hardware and runs the programs

applications software – software designed to do a particular type of job

package – sometimes called an applications package. A set of programs, with documentation, used to perform a task or a set of tasks

Operating system software

Operating systems are programs that control the computer hardware directly. Examples of operating systems include:

Windows XP
Windows 2000
Linux
Windows NT
Unix

The operating system needs to be loaded *before* the **applications software**.

Applications software

Applications software is used to perform a specific task. Applications software varies from wordprocessing packages used to write letters, prepare reports, etc. to specialist applications **packages** used only within one industry.

Examples of applications packages include:

- wordprocessing software, such as Word and WordPerfect
- spreadsheet software, such as Excel and Lotus 123
- database software, such as Access.

Some businesses buy software packages. Software packages are cheap and they have been well tested by other users. The costs of the development of applications packages are spread among all the users.

Businesses sometimes cannot find a suitable applications package so they have to get one written specifically. This type of applications software is said to be tailor-made because it fits the purpose exactly. Developing this type of software is expensive and is usually restricted to large businesses and organisations.

Getting data into the computer: input devices

Input devices are used to get data into a computer. It may first need to be converted into a form that can be read by the computer. Data can enter the system through a range of input devices. The main aim of an input device is to input data automatically without a human needing to be there. Also the method needs to be accurate, quick and low-cost. It is hard to find an input device that fulfils all of these requirements. Here is a list of the input devices that you may come across.

Keyboard

Here are some important points about keyboards:

- Keyboards are cheap and come with all computers.
- Not everyone can use a keyboard (e.g. people with physical disabilities).
- They are a very slow way of inputting data.
- Errors can easily be introduced into the system when using keyboards (it is very easy to make a typing mistake).

The standard **QWERTY** keyboard (called this because of the first six letters on the keyboard) comes with almost all computers, but there are plenty of other types. Here are some specialist keyboards for use by disabled people:

Braille keyboards make it easy for blind users to input data into a computer.

THE JARGON DRAGON

QWERTY – the arrangement of the letters on a standard keyboard

A Braille keyboard. Notice that it has fewer keys than a QWERTY keyboard

For those users who have failing vision, there are also keyboards that have large coloured keys that are easier to see. Each key is about one-inch square.

A large-keyed colour-coded keyboard for the visually impaired

Mouse

The mouse is used mainly to make selections on the computer screen. It is still classed as an input device.

Scanner

Here are some important points about **scanners**:

- They are used to scan in photographs and other images to put into documents or web pages.
- They can also be used to scan text into a wordprocessing package.

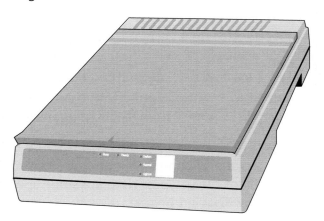

Scanners are used to scan both pictures and text into a computer

Optical character recognition (OCR)

Here are some important points about optical character recognition:

- Optical character recognition (**OCR**) uses a scanner and special software.
- OCR allows individual characters (letters of the alphabet, numbers, punctuation marks, etc.) to be recognised
- It is an ideal method for getting lots of text into a wordprocessing or desktop publishing package without the need for re-typing.
- It is sometimes used for recognising account numbers on bills.

Optical mark recognition (OMR)

Here are some important points about optical mark recognition:

- The hardware device used is called an optical mark reader.
- An optical mark reader can only read marks on specially designed documents.
- It is a very fast way of inputting data.
- **OMR** is ideal for reading the data from questionnaires, answers to multiple-choice examination questions, menu choices in hospitals, football pools and lottery tickets.

THE JARGON DRAGON

scanner – a hardware device used to scan pictures or text into a computer system

OCR – optical character recognition. A combination of software and a scanner which is able to read characters into a computer

OMR – optical mark reader/ recognition. A reader that detects marks on a piece of paper. The computer detects shaded areas and is able to interpret the information contained in them

- It has a high reject rate if documents have been folded.
- A problem with OMR is that a lot of marks are needed to capture a small amount of data.

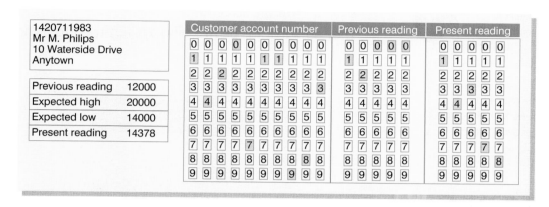

An example of a document that is read using optical mark recognition

Magnetic ink character recognition (MICR)

Here are some important points about magnetic ink character recognition (**MICR**):

- The input device reads characters written in magnetic ink.
- These are the funny-looking numbers found on the bottom of a cheque.
- They are used for account numbers, sort code numbers and cheque numbers on a cheque.
- Magnetic ink character readers are very fast but very expensive devices.

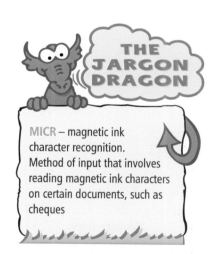

THE JARGON DRAGON

MICR – magnetic ink character recognition. Method of input that involves reading magnetic ink characters on certain documents, such as cheques

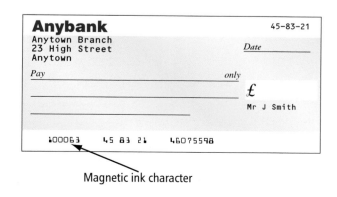

Magnetic ink character

Magnetic ink characters are read by a magnetic ink character reader at high speed

touch screen – a special type of screen that is sensitive to touch. A selection is made from a menu on the screen by touching part of it

magnetic stripe reader – reads the data contained in magnetic stripes, such as those on the back of credit cards

Touch screen

Here are some important points about **touch screens**:

- Touch screens are a special type of screen that is sensitive to touch.
- A selection is made simply by touching part of a menu or a picture on the screen.
- They are ideal for people who are not used to using keyboards.

A touch screen is probably the easiest input device to use

Magnetic stripe reader

Here are some important points about **magnetic stripe readers**:

- They are used to read the information coded in magnetic stripes.
- Magnetic stripes can be found on the backs of credit cards, membership cards and store loyalty cards.

Magnetic stripe

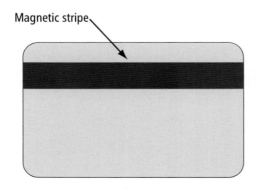

Magnetic stripes hold data on credit/debit cards, loyalty cards and membership cards

A magnetic stripe reader

Voice recognition

Here are some important points about **voice recognition**:

- You speak directly into the computer using a microphone.
- You can either give instructions or dictate text.
- It is used for voice mail where a message is digitised and stored on a magnetic disk.
- Voice recognition is becoming a popular input method and is used with mobile phones and also with some operating systems.

THE JARGON DRAGON

voice recognition – the ability of a computer to 'understand' spoken words by comparing them with stored data

barcode – a series of lines on labels on goods, luggage, etc. used to encode information

barcode reader – an input device used to scan a barcode

Barcode reader

Barcodes are the series of dark and light lines you see on the labels of goods on a supermarket shelf. **Barcode readers** are able to read a numerical code on the goods and it saves having to type this long code in using a keyboard. As well as being used in shops for recording goods sold, barcodes can also be used in library systems. In a library, there is a barcode on each book and also on each borrower's library ticket. When a book is borrowed the computer links the book number to the borrower number. These numbers are stored together with the date, and this information can be used to send letters to borrowers if their books are overdue.

Barcodes are not just on labels on goods in shops. You can find them on library tickets (and in the books), luggage labels, parcel labels, etc.

If a barcode is damaged, then the number under the barcode can simply be entered into the system using the keyboard.

Information on barcodes and barcode readers can be obtained from: `http://www.barcodehq.com`.

Digital camera

Digital cameras are becoming very popular for a number of reasons:

- No film is needed.
- There are no expensive developing costs.
- You can put photographic images directly into a document without the need for a scanner.
- The pictures, since they are in digital form, can be sent over the Internet immediately.
- You can size (enlarge and reduce) the image as well as crop it (cut out the part of the photograph that you want) yourself.

THE JARGON DRAGON

digital camera – a camera that takes a picture and stores it digitally

web camera – a digital camera used to capture still and video images

Digital cameras look just like traditional cameras except they have no film. Instead they have light sensors and a memory which stores the image. The amount of storage taken up by a picture depends on the resolution of the image. The resolution is determined by the number of dots that make up the picture. The greater the number of dots, the clearer the picture and the better the resolution of the image.

Digital cameras are ideal for:

- website designers
- estate agents, for taking pictures of houses and rooms within a house
- schools, for taking pictures of their pupils to be included in a pupil database.

Web camera (web cam)

A **web camera** (web cam) is simply a digital camera that is used to capture still images and video images (i.e. moving images). These images can then be transmitted to a computer where they are stored in a suitable graphics format. If required, the pictures can be used on a website.

Web cams are often included with complete computer set-ups, with the camera placed on top of the monitor. Such a system allows videoconferencing.

Web cams are good fun because you can see the person you are talking to

Web cams are not, however, restricted to the tops of computers. There are web cams everywhere. Here are some of their uses:

Advertising
Cruise companies place web cams around their ships so that potential customers can see what is going on onboard and where the ship is at a particular time.

Checking on children in nurseries
All parents worry about child abuse. When they put their children in nurseries that want to be sure that they are looked after properly. Some nurseries have web cams set up so that parents can see their children on the computer while they are at work.

Checking on the weather in another part of the world
There are web cams just about everywhere. You can see what the weather is like anywhere in the world using a picture from a web cam.

Data captured using sensors
Sometimes the input to a system is in the form of a series of electrical signals. For instance, in voice recognition systems, a person's voice is converted into electrical signals which are then entered automatically into the computer. There they are analysed and eventually acted upon. Voice recognition systems are used by solicitors, who use the system to dictate letters straight into the wordprocessing system without the need for any typing.

Data can enter a computer directly from **sensors**. For example, a burglar can be sensed in a room and a signal sent directly to

THE JARGON DRAGON

sensors – devices which measure physical quantities such as temperature, pressure, etc.

the police station for further investigation. If you wanted to find out about traffic flow along a road then you could use pressure sensors that detect vehicles as they pass over them. The data from these sensors is then sent to the computer for processing.

Sensed data is also used in control applications. Sensors detect a certain physical property and feed the data in the form of electrical signals back to the computer where the computer can decide on the relevant action. For example, with a central heating system, a temperature sensor called a thermistor samples the temperature at pre-determined intervals and feeds the data back to the microprocessor. If the temperature is too low the microprocessor switches the heating on and if it is too high then it switches the heating off. In this way the temperature of the room is kept constant.

THE JARGON DRAGON

CPU – central processing unit. The computer's 'brain'. It stores and processes data. It has three parts: the ALU, the control unit and the memory

Processing the data

The central processing unit (**CPU**) is often simply called the processor. The CPU processes the raw data which enters a computer through the input devices and turns it into information. Processors are continually being improved to offer faster data processing.

Output devices

Once the input data has been processed, the results can be output. In many cases the results are printed out on paper using a printer. In other cases a screen can be used to output a simple answer. For example, a customer at a travel agency may want to find out if a particular holiday is available. The answer can be displayed on the screen and only if the customer makes a booking will a printout be produced.

Monitor

Monitors are ideal for displaying results where no printouts are needed. For desktop publishing or computer graphics work, the screen needs to be as large as possible. LCD (liquid crystal display) monitors are the thin screens that you get with laptops. They are popular because they do not take up much desk space.

Laser printer

Laser printers offer high-speed printing and high-quality printing. Most people use laser printers that only print in black and white. Colour laser printers are very expensive and are used for producing adverts, samples of website designs, etc.

Ink-jet printer

Ink-jet printers spray ink onto the page and they can print in black and white or colour. They are a low-cost way of printing in colour and are ideal for printing photographs and other artwork. Although ink-jet printers are cheap to buy they are expensive to run because the ink-jet cartridges are expensive.

Voice output (speech synthesis)

Visually handicapped people find synthesised speech from a computer invaluable. For instance, when they use special software with a wordprocessor they can hear on headphones each letter as it is typed, and if they go to the start of a word they can hear the whole word.

Electric motors

Signals from the processor can be used to operate electric motors. These motors can be used for all sorts of things. They can open a window in a greenhouse or close a valve to shut of the flow of liquid in a chemical process.

Ports and cables

Ports and cables are used to connect devices such as scanners, joysticks, keyboards, etc. to a computer.

Cables

Cables are needed to connect hardware devices such as keyboards, monitors, scanners, mice and other devices to a computer. If a network is used, then cables are often used to connect the terminals together. These cables could consist of metal wires or fibre-optic cables.

Ports

Ports are external connection points on a computer where you can connect input and output devices. If you follow the cable from your keyboard back to your computer you will find a port.

Ports are either serial or parallel. Parallel ports allow data to be transmitted side-by-side at the same time along a cable. Serial ports only allow data to travel through the cable in single file.

THE JARGON DRAGON

port – an external connection point on a computer where input, output and other devices can be connected

Serial ports are used for keyboards and for transmitting data over a communication line. Parallel ports are used to connect disk drives and printers.

Universal serial bus (USB)

USB is a way that allows external devices such as printers and scanners to be connected easily to a computer.

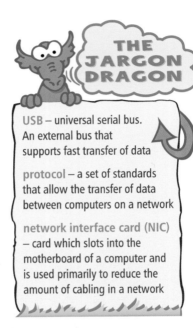

THE JARGON DRAGON

USB – universal serial bus. An external bus that supports fast transfer of data

protocol – a set of standards that allow the transfer of data between computers on a network

network interface card (NIC) – card which slots into the motherboard of a computer and is used primarily to reduce the amount of cabling in a network

Network protocols

When people communicate with each other, they have a set of rules which they use. Although we do not think about them when we are holding a conversation, they still exist. For instance, we wait until the other person has finished talking before we say something and usually acknowledge that we have understood what has been said by nodding occasionally. In other words, there is a **protocol** between the two people.

We also have protocols in telecommunications. Protocols ensure that each computer behaves predictably and provides information in an understandable way.

A gateway changes the protocols between computers so that different computers are able to communicate with each other.

Before sending data, a computer performs what is called a handshake. The handshake is an exchange of signals which establishes the communication between the devices.

Network interface cards (NIC)

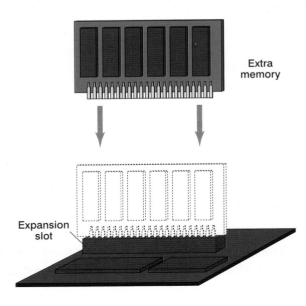

Extra memory

Expansion slot

A network interface card (NIC)

Network interface cards are circuit boards that plug into the main circuit board of a computer. They basically turn a stand-alone computer into a terminal that can be used in a network. Network interface cards are needed to turn the data from the form in which it is used inside the computer into a form that can be passed along a cable.

Storage devices

Data needs to be stored until it is needed by the computer. There are various places in the computer where data can be stored.

Storage in chips: RAM and ROM

Computers store data either in chips inside the computer or on other media such as magnetic disks, tapes or optical disks. Storage in chips may be in either **RAM** (random access memory) or **ROM** (read-only memory). When data is stored in a chip it is immediately accessible by the processor. There is no delay while the data is loaded.

When data is held in RAM it is only held temporarily. This means that the data disappears when the power is turned off. RAM is normally used to hold data and program instructions during processing.

ROM is used to hold data that cannot be changed by the user. In most computers the program used to start up the computer (called the boot program) is stored in ROM. Since data is stored in ROM permanently, it will remain in ROM even if the power is removed.

THE JARGON DRAGON

RAM – random access memory. A fast, temporary memory area where programs and data are stored only while a computer is switched on

ROM – read-only memory. Computer memory whose contents can be read but not altered

Hard disk drive

A hard drive consists of several disks on a single spindle. Each disk can hold data stored in a magnetic pattern on its surface. Read/write heads move over the disk surface, either recording data onto the disk or reading it off the disk. Hard disks come in a range of sizes, with a size of 40 GB (40,000 MB) being typical for a modern personal computer.

It is possible to buy removable hard disk drives. These are useful for backing up data because they can be removed and placed in a locked fireproof safe to protect against theft and damage by fire.

Floppy disk drive

Most computers come with a 3.5 inch floppy disk drive. These magnetic disks are very cheap to buy but are only useful for storing small amounts of data. A typical 3.5 inch floppy disk holds 1.44 MB of data.

CD drive

Data is stored on a CD digitally, and data stored on the disk is read optically by a laser. CDs have a high storage capacity (typically 600 MB) and are ideal for distributing programs where lots of floppy disks would be needed. CDs are used to hold clip art libraries, encyclopaedias, photographs and all sorts of reference material.

CD-ROM drives only allow data to be read off a CD. **CD-RW** (Read/Write) enables you to store data onto the CD as well as read data off it. If you have a CD-RW you can store data on special CDs. This is useful for making backup copies of important data.

DVD drive

DVD stands for digital versatile disk. DVDs look the same as CDs except they are able to store a lot more data. They have exactly the same uses as CD-ROMs but because of their much higher storage capacity (typically 4.7 GB to 17 GB) they can be used to store films.

Read/write DVD drives are now available so you can put your own data onto DVD. Like CDs, DVDs are a popular way of storing multimedia programs and presentations.

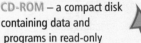

THE JARGON DRAGON

CD-ROM – a compact disk containing data and programs in read-only memory

CD-RW – a CD that can be used in a similar way to a floppy disk

DVD – digital versatile disk. Disk with a larger storage capacity than a CD-ROM. Set to replace CD-ROMs. Recent models allow the user to write data to the disk

RESEARCH TASK

Designing an estate agent database
An estate agent wishes to keep details of her houses in a database. As part of this database she would like to keep some internal and external photographs so that prospective purchasers can see what the property looks like before they go to view it.

You have been asked to research suitable hardware for the estate agent. She has four sales staff and sometimes all of them can be occupied with customers, so it is important that they have a terminal each so that they can view the database.

Task one

For this task you are required to produce a list of the main components that the estate agent would need for her proposed system. For each item in your list, you should explain briefly why it is needed.

Task two

The estate agent would also need some applications software to run on the hardware.

Write a list of the applications software you think the estate agent should use. You should divide your list into two: essential software and desirable software.

It would be a good idea to go into an estate agent's office and pick up a few sales details of houses that are up for sale. This will give you an idea of the output that is needed from the system and also what needs to be input.

FIND IT OUT

Did you consider backup devices in the research task above? Remember that digitised photographs take up a lot of storage space so floppy disks would be no good for backing up.

In your list of software, did you consider software that protects against viruses or software that can be used to get data back that might have been accidentally lost?

Think IT THROUGH

Graphical representation of systems

A system is a group of operations or objects that are connected. For example, you probably have a set system for getting up in the morning. Your system may be different from that of another member of your family. We can describe systems in various ways.

In ICT we often draw diagrams to help explain how ICT systems work. These diagrams include block diagrams and flowcharts. The simplest view of any ICT system can be represented as three boxes representing input, process and output.

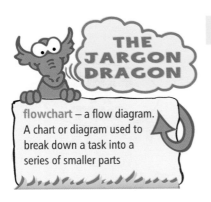

THE JARGON DRAGON

flowchart – a flow diagram. A chart or diagram used to break down a task into a series of smaller parts

Flowcharts

When you are planning how to solve a problem, a good way is to break the problem down into a series of small steps placed in the correct order. Rather than just listing the steps, we can show them in a diagram. This type of diagram is called a **flowchart**.

Flowcharts are made up of boxes connected by lines and the steps are written inside the boxes. The main flowchart symbols (i.e. the boxes) are below.

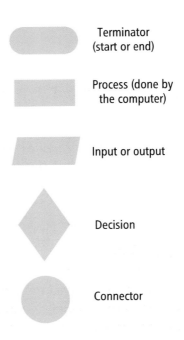

Terminator (start or end)

Process (done by the computer)

Input or output

Decision

Connector

Stop and start boxes

These symbols are used at the start and end of the flowchart. Notice the way that the flow lines go into or out of the boxes and that the name of the box is placed inside.

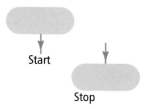

Start

Stop

Process boxes

A process is something that is done. This could be:

- a calculation (e.g. calculate VAT)
- finding some data (e.g. on disk, in a file, etc.)
- an activity that someone has to do (e.g. contact customer, fill in form, etc.)
- an activity that can be performed automatically (e.g. measure temperature, open window, etc.)
- storing data (either manually or using the computer)

Below are some process boxes with the names of the processes inside.

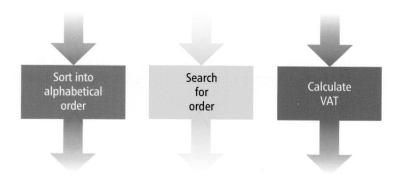

Examples of process boxes

Input and output boxes

Data needs to be input into a system before it can be processed. If a calculation needs to be performed then the input will need to be some figures. If you are replying to a job advertisement, then the input would be the job advert itself.

The output is the results of processing. A printed list of all the members of a certain class is an example of output.

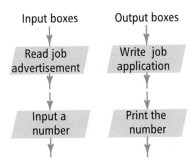

Decision boxes

These boxes are used to ask questions to which there are two answers: yes or no. 'Yes' and 'no' must be written by the paths to be taken for each answer.

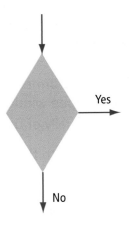

Decisions choose between two routes depending on whether the decision inside the box is true or false

One flow line goes into the decision box and two lines leave it. The question inside the box must be one which has the answer yes or no. Some examples of decision boxes are shown below.

A question is asked inside the box that has a yes or no answer

In decision boxes, one of the flow lines can come out of the decision box to either the right or the left. The line coming out of the right or the left of the flowchart may eventually join up at a place further along the flow line.

System flowcharts

In order to understand how best to proceed when a new system is to be developed, you need to understand how the old system worked.

The people who develop new systems, called systems analysts, use diagrams a lot. They use them to explain how the task is done now and how it will be done using the new system that they are going to develop.

A system flowchart shows what happens to data when it is input, processed and output by the computer system. It shows a more general view of a whole system than a flowchart, which looks in detail at a particular area. The flow lines in a system flowchart show the flow of data in the system rather than the order in which the steps should be carried out.

System flowcharts show us the types of input and output methods and also the type of backing store used. The process boxes tell us what is happening to the data during processing.

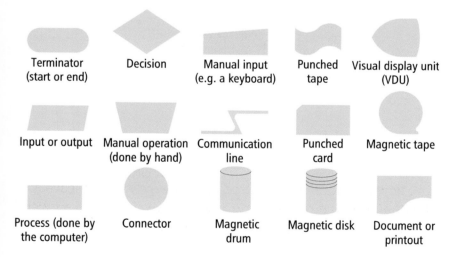

Symbols used in systems flowcharts

A computerised theatre/concert booking system

In a typical system, the booking agent types into the computer the venue number, concert date and concert time. The records of all the concerts are held on disk and, because they are on-line, these are accessed by computer very quickly. The computer then outputs the availability of seats. The details are entered into the system and the computer updates its files by reducing the number of available seats. Then the computer confirms that a booking has been made and the tickets are printed. It is then up to the booking clerk to collect the money (cheque, credit/debit card or cash).

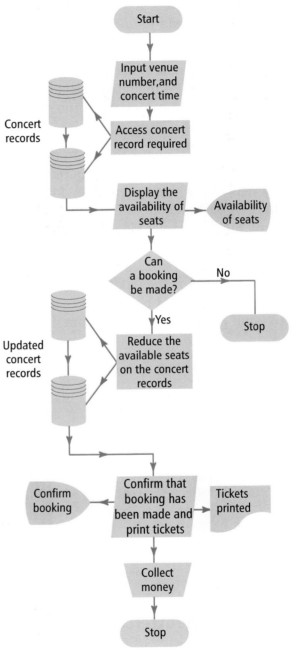

The system flowchart for a theatre booking system

Structure diagrams

Structure diagrams can be used to describe information systems. An overall task is broken down into smaller, more manageable tasks. These may then be broken down further into smaller tasks. This way of describing tasks is described as the 'top-down' approach.

The top-down approach

Let's take a look at drawing a structure diagram for a task we are probably all familiar with: doing the weekly shopping.

First we place the overall task at the top and we write a brief description of the overall task in the box, i.e. do the weekly shopping (see opposite).

Do weekly shopping ← Overall task

This task is then divided up into a series of tasks that make up the main task. For instance, to do the shopping we may have to:

- prepare a shopping list
- do the shopping
- put the shopping away.

So, we now have the structure shown below.

Prepare list | Do weekly shopping | Put shopping away

Again this second set of tasks may be split up as shown here.

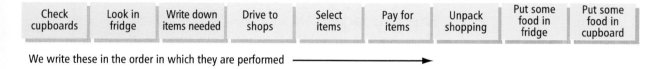

Check cupboards | Look in fridge | Write down items needed | Drive to shops | Select items | Pay for items | Unpack shopping | Put some food in fridge | Put some food in cupboard

We write these in the order in which they are performed ⟶

We can now put all the stages together to produce the final structure diagram shown below. Don't worry, when drawing structure diagrams, if yours looks different from other people's. They are rarely the same.

We write these in the order in which they are performed ⟶

As you can see, the purpose of a structure diagram is to show the tasks in more detail as you move down the diagram. The top box is the overall view (doing the weekly shopping), hence the term top-down approach. You can carry on breaking each task down until they contain as much detail as you need.

Dataflow diagrams

Dataflow diagrams are used to look at the data without considering the equipment used to store it. They are the first step in describing a system. They show where the data comes from and what data is needed for the processes in the system. Four symbols are used in these diagrams and these are described below.

The box
The box is either a *source* of data, such as an order form from a customer, or a part of the system which uses or consumes the data, called a *sink*. We are not concerned with what happens to the data before it reaches a source, or what happens to it after it goes past a sink.

The sausage
The sausage is replaced by a circle on some dataflow diagrams, and is used to denote a process performed on the data. A process is something that is done to the data, like a calculation. The process might be sorting the data or combining it with some other data. A brief description of the process should be placed inside the box.

The open rectangle
The open rectangle represents a data store. This is where the data is held. It could represent the data being held manually or on a computer. Basically, a data store is a logical collection of data. A description of the store can be placed inside the box.

The arrows
The arrows are used to show how the other symbols are connected. The show the data flow around the system.

Let's now draw a series of dataflow diagrams for a system for a video library. The first diagram follows the data flow that takes place when a new member joins the library. To join the library it is necessary to fill in an application form and to show certain documents to provide proof of identity. If the potential member does not have this documentation, then the library manager will refuse them membership.

After the membership details have been checked (or validated) a membership card is produced and given to the new member and the member's details are recorded. If the member borrows a video or if the manager wants to know whether a particular person is a member, then the details can be found. The figure below shows the dataflow diagram for this part of the system.

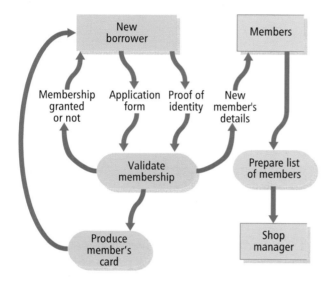

A dataflow diagram for a video library

Now we can look at the dataflow diagram for a video being added to the library. This is a simple system, with the details of the video, such as name, price, etc. being recorded and then stored. The following figure shows this part of the system.

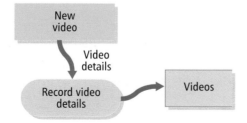

The dataflow diagram for adding a new video to the library

Below is the dataflow diagram for the process of borrowing a video. Notice that the member data and video data are needed because the loans store of data will only contain the video number and the membership number. This is done to save space. By storing the video and membership numbers together it is possible to find out a member's details and the video details if they are needed.

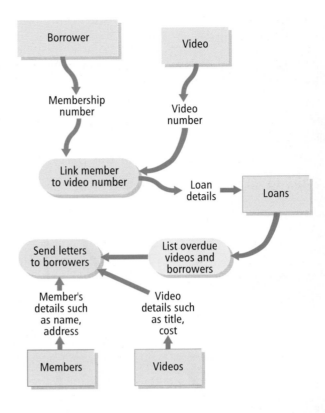

The dataflow diagram for borrowing a video

We could, if we wanted to get an overall view of the system, join these diagrams together but it is much easier to draw them for each part of the system and then to draw a diagram with them all joined.

College enrolment system
A college needs to keep records of the students on all of the courses. It needs to keep information about its students. This data is collected when the students come to the college to enrol on courses. Here are the procedures that take place when a student enrols on a course:

1. *The student fills in an enrolment form.*
2. *The course tutor fills in details about the course such as the course number (each course has its own unique number), the number of hours, etc.*
3. *The student takes the enrolment form to the college office.*

4   The student is allocated a unique number, called the student number, by the college office.

5   The details such as name, address, telephone number, date of birth, National Insurance number, etc. are keyed in by the enrolment officer.

6   The enrolment officer looks to see if the course is free. If not, they look at a course fees booklet for the fee for the course. The student pays the course fees if applicable (many courses are free).

7   A photograph is taken of the student using a small digital camera.

8   A plastic card with a photograph of the student, the student name, student number and expiry date is printed. This is called the student ID card. There is also a barcode on the card that can be used to input the student number into any of the college systems. This card can act as a library card or a card to gain entry to certain college rooms.

9   A receipt is printed and given to the student with their student number printed on it.

Draw a dataflow diagram to illustrate this part of the enrolment system.

How ICT systems are designed and implemented

This section looks at how you would go about designing and implementing an ICT system that you produce yourself.

Designing your own system

By now you will have seen how ICT is used in a variety of organisations. You will also have seen how each organisation uses a number of ICT systems. Once a system has been developed, the organisation needs to constantly look at it to see if it needs any improvement. Sometimes, a new system is needed to do a job that was not done before. For example, a store may wish to start a loyalty scheme and it would need a system to administer this.

After you have investigated and understood the use of ICT in lots of different contexts (e.g. personnel, stock control, payroll, etc.) you will understand how ICT systems can be used to solve problems. You can then investigate and develop a system for yourself. The system you develop can replace an existing ICT system or it might take the place of a manual system that cannot cope with the workload.

You could decide to develop one of the following types of system:

- You could design a computer system to replace an existing manual system.
- You could design a new improved computer system to replace an older computer system.
- You could produce a new system for a task that is not being done at the moment.

Whichever one you choose, you will need to find out about either the existing system or the way the new system is to work. In other words, you must understand thoroughly the problem that you are trying to solve. Finding out about an existing system is called fact finding. Although it is important to collect as much information as possible before starting on the design of a new system, fact finding can be done at any stage when more information is needed.

Identify the user requirements

Once you have decided on a system to develop you need to find out some information about the way the system works at the moment. If it is a brand new system, you will need to consider how the system should work. If possible you should ask the potential users of the system what they want the system to do. This is called identifying the user requirements. It is always important to develop a system that the user wants and not the system you think they want.

In order to identify the user requirements it is best first to assemble some facts about the area of the business you are going to look at. If there is an existing system it is useful to find about it by using a fact find.

Fact finding

There are four main ways of finding out about a system:

- asking questions by interviewing people
- letting people fill in carefully designed questionnaires
- sitting with various people to observe how the job is done at the moment
- inspecting any paperwork, screen displays and files used in the present system.

If there is no existing system then you will have to produce a new system from scratch. Suppose you decide to develop a personnel system based around a database. You would need to find out about what information such a system would normally hold. There are many ways you could do this, including:

- Ask friends and relatives who work in an organisation where they can find the information for you.
- Use the Internet. You could, for instance, look for companies that supply personnel software packages. This will give an idea of the sort of information that is normally needed.
- You can use textbooks. Do not restrict yourself to just ICT books. You may find the information you need in business studies textbooks. There may also be specialist books available in your local or main city library. Make use of librarians to help you find the information.
- Contact a local organisation yourself. This is quite hard to do, as people are very busy and may not be able to spare you much of their time. It is still worth a try though.
- Get your teacher to arrange a visit to a nearby company or organisation.

Produce a design specification

The next stage is to start to consider the design of the system. When the design is complete, a document called a design specification is produced. The design specification will say what inputs, processes and outputs are needed. It will also say what software is needed. In the design specification, any choices of inputs, processes, outputs and software need to be justified.

We will now look at each part of the design specification in more detail.

Information sources

Information or data is needed to supply the system. There needs to be a system in place to supply this. Sometimes the information will come from a customer via a phone call or an order form. When designing a system you need to consider where the information coming into the system comes from. When you draw your dataflow diagrams you will have to consider where the data comes from.

Output requirements

The outputs are the results from the computer system. Outputs need to be looked at first because they determine what input and processing needs to be done. You cannot get useful information out of a computer unless it can be obtained from the input data.

In this part of the design specification you need to look at:

- What output is needed? For instance, you may decide that, for your system, you need the following:
  - an invoice (bill) which is sent out to each customer
  - a copy of the invoice to be sent to the accounts office
  - a dispatch note to be sent with the goods
  - a picking list for the storekeeper
  - a screen display so that you can find out if a particular item is in stock.
- What needs to be on these documents and screens.

Process requirements

Process requirements are all the clerical and computer procedures needed to produce the output. Once the data has been entered into the system it will be subject to various processes. Processes are things that the processor does to the data to produce the output. For example, in a payroll system it multiplies the hours worked by the hourly rate to give the gross pay. It then calculates National Insurance and tax deductions.

Processing is not just calculating. Searching, sorting and storing are all classed as processes.

Dataflow diagrams can be used to define in more detail the processes that are needed. Any calculations or decisions that need to be made should be identified.

You can look at the processes that are in your dataflow diagram and describe them in more detail by writing the process as a series of steps. This is called a process description.

Input requirements

Here are some questions that you will need to answer about the inputs to the system:

- Where does the data come from? How does the data arrive in the organisation?
- What data needs to be input to the system? Look at what output is needed to make sure that you have the right inputs to produce the output.
- How much data needs to be entered and how often does it need entering?
- Which input device should be chosen? This really depends on how much data needs to be entered. Your system is likely to be small, so in most cases the input device will be a keyboard. It is important to remember that you are going to develop the project, so don't use an input devices you don't have access to in your school/college.

You will also need to design input screens to make it easy for users to enter information.

The types of applications software needed

This part of the design specification outlines the applications software needed. It is important to give reasons why a particular type of applications software was selected.

As well as giving the brand name of a package you should give the name of the type of package that you are using (i.e. wordprocessing, spreadsheet, etc.).

Implement the system

In this section you will put your design specification into action by starting to build the system. Building the system and getting it to work with the users' data is called **implementing** the system. If the new system replaces a manual system, then any

THE JARGON DRAGON

implementation – the process of converting to a new system

data on paper files will need to be input to the computer system.

It is important to make sure that the system you build is exactly what the user wanted. It is important to compare the system with the user requirements to make sure that they match.

Output

The output is the results you get from the system. It might be an invoice (another name for a bill), it might be the monthly repayment figure for a loan or it could be a list of people arranged in alphabetical order.

The output is usually displayed on the screen, printed out or both. The output is usually considered first, because from the output you can determine what data needs to be input. You cannot output anything that has not been input or cannot be calculated from the input data.

If you are going to use database software, then the output is often called a **report**. Reports include telephone lists, lists of orders, invoices and account statements.

Screen reports are reports that are simply displayed on the screen. Usually there is the option to print them out although in most cases this is not needed. They can be used for answering enquiries such as:

THE JARGON DRAGON

report – the production of output from software such as a database for a specific purpose

- Is a particular book in stock?
- When is the next train from Manchester to London?
- How much is the cheapest flight from Barcelona to London?
- I would like to pay off my credit card balance. How much do I owe?

If a document is needed that can be taken away and studied, then a printout on paper is better. Printed reports would include the following:

- lists of goods on order
- lists of customers with overdue accounts
- lists of members of a video hire store who have not brought their videos back
- lists of students enrolled on a college course.

Data capture

Data capture involves getting the raw data into a form that can be processed by the computer. Unless your school has a barcode reader or OCR software and a scanner, then you will use a keyboard for your data capture.

Verification and validation

Only accurate data should be processed. If mistakes are made when the data is entered into the computer, then the wrong data will be processed. The results (i.e. the output) from the system will be wrong. Wrong output causes all kinds of problems. Some of these are shown below.

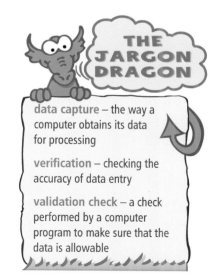

THE JARGON DRAGON

data capture – the way a computer obtains its data for processing

verification – checking the accuracy of data entry

validation check – a check performed by a computer program to make sure that the data is allowable

Here are some possible errors that you need to consider when designing and building your system:

- typing the same information twice
- leaving a field in a database blank when it should contain data
- transposing words, letters and numbers (i.e. putting them in the wrong order)
- misreading a word or number from a document you are copying.

Verification simply involves checking that the data being entered matches exactly the data on the document used to supply the information. This document could be a bill, an order, an application form and so on. In other words, verification checks that no errors are introduced during typing.

Verification in many cases involves proof-reading what has been typed in by comparing it against the original source of the information. Any document should be proof-read before it is used by someone else.

Validation is a check that is performed by the computer program. When creating the structure of a database you can make up validation checks which restrict the data that can be entered, to particular values or a range of values.

Testing the system under a range of conditions

Before a new system is used, it must be tested thoroughly. The testing of a system can be broken down into four stages:

1 The system is tested with data that contains no errors to see if it produces the correct results.
2 Known errors are introduced into the data to see how the computer processes them. It is important to know what should happen when an error occurs, and compare this with what actually happens.
3 The output is produced and checked to make sure that the results are as expected.
4 Extreme data should be entered to make sure that the range checks included as part of the validation checks are working.

Test plans

To make sure that the system is tested thoroughly, a test plan is produced. Test plans should be comprehensive. A good way of making sure that they are is to:

- number each test
- specify clearly the data to be used in each test
- state the reason for each test
- state the expected result for each test
- leave space for the actual result and/or comment on the result, and a page number reference to where the hard copy evidence can be found.

Here is a test plan to test a spreadsheet for analysing the marks in an examination. A mark is input next to each candidate's name. The mark is a percentage and can only be in the range 0% to 100%. In this exam, half marks are possible.

Test no.	Test mark entered	Purpose of test	Expected result	Actual result
1	45.5	Test valid data	Accept	
2	100	Test extreme data	Accept	
3	0	Test extreme data	Accept	
4	123	Test out-of-range data	Error message	
5	−3	Test out-of-range data	Error message	
6	45D	Test invalid characters	Error message	

The 'actual result' column would be filled in when the test mark was entered. If the expected results and the actual results are all the same then the validation checks are working correctly. If the two do not agree, then the validation checks need to be modified and re-tested.

Produce user documentation (or user guide) for the system

A user guide or manual is **documentation** that the user can turn to for learning a new procedure or for dealing with a problem that has arisen. The guide should cover advice like how to load the software, how to perform certain functions, how to save and how to print. It is a good idea to include examples and exercises to help the user understand the system. Since

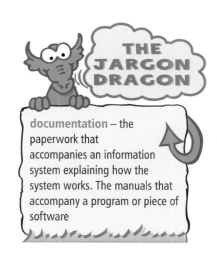

THE JARGON DRAGON

documentation – the paperwork that accompanies an information system explaining how the system works. The manuals that accompany a program or piece of software

users are usually non-technical, any specialist, technical language should be avoided or defined.

The guide should detail what to do in exceptional circumstances. For instance, if the system fails to read a disk or data is sent to the printer without it being switched on and the machine is locked, a user will need to know what they have to do. You should also include backing up and closing down instructions.

As always, users have the best view of a system and so should be asked to evaluate any proposed user guide. Their comments should be incorporated into the guide. You have probably used manuals yourself so you will know how important it is to be able to find the information you need easily.

Evaluate the design and implementation of the system

As soon as a system is developed it should be checked against the user requirements to make sure that the system does everything the user wanted. To do this, you can produce a list of the user requirements and then tick them off once you are sure they have been met.

After a project has been implemented it should be reviewed periodically to make sure that it is still meeting its objectives.

A good way of evaluating a system is to ask the users. They are able to tell you if a system does what they originally wanted or if there are any improvements needed. It is a good idea to produce a user questionnaire to find out what each user thinks of the system. You could, for example, ask them how easy they found it to use. You can then use the answers to the questionnaire to make modifications or improvements to the system.

The form on the next page was used to get the users' opinions on a template used to produce a leaflet on conferences at a country house hotel. The main aim of the template was to look good and to make it easy to change the information in the leaflet that varies, such as title of conference, date, room, etc.

There are always constraints placed on the system and these might include time, money and the lack of qualified staff involved in the project. All solutions have some limitations placed on them. For example, you may have been limited by the hardware or software that your school/college has. It is important to describe how you could have improved on the system had the resources been available.

Feature of template	User's comment
Do you think that the template is easy to use?	
Did you find it quick to produce a final leaflet?	
Do you think that the information is easy enough to change?	
Did you find the user guide easy to understand?	

RESEARCH TASK

Video hire store

This task refers to the video hire store described in the case study at the end of this unit. In this task you will design and develop a new system to replace the existing manual one. You will also have to evaluate and test the system.

Here are instructions for each task in more detail.

Task one

Briefly outline each of the following:

- *the purpose of the system*
- *the benefits of the system*
- *the information requirements of the system.*

Task two

Produce a dataflow diagram for the computerised system for the video hire store. You can use the example in the dataflow diagram section to guide you, but this system is slightly different so do not simply copy it.

Task three

Produce a list of the user requirements for this system. This is a list of what the system must do. You will use this list later to make sure that your system does all the things you intended to do.

Task four

This task involves creating the database. Here are the steps involved in doing this:

- deciding on the fields in each of the tables
- creating the structure of each table and including some validation checks
- creating the relationships between the tables
- creating forms so that the data can be entered into each table
- entering data into each table (a minimum of 30 records should be entered)
- creating queries and reports.

You should provide an outline of how you have created the database. Include any screenshots to help illustrate your description. Also include copies of any output (screenshots or printouts) from the system.

You should also produce a brief user guide for the system.

Task five

In this task you have to test the system.

The testing should include:

- a test plan
- making comments about improvements you've made to the system.
- checking that your system matches the user requirements (you can include the list of user requirements here and tick them if they have been met)
- putting valid and invalid data into the tables to check that the validation checks are working properly.

Task six

This task involves evaluating the system. This section should include:

- an evaluation of how your solution met the user requirements
- a questionnaire or similar form to determine from the users what they thought about the new system.

Cozy Plastics is a large company which manufactures plastic kitchen items such as bowls and buckets. It employs around 380 staff.

The manual personnel system

A manual personnel system is used at present, and it is having problems supplying the information needs of the company. Each employee has a file and all the employee files are kept in a series of filing cabinets. The main problems with the existing system are:

- Updating the manual files involves crossing out the old information and writing the new information at the side, if there is enough room. The employee records start to look very messy if lots of changes are made.
- Since the company is expanding and employing more staff it is becoming harder to keep track of absences due to holidays, sickness, etc.
- The manual records are organised in alphabetical order according to surname. Sometimes information such as 'how many disabled people do we employ?' needs to be extracted and this involves looking at each record and making a note of the relevant information. This is very time consuming.
- Sometimes a file is found to have been removed by someone from another department. This causes a problem if it is needed by the personnel department.

The purpose of the new computerised personnel system

Here are the main purposes of the new system:

- To hold comprehensive and up-to-date records about all the personnel employed by the company.
- To provide links to the payroll system so that it is possible to find up-to-date information about how much each person is paid.
- To record the details of all absences from work, along with the reasons for those absences, e.g. holidays, sickness, jury service, maternity leave.
- To record details about training courses attended and extra skills and qualifications obtained.
- The database system should also provide a link to wordprocessing software so that mail-merged letters can be produced.

Information requirements

Much of the information for the database will come from the application forms and references obtained when employees join the company. Some information will come from the payroll department and there will need to be a network link to this department. To keep the information up to date the employees will need to fill in a form with the latest information on it.

Advantages and disadvantages of the new system

Advantages

1   The information from the new system will be more comprehensive, so staff with certain qualifications can be found quickly.
2   The information is available at all times to every user (unlike the old system where if a file was removed it could not be used by anyone else).
3   It is easy to collect statistical information using the system (e.g. What is the average age of an employee? Which staff are qualified first-aiders?).
4   Printouts (called reports) are obtained easily.
5   Several people can access the same data at the same time using the network.
6   E-mail makes it easier for the personnel department to communicate with staff and their managers.
7   Searches can be performed quickly.

Disadvantages

1   The personnel staff will need to be trained to use the new system.
2   All the staff must cooperate by keeping the department informed about changes that need to be input to the system (e.g. changes in address, changes in job, etc.).

Main components

Three terminals are to be used in the personnel department to access the data held in a database on a file server. A laser printer is shared between these terminals and these terminals can also be used to send e-mail to any of the terminals in the building.

Data is typed into the personnel system using a keyboard.

The data is verified by the person who is keying in the data by carefully proof-reading it against the data on the form. Access to the Internet is provided for all the staff in the department so that they can contact other staff members by e-mail as well as telephone. Many potential applicants for jobs have e-mail addresses and the personnel department would like to send these applicants electronic forms to fill in using e-mail.

Working practices

Because the personnel system holds personal details about individuals, the use of the system has to be registered with the Data Protection Commissioner according to the 1998 Data Protection Act. The data subjects (i.e. the people who the personal data is about) are allowed to see the data held, so the company will have to make sure that the data held is correct. They must also make sure that the information is not disclosed to anyone outside the department.

Verfication of data

Data in the personnel database has to be accurate. If it isn't, then staff could be paid incorrectly or details about jobs could be sent to the wrong address.

When details about employees are typed into the system, they should be verified by carefully proof-reading them against the form used to supply the details. Sometimes, the employee will be asked to read the information on the computer screen to check its accuracy.

Validation of data

The database should have validation checks built into it. These will make sure that the data entered is only accepted if it is valid. For example, an employee's date of birth cannot be a future date. There is a limit to the amount of wages paid by the company.

There are also simple checks to make sure that letters are not placed where numbers should go and vice versa. Examples of the data should be supplied to the database designer so they know what type of data is valid.

Tests can be performed by the database designer to ensure that the validation checks work. The tests and their results are kept so that they can be referred to if there are any problems in the future.

File security

The files are to be stored on the main file server for the company, along with all the other files in the company. These files are backed up automatically at regular intervals throughout the day. Each night the backup copies stored on removable hard disk drives are removed and locked away in a fireproof safe.

Security of the new system

To gain access to the personnel system, a user name and password have to be input. The user name identifies the user of the system. The password is then input and this password must be changed every two weeks. The system will not allow you to use the same password more than once.

The database itself

The personnel database consists of three tables and these are:

- the personal details table
- the absences table (for absences other than planned holidays)
- the holiday table (for absences due to annual leave).

Changes in working practices

There are a number of changes in working practices that are necessary for the smooth running of the new system.

These include:

* Forms must be filled in at regular intervals so that the personnel department can ensure that their records are kept up to date.
* All the staff must cooperate by returning forms (for absences, changes of address, etc.) at the correct time.
* The personnel staff must make sure that their terminals are not left unattended whilst displaying personnel records on the screen.

Costs of the system

Although the system will cost £5,000 to design and implement, it will enable accurate information to be obtained quickly. Use of the Internet to send out job details means that postage costs will decrease. Some of the personnel staff can be moved to a more profitable part of the business.

Future trends

All staff will eventually have access to the Internet. This means internal jobs, courses, holidays, sickness, etc. can be notified directly without the need to visit or phone the personnel department. A company newsletters produced by the personnel department is currently printed and distributed to each member of staff. This could be replaced with an on-line version, and this will reduce the printing and distribution costs.

Questions

1 *Explain the difference between the terms 'verification' and 'validation'.*

2 *Describe two ways that communication will improve because of the introduction of the new system.*

3 *Explain briefly how data is:*
   (a) verified
   (b) validated
   in this system.

4 *Draw a dataflow diagram to show the system when a new employee joins the company.*

5 *Give one example of a working practice that will change due to the introduction of the new system.*

Groovy Movies

Groovy Movies is a video hire store that hires out videos from a shop on a high street. It employs three part-time and one full-time members of staff. It currently uses a manual system to store the details about members, videos and rentals. The manual system is paper-based which means that details are written down on paper.

There are many problems with this manual system, including:

- Since details are written down, the system relies on everyone being able to understand each other's handwriting. Sometimes it is hard to read handwriting.
- Films thought to be available are actually on loan because the rental details have not been recorded properly.
- Late returns are sometimes not noticed by staff, resulting in money lost for the store.
- Letters to members who have outstanding videos are often not sent soon enough. This makes it hard to recover the late videos, as members feel embarrassed to bring them back if they are extremely late.
- It is hard for the staff to know which videos are being rented the most often.
- It is hard for the staff to identify those videos to get rid of to make room for the latest videos.

All this means that the customer is not getting a good level of service. The staff waste too much time recording details rather than helping the customer.

The current system
When a new member joins, they fill in a brief application form. Two forms of identification are needed. One important item of information needed is their date of birth. Date of birth is needed because it can be used by the shop to prevent customers renting videos they are too young to watch.

A card is filled in with the details on the application form. A membership number is added to the card using the next number in the sequence. This number is written on a membership card given to the customer.

The cards containing each member's details are put into a card box file arranged alphabetically according to surname.

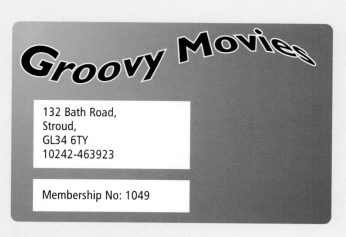

The front of the membership card given to all members

When a new video is bought, its details are recorded on a card. These cards are all numbered and filled in the sequence. The number is also added to a label on the side of the video case.

Rentals

Rentals are recorded in a diary that uses two pages for each day. The figure below shows a sample page for the date 5 March.

5th March 02

Membership Number	Video Number	Days Rented
1092	1023	1
1100	0451	1
0023	0071	2
0721	0912	1
0021	0234	1
0109	1189	

Information kept in the rentals diary

Most videos are hired for only one day. When a video is returned, the member of staff looks back through the diary for the video number, and checks to see if the video is late. If it is late then they work out the fine payable. If it is on time then the member of staff highlights the entry in the diary. Looking at the diary for 5 March on 7 March we can see that video 1189 is overdue and that video 0071 is due back today.

case study

Groovy Movies

5th March 02

Membership Number	Video Number	Days Rented
1092	1023	1
1100	0451	1
0023	0071	2
0721	0912	1
0021	0234	1
0109	1189	

The shaded entries in the diary show the videos that have been returned

When the shop is quiet, a member of staff looks through the diary to see if there are any videos overdue. They do not get in touch with members with overdue videos unless they are three or more days late. A member of staff will first contact them by phone or letter. The letters take a bit of time to produce, as they are handwritten.

The process of sending letters is quite complicated. From the diary the member of staff only knows how many days late the video is, along with the membership number and video number. To send the letter or speak to the member on the phone they need to obtain their details from the membership file. As the cards are in order of membership number, the card can be found and the personal details noted. They then find the title of the video from the video file, which is ordered according to video number. The letters can then be produced.

Which old videos should we get rid of?

The manager of the store has to make room for new videos by getting rid of old ones. It is hard for the manager to decide which videos to replace. One way is to select a video that they think is not borrowed very often and take a quick look through the diary over the last couple of months to see if the video number appears in the rental entries. This is very time consuming.

The new system

A computer consultant has taken a look at the shop and has suggested that a database be used. A database system will link customer records and video records to video rental records. The links will mean that the system can calculate fines for late returns of videos, and produce lists of the members who have not returned their videos. Ideally, the system will also be able to monitor trends so that the manager can decide which videos to get rid of and which to buy more of. The consultant who will be developing the new system sits down with the staff and asks them what information they need to know about the following:

- videos
- members
- rentals.

It is decided that the members file/table should contain the following fields:

Membership number
Surname
Forename
Street
Town
Postcode
Land telephone number
Mobile telephone number
E-mail address
Date of birth

The date of birth field is included so that staff can make sure that youngsters cannot rent videos that are only suitable for adults. The computer calculates a member's age by finding the difference between their date of birth and today's date.

The other files/tables are designed in a similar way.

The main components of the new system
The new system consists of a single computer connected to a laser printer.

Here are the main hardware components:

- input devices – keyboard and mouse
- processor – Pentium 4, 1.4 GHz
- output devices – 17 inch monitor, laser printer (black and white)

- ports and cables
- storage devices – 256 MB memory, 30 GB hard disk drive, CD-RW drive, floppy disk drive.

Here are the main software components:

- operating system – Microsoft Windows XP
- applications software – Microsoft Office XP. This includes Word (the wordprocessor), Access (the database) and Excel (the spreadsheet).

Future improvements

No system is ever perfect and there is always some room for improvement. Here are some improvements that could be made to the new system:

Using a barcode reader

One problem with the new system is that the staff type in the membership numbers and video numbers. Both these numbers are important and there are problems typing them in. When the shop is busy, staff make typing mistakes. This means that wrong rental details are stored. Members have complained about letters sent to them requesting them to return videos they have never borrowed.

A way around this is to use a barcode reader to record a barcode number on the video and another on the member's membership card. This will input the two numbers quicker and more accurately.

Using e-mail to keep in contact with members

A member's e-mail address is stored with their personal details in the members table. This could be used to send members details of special promotions. It is much cheaper to send the same e-mail to lots of members than to send them the same details in a letter through the post.

Using a simple network so that more than one person can access the database at the same time

At present there is only one computer. If someone is using it nobody else can access the database. In the future, the store would like to have another two computers connected to the original one, so they will need a simple network.

Networks are quite expensive to set up and run so this may not be practical until the business expands.

There is a current trend toward video-on-demand, where customers can pay as they view films and sports events. The video library may therefore need to move into this new area.

Groovy Movies

case study

This unit will help you to:

- understand how much ICT systems affect everyday life.
- understand how, through examples, ICT systems can improve our lives.

The unit will focus on how ICT has changed the way we live and work for individuals, families, clubs and societies, work teams and community groups.

ICT affects most people in their personal, social and professional lives; even people who do not have access to ICT are still affected by it. We will look at how work has changed due to ICT and how it creates some difficulties as well as improvements.

New ICT products and applications are constantly being developed and the pace of development is very fast. The unit will look to the future to try to see how our lives may still change, probably beyond all recognition.

Society is made up of different groups, all with their own needs for using ICT. In this unit we will look at how the needs of each of these groups influence their choice of ICT systems.

There are many positive effects of ICT, but there are also a number of negative effects, and these will be looked into.

You will examine ICT developments in the following areas and look at how the developments continue to be influential in these areas:

- business
- working styles and new employment opportunities.
- legislation
- entertainment and leisure
- personal communications.

ICT and society 3

In this unit you will learn about:

Available technologies	226
How ICT is used in business	247
How ICT has affected work styles	260
Legislation	267
How ICT has affected personal communications	279
How ICT is used in community activities	293
ICT and people with special needs	300

Available technologies

Internet technologies

The Internet can be described as a network of networks. When your own computer is connected to the Internet it becomes part of the Internet, and the size of the Internet has increased by a tiny amount.

The Internet

The Internet is a global network and anyone who has access to it can contact websites throughout the world, and correspond with anyone connected to it by using e-mail. Almost any kind of information can be found on this network. You can access anything from the latest news and sports results to research information on a certain illness.

World Wide Web (WWW)

The World Wide Web is part of the Internet where graphics, sound, video and animation are used as well as text. The word used for this type of media is 'hypertext'. Special hypertext links are built into the World Wide Web to allow the user to move around the Internet by using the mouse to click on words or graphics on the screen. Special software, called web browser software, is needed to take full advantage of the World Wide Web.

Websites

Websites allow communication between an organisation or individual and the outside world. For commercial organisations, it allows potential customers to learn about the organisation, its products or services. Some websites allow the user to place electronic orders. The cost of conducting business on the web is low compared with other more traditional methods. Individuals often produce their own website so that people who have similar interests can contact them. When you make your own website, it is stored on space that has been allocated to you by the company that provides you with your Internet connection (called an **Internet service provider**).

THE JARGON DRAGON

Internet service provider (ISP) – a company that provides a permanent connection to the Internet

E-mail

Electronic mail, called e-mail for short, is used to send messages from one terminal to another. The message can be sent to another terminal in the same building, or to one in a completely different part of the world.

To communicate using e-mail you need to have an e-mail address of your own. If you are not connected to an internal e-mail system then you need to be connected to the Internet. You also need to know the e-mail address of the person who will receive the e-mail. You can then write the e-mail message using special software that is normally provided as part of your Internet connection. Then the e-mail is then sent and stored on the **file server** of the recipient's Internet service provider. As soon as the person to whom you have sent the message logs onto the system they can access their mailbox and read any messages that have been sent to them.

THE JARGON DRAGON

file server – a network computer used for storing all the users' programs and data

Writing e-mail off- and on-line

If you want to write an e-mail message then you can simply log on to your system and write it. In this case you are said to be writing the e-mail on-line. If you have to pay a telephone charge (though many Internet service providers charge a fixed monthly fee and all the calls are free), then you will be charged for the telephone call as you are writing your message/letter.

If you have to pay for your telephone calls then you can write your e-mails off-line and then just go on-line to send it.

E-mails are usually short, to-the-point messages. If you want to write a long letter then you should use your wordprocessor to write it, and once it has been checked you should save it. You can then write a short e-mail explaining to the person receiving the letter that the file is going to be attached to the e-mail. You will also need to mention what wordprocessing package and version you have used. If you know the recipient has a different wordprocessing package, then you can always save it as a text file, as all wordprocessors can read these.

You then need to attach the document file to the e-mail. We will look at how file attachments are made a bit later on.

Replying to an e-mail

When you receive e-mail you will notice that there is a button to click for your reply. All you have to do is then type in your reply, as the e-mail address is included automatically. You can also send the message that was sent to you so that your reply is set in context. It also means that the receiver does not have to look for their original letter.

The figure below shows the e-mail preparation screen from AOL. Notice that you can format the text (bold, italics, etc.). Notice also that there is an address book and you can attach files using Attachments.

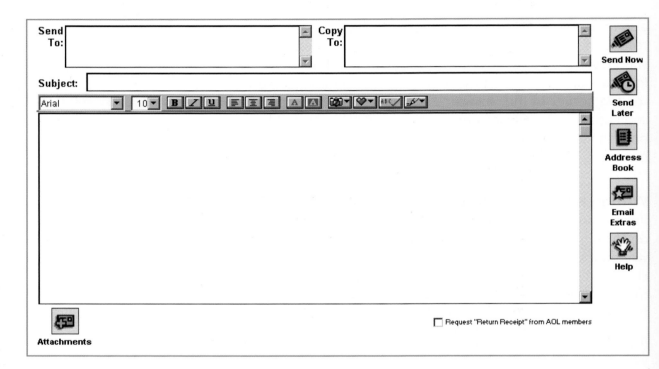

Address book

Internet service providers have a feature called an address book for managing your e-mail addresses. In the address book are the names and e-mail addresses of all the people whom you are likely to send e-mail. Instead of having to type in the address when writing an e-mail, you just have to click on the e-mail address or addresses in the address book.

Mailing lists

Mailing lists are lists of people and their e-mail addresses. They are used when a copy of an e-mail needs to be distributed to people in a particular group. For example, if you were working as part of a team and often needed to send each member of the team the same e-mail, then you would set up a mailing list. Every time you needed to send the members of the team e-mail, then you could use the list to save time.

File attachments

You can attach files to e-mails. For example, you could attach a file containing a photograph of yourself obtained from a digital camera, a piece of clip art, a picture that you have scanned in, a long document, etc. Basically, if you can store something as a file, then you can attach it to an e-mail.

You can attach more than one file to an e-mail, so if you had six photographs to send, then you could attach them and send them all at once.

Before you attach a file, you must first prepare an e-mail message to send explaining the purpose of your e-mail and also giving some information about the files that you are sending (what their purpose is, what file format they are in, etc.).

Once the e-mail message has been completed, you click on the File Attachment button. A box will appear to allow you to select the drive, folder and eventually the file that you want to send.

If you want to send more than one file, repeat the file attachment process. Usually, if there is more than one file to send then the files will be compressed to reduce the time taken to send them.

Is an e-mail private?

E-mail is not as private as ordinary mail. With ordinary mail you can usually tell if the envelope has been opened and stuck down again, but with e-mail it is impossible to tell if somebody has read it. Because of the way e-mail is distributed over the Internet it is possible for others to copy, forge or intercept messages. You should never divulge passwords or credit card details using e-mail, even if the request for the information looks official.

Advantages and disadvantages of using e-mail

In America, more e-mails are sent than traditional letters, and this will soon happen in the UK. Here are the advantages and the disadvantages of using e-mail compared with using traditional letters.

Advantages

1   It is very fast, as mail is sent immediately and a reply can be sent as soon as the receiver checks their e-mail. Ordinary post takes several days.
2   E-mails are quick to write because they lack the formal structure of a letter.

3 You can attach a copy of the sender's e-mail with your reply, so this saves them having to search for the original message.

4 E-mail is cheaper than a letter. No stamp, envelope or paper is needed. There is also a time saving, so this also makes e-mail cheaper. Even if the e-mail is sent across the world it will not cost any more than a local e-mail.

5 You do not have to go out to a post box.

6 You do not have to waste time shopping for stamps, envelopes and paper.

Disadvantages

1 Not everyone has the equipment to send and receive e-mail. However, with Internet access from televisions, land line phones and mobile phones it will soon take over from traditional post.

2 Junk mail is a problem. You can waste time looking through e-mails that are just adverts.

3 E-mails are not as secure as traditional letters.

4 The system relies on people checking their e-mail regularly.

5 The technology involved may deter non-technical people from using e-mail.

6 The equipment to send and receive e-mail is quite expensive compared with traditional methods.

THE JARGON DRAGON

multimedia – software that combines more than one medium for presentation purposes, such as sound, graphics and video

interactive – a program or system that allows the user to respond to questions from the computer (and vice versa) and the computer immediately acts on the answers

Multimedia

Multimedia is the mixture of text and graphics with motion and sound, including video, audio, animation and photographs. Multimedia is **interactive**, which means that the user can decide on different routes through the software. The paths taken are usually controlled by moving and clicking a mouse. Multimedia is ideal for learning because you can control the program to work as slowly or as quickly as you like, and it will not tell you off if you get things wrong. In a way, multimedia is an ideal teacher. Learning topics you find boring can be made more fun using multimedia. Nearly all computers today are capable of running multimedia. Multimedia software is distributed on either CD-ROM or DVD.

Encryption

Encryption is about keeping data secret.

Can you keep a secret?

If you want to send a letter to another person and its contents are to be kept secret, then you could write your letter in a secret code. If someone other than the intended recipient opens the letter and reads it, it will make no sense to them. The proper recipient will know how to decode it so it will make sense to her.

A simple code might be to reverse the letters of the alphabet like this:

Letter	Code	Letter	Code
A	Z	M	N
B	Y	N	M
C	X	O	L
D	W	P	K
E	V	Q	J
F	U	R	I
G	T	S	H
H	S	T	G
I	R	U	F
J	Q	V	E
K	P	W	D
I	O	X	C
		Y	B
		Z	A

Once both the sender and the recipient of the message have the 'key' to the code (i.e. the method used to code and decode) then they can 'scramble' the message:

Meet me outside the embassy

becomes:

Nvvg nv lfghrwv gsv vnyzhhb

Is this a good code? It is a very obvious one and anyone used to dealing with codes and intent on reading your message could soon work out how to decode it. They could use the average frequency of common letters to find out, for example, which letters are the vowels such as 'a' and 'e'.

If you want a code that is hard to decipher, then you will have to make it more complicated than this.

You can see that a code is only of use if both the sender and recipient can code and decode the message. The way that this is done is called the key. This is how secret or confidential data is coded before sending it electronically, but in this case the computer takes care of the coding and decoding.

Are e-mails confidential?

E-mail is a very popular method of communicating but can it be read by people other than the recipient? The answer is yes, if they really want to. Some people say that communicating using e-mail is like sending a postcard – everyone who handles the postcard can read what it says on it. Perhaps what you are communicating would not be that interesting to others, but if you were a famous pop star, actor/actress, footballer or member of the royal family, for example, then many people (including the tabloid press) would be interested in reading your private messages.

You should always be careful that you do not disclose any personal details in an e-mail. You should never divulge credit card details even if you are asked to using e-mail. Credit card details should always be transferred over a link using encryption.

encryption – scrambling data so that it can be read only by the authorised sender and recipient

What can be done to keep private data private?

One thing a user can do is to use a method called encryption where messages sent over the Internet are encrypted (i.e. turned into a secret code). The **encryption** is done by the computer, and the code is then decrypted (decoded) by the receiver's computer. Encryption systems are so secure that they are used for transferring credit card information when a user buys goods using a credit card over the Internet.

One such encryption program is called PGP (pretty good privacy) and it is the main encryption program used worldwide. It is very popular because it is completely free and readily available. You may think that if so many people use PGP, then won't they know how to intercept and decode data sent by others? The answer is that it is much more complex than the simple example of a coding system mentioned before, and the data cannot be read by anyone while it travels from place to place on the Internet.

Encryption sounds a great idea but are there any problems with it?

One problem with encryption is that, because nobody other than the recipient (i.e. the person to whom the message is sent) is able to read the message, information that may be damaging to others can be sent in complete secrecy. The police, MI5 and government departments cannot intercept the message and read it. For example, the police may want to monitor the correspondence of a person they suspect of drug dealing. The suspected drug dealers may use e-mail to arrange drop-off points for drugs shipments. Terrorist organisations may keep in touch with their members and plan bombings all with the help of encryption, safe in the knowledge that their e-mails are completely private.

If we have nothing to hide, why does it matter if people read our e-mails?

You may think that if you have nothing to hide, then you do not need to worry about others reading your e-mails. Most people will agree that freedom of speech (i.e. the freedom to say what you like without the fear of persecution or imprisonment) is fundamental to everyone's happiness. In some countries freedom of speech is not a right and you cannot disagree with the government. If you are found saying things the government doesn't like, you could be imprisoned or even killed. If you lived in such a country then there would be no way of letting people in other countries know what was going on. You couldn't send a letter because all the letters going out of the country are read, and e-mails are also monitored. Encryption would be the only way of letting others know how bad things were.

1   *Explain what is meant by the term 'privacy'.*
2   *Give an example of why freedom of speech is so important.*
3   *Why is it important that the government is able to read e-mails even when they are encrypted?*

ACTIVITY

Internet connections

This section covers the methods you can use to connect your computer to the Internet.

Modem

A **modem** (short for modulator/demodulator) allows data to be passed along telephone lines from one computer to another. This device converts the digital signals produced by the

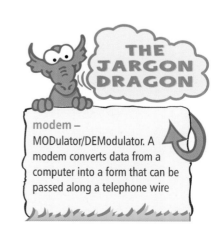

THE JARGON DRAGON

modem –
MODulator/DEModulator. A modem converts data from a computer into a form that can be passed along a telephone wire

computer into analogue signals. These analogue signals are sent along a telephone line to another modem, where they are converted back into digital signals for the receiving computer.

The speed at which data is transferred is measured in bits per second (bit/s or bps for short). The faster the modem, the quicker the data can be transferred and it is possible to get up to speeds of around 56,500 bits per second.

Bandwidth

Bandwidth is a term used to measure a communication channel's capacity for passing data from one place to another. A page of text (ordinary letters, numbers and punctuation marks) requires less bandwidth than a photograph, if each is transmitted in the same time period.

Bandwidth is how fast the data flows on a given transmission path, and all data has a bandwidth. With a digital system, the bandwidth is expressed as the data transmission speed in bps (bits per second) so a modem with a speed of 28,800 bps has half the bandwidth of a modem operating at 57,600 bps.

The bandwidth requirement for digital video is very high because the signal consists of data, images, sound and voice.

ISDN (Integrated Services Digital Network)

The trouble with modems is that they are slow at transferring data. **ISDN** does not need a modem. Instead a device called an ISDN terminal adapter is used. ISDN is still able to use the existing telephone cables so there is no need to dig up your path or garden to lay a new cable.

Connection to a site on the Internet takes around 15 seconds using a modem, but using ISDN this time can be reduced to about 0.075 seconds making use of two ISDN channels. If you downloaded a file using ISDN then the download time would be around one tenth of the time it takes to download the same file using a modem.

Deciding on whether to use ISDN or a modem depends on two main factors:

- the speed of data transfer
- the cost of transferring the data.

The speed of data transfer might be extremely important in some applications. For example, an X-ray photograph may need to be sent quickly to a doctor in another part of a hospital. In

THE JARGON DRAGON

bandwidth – the factor that determines how fast data can be passed along a communication channel

ISDN – Integrated Services Digital Network. A communications standard for sending voice, video and data over digital telephone lines. It is much faster than sending data using modems

videoconferencing systems, pictures, sound and data (documents, charts, etc.) need to be sent simultaneously, so speed of transfer is very important. In both of these cases ISDN should be used. If data is downloaded only occasionally, then a modem would be sufficient.

Since ISDN makes use of two channels, a single phone line can be split in two, so you could surf the Internet and have a telephone conversation at the same time.

Broadband

Broadband can be thought of as a wide bandwidth and is a method used to transmit more data along a single cable. It does this by using channels, with each channel being used for data. These channels can be used for voice communication (i.e. telephone conversations or voice mail), still images (diagrams, charts, photographs, etc.) video pictures and other types of data. Basically, instead of the single cable carrying a single signal, broadband divides the capacity of the cable in a way that allows multiple signals to be passed. You can think of broadband as a motorway with lots of lanes and, like the traffic, the data is able to travel in these separate lanes, which speeds up the flow.

broadband – a very high-speed Internet connection (usually cable)

The main features of broadband are:

* it is extremely fast
* it is always 'on' which means that you do not spend time dialing up and waiting for a connection.

Transferring data using a modem is like transferring water along a narrow pipe with a tap on it. The narrowness of the pipe means that it is hard to get a lot of water through it. To make the water flow you have to turn the tap on.

With broadband the pipe is much fatter so lots of water can flow. The water flows all the time so you do not have to wait for the tap to be turned on

DSL and ADSL

DSL (Digital Subscriber Loop) is a broadband service that combines separate voice and data channels over a single cable.

One type of broadband, called ADSL (Asymmetric Digital Subscriber Loop), allows greater bandwidth for the downstream traffic (i.e. the data from the site you are accessing to your computer) at the expense of lesser bandwidth for the upstream traffic.

Broadband offers 'streaming media' which means that you can send video directly over the link. This has led to video on demand, where you can simply choose a video and have it downloaded to your TV or special TV set as you watch it. It also allows video Internet commercials where you can see videos of products being used rather than just still pictures.

As more companies get involved in making the Internet more accessible by the merger of television and Internet technologies, working from home and lightning-speed Internet access are becoming a reality.

Some of the applications of broadband are:

- You can watch trailers for films straight from Hollywood, long before they appear in the UK.
- You can listen in high quality FM stereo to thousands of radio stations around the world.
- You can listen to **MP3** files of up-and-coming bands.
- You may be able to work from home, making use of videoconferencing which, up until now, has been poor in terms of quality of voice and pictures.
- You can have lightning access to the Internet, making trips to libraries for research a thing of the past.
- You can use a web camera in your house and set it up to e-mail you if anything moves in the house after your alarm has been set. You can also access any of the thousands of web cameras anywhere in the world.
- Parents who have to work away can keep in touch with their children using a web camera and the Internet.

THE JARGON DRAGON

MP3 – a file format for music files that makes use of compression

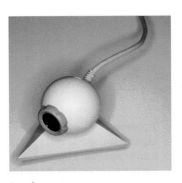

A web cam

Times taken to deliver a 1.5 megabyte file

Here is a table showing the times various connection methods take to transfer a 1.5 megabyte file. A 1.5 MB file is slightly more data than you can get on a completely full floppy disk.

Connection method	Time taken to transfer 1.5 MB file
56k Modem	3.5 minutes
ISDN	1.5 minutes
ADSL	25 seconds

A person is using a modem at present to connect them to the Internet. Because they spend a lot of time using the Internet, they would like to be able to surf the Internet faster.

1 Explain what the term 'surf the Internet' means.
2 Explain why broadband would be better than using a modem.
3 Broadband offers 'video on demand'. Explain what this means.
4 Give the names of two things that can be done using broadband that would be difficult to do using a connection via a modem.
5 Why is bandwidth so important when you are transferring large files from place to place?

Mobile telephone technologies

Mobile phones are one of the most popular modern-day inventions. Many people would be lost without them. When they were first developed they were simply the mobile equivalent of an ordinary telephone, so their only use was for having telephone conversations. The development of the Internet and other messaging systems means that mobile phones can now offer many new ways of communicating.

SMS (Simple Message Service)

Simple Message Service (or **SMS**) is the service that is commonly used to send and receive text messages using mobile phones. The message has to be basic text and is restricted to a message length of 160 characters (a character is a letter of the alphabet,

THE JARGON DRAGON

SMS – Simple Message Service. Service that mobile phones use to send and receive text messages

a number or a punctuation mark). When a text message is sent from your phone it will let the receiver know there is a message by causing their phone to give out a noise when it arrives. The message is then stored in the receiver's phone until they have a chance to read it.

WAP (Wireless Application Protocol)

WAP mobile phones are able to connect up to the Internet. Using a mobile phone with **WAP** allows you to receive text and simple images over the Internet. You can send and receive e-mail and text messages, as well as obtain limited Internet services that allow you to check the latest news, receive football results, order goods and services from e-commerce sites, etc. WAP banking allows you to check your balance, pay bills and transfer money, all from a special mobile phone.

WAP is quite difficult to use and many people find it frustrating and would prefer to wait until they have access to a personal computer. This is soon to change, as a service called 3G is set to replace WAP and make the Internet as easy to use on a mobile phone as it is using a PC.

THE JARGON DRAGON

WAP – Wireless Application Protocol. A mobile phone service that allows the phone to access the Internet

'This is the latest WAP-enabled, full-screen LCD, QWERTY keyboard, SMS, personal digital assistant, organiser mobile communicator. It has a flashing light on the top so that everyone notices how cool you are when you are using it!'

Task one

You are required to produce a report on the latest mobile telephones. In your report you will need to cover the following:

- the names and prices of the phones
- a list of the features that you would normally expect a mobile phone to have
- a list of the latest features and a brief description of how they can be used.

Task two

Produce a brief essay outlining how mobiles phones have improved society.

RESEARCH TASK

FIND IT OUT

Look at adverts for the latest mobile phones in newspapers or magazines. Find out what facilities they offer. You could also pick up some leaflets from mobile phone stores.

Try to find out some statistics on how many people now own mobile phones. Use the Internet for this research. Try to consider other members of society such as the disabled or senior citizens who may use a mobile phone as a lifeline in case of difficulties.

Think IT THROUGH

Consider how mobile phones are starting to offer a lot more than voice and text messaging. Try to find out what future developments are planned for mobile phones. You can use the websites of mobile phone manufacturers to get information. To find the names of manufacturers, use Index or Argos magazines, or look in the tabloid newspapers for adverts. Another way would be to ask all your friends who made their mobile phones.

You can also search the sites of computer/lifestyle magazines for further information.

Digital broadcasting

Television signals can be received by using an aerial or satellite, or by cable. In the future, television will be entirely **digital** and will offer a lot more than just television sound and pictures.

In the near future, all TV programmes will be transmitted digitally

THE JARGON DRAGON

digital – stored as a series of binary digits (0s and 1s)

interactive – a program or system that allows the user to respond to questions from the computer (and vice versa), and the computer immediately acts on the answers

broadband – a very high-speed Internet connection (usually cable)

MP3 – there are lots of ways to compress a music file but the most popular way is by using MP3

Interactive digital television combines the latest TV, computer and communications technology. This type of television allows users to interact with the broadcaster. For example, they can have full access to the Internet, home shopping, home banking, etc.

Video on demand is also possible. You simply log on to the system and the video you choose is sent via a cable straight to your TV set. A trip to the local video library to rent a film will be a thing of the past.

Cable systems provide what are known as **broadband** services. They are called broadband because huge amounts of data can be sent along the cable. This enables lightning-fast Internet access. Compared with using an ordinary modem, cable Internet is about nine times faster. Because of the high speed at which data can be transferred, you can play fast-action games and look at high quality video pictures over the Internet. You can also download music tracks in a special compressed format called MP3. With an ordinary modem it takes 14 minutes to download just one track, but with cable it takes around one minute.

RESEARCH TASK

You are required to research broadband services and write a small piece about them.

In your piece you will need to mention:

- *what broadband is*
- *the advantages that it gives compared with the use of a modem*
- *who provides broadband services and how much they charge.*

FIND IT OUT

Further information about broadband services can be found from the following website:

`www.askntl.com/broadband`

One of the companies which provides broadband is called Telewest, and its broadband service is called BlueYonder. See if you can find further information from their website.

Personal digital assistants and organisers

THE JARGON DRAGON

PDA – personal digital assistant. A small computer used mainly for organising a busy schedule

Personal digital assistants (**PDAs**) are small, hand-held devices that you can use if you need to organise a busy schedule. Their main advantage over a small PC, such as a laptop, is their small size. Most of them are little bigger than a diary or large calculator.

PDAs allow you to do the following:

- You can keep track of appointments and things you have to do on certain days.
- You can store the names and addresses of your contacts and friends.
- Many PDAs are able to download e-mail from your personal computer that you can then read off-line on the PDA.
- They have calculating facilities similar to those of a fully featured calculator.
- You can prepare, edit and send faxes, and also receive them.

A personal digital assistant (PDA)

Personal digital assistants (PDAs) are portable devices that keep track of your calendar, contacts and e-mail. They can also exchange information with PCs and other PDAs, download music, allow you to surf the Web and more.

The Nokia 9210

The latest mobile phones are able to do many of the things PDAs can do. Notice that this one has a full QWERTY keyboard located on either side of the display.

Storage media

Information storage systems are places where data is held. In the past most commercial information would have been stored on paper kept in filing cabinets. Now information is usually stored on magnetic or optical disks. A computer program helps you retrieve this stored information.

In the past music was stored in grooves on plastic records. These records took up a lot of space and the music quality went down as the records became scratched over time. Cassettes containing magnetic tape are smaller, but the quality of the sound is still low compared with CDs. It was not until the development of the CD player that music could be stored digitally. Digital music offers very high sound quality reproduction.

There have been large increases in the storage capacity of storage media (i.e. optical and magnetic disks). Storage media, and the devices to read the data stored on them, have also got a lot smaller. This has resulted in lots of new products that it would not have been possible to produce before. Portable DVD players, that allow you to play movie DVDs when you are on a long journey, are an example. DVDs enable devices to store huge quantities of information. Different language versions of a film can be stored, and they are also used to distribute course material for use on a computer.

Minidisks are used to store large amounts of music on minidisk players.

DVD drives

DVD disks look identical to CDs except they are able to store a lot more information. Like CD-ROMs, they can be used to store computer application programs, multimedia programs (e.g. encyclopaedias) and full-length films. Computer software packages are often supplied on six or seven CD-ROMs – these CD-ROMs could be replaced by a single DVD. This is because CD-ROMs typically store 650 MB (megabytes) of data whereas a DVD stores between 4.7 GB (gigabytes) and 17 GB (i.e. between 4,700 and 17,000 MB).

DVD read/write drives are now available. These allow you to record onto special DVD disks. Using these disks a massive 4.7 GB can be stored, and DVD read/write drives are set to replace the video-cassette recorder that we are all familiar with. DVDs produce much better pictures and sound compared with a normal video tape. A film stored on DVD can even be offered in a choice of several languages.

Touch screen technologies

Touch screen technology can be seen in many different places, such as:

THE
JARGON
DRAGON

touch screen – a touch screen is a special type of screen that is sensitive to touch. A selection is made from a menu on the screen by touching part of it

- banks
- building societies
- quiz machines in pubs
- information on special offers or loyalty schemes in supermarkets
- in large stores, for customers to locate CDs and videos.

Touch screen technology is ideal where customers or users are not used to keyboards. These customers can find out information simply by touching an area on the screen to make a selection. Touch screens are less affected by dirt than keyboards.

THE JARGON DRAGON

virtual reality – computer technology that creates a simulated multidimensional environment for the user

Virtual reality

Virtual reality is being used to help understand how the human heart works. The heart beats once every second, but when it stops there are four minutes before the person dies. To understand what happens when the heart fails, scientists need to understand what is happening to the heart during these four minutes. To do this, scientists have used a computer program to model the heart in 3D. This takes a huge amount of computer power, and to model just ten seconds of the heart's activity took scientists six months. Once a 3D model of the heart has been produced, surgeons will be able to feed a patient's details into the computer and use it to work out the best treatment for them.

Another use for virtual reality is to give medical students experience of what it is like to be exhausted due to a serious medical condition. When patients undergo chemotherapy for cancer it makes them extremely tired. To get an idea of what this is like, the potential doctors are sat in a chair with foot pedals, wearing a head-mounted virtual reality headset. Through the headset they can see the layout of a typical house. If the doorbell goes then they use the pedals to move around the rooms to answer it. The pedals are made hard to move, and this gives the medical students an idea of how difficult it is to do simple things. They can also alter the image in the headset to make it blurred, which gives the students the impression of dizziness. It is hoped that the system will make the potential doctors more aware of the problems that some patients face.

A 5 Series BMW is driven into a concrete wall and the driver moves forward against the seatbelts and into the airbag. The car is travelling fast and the bonnet is crushed completely. This crash is not happening in real life, it is happening on a computer screen. The engineer uses the computer to **model** the crash.

The damage inside the car can be seen by a click of the mouse. The inside of the car is revealed to see how the various parts have been affected by the crash. Most importantly, the engineers can see the effect on the driver of the car. If the car has been well designed, the part where the driver sits will not collapse so the driver will not be injured.

Before a new car is built it will have been 'crashed' over a hundred times in different directions. A powerful computer takes days to work out the damage of just one crash because of the millions of calculations it needs to make. The effect of the crash can be seen in slow motion and the designers can make alterations to the design of the car if needed. In the past they would have had to make prototypes (almost complete cars) costing as much

THE JARGON DRAGON

model – a computer program that mimics a real situation. Flight simulation software would be an example of a model

as £500,000 each, and then crash them. A very expensive process, bearing in mind that several cars would be needed! A crash using the computer costs as little as £250.

A BMW 5 Series prototype that has been crash tested (© MIRRC, Thatcham57)

Questions

1 *The crash testing system used by BMW is an example of virtual reality. Explain what is meant by the term 'virtual reality'.*

2 *Certain details about the car need to be input to the computer before the crash takes place. Give three inputs that might be needed.*

3 *Give two advantages of using the virtual reality system rather than a real car to find out what happens during a crash.*

How ICT is used in business

ICT is used in most businesses and other organisations to make them more efficient. Businesses remain competitive by making use of the latest ICT equipment. Customers notice the improvement that ICT brings by a decrease in the time needed to complete a transaction (a transaction is a piece of business). They also notice the speed with which goods arrive after being bought using ICT. In this section we will look closely at how businesses use the power of ICT.

Home shopping and e-commerce systems

Most goods or services can now be bought from the comfort of your own home. Home shopping services allow you to choose goods from a catalogue, then ring up a call centre and speak with an operator to give your order. Payment is organised (usually using a credit card) and the goods are then sent to you.

E-commerce goes a step further. You do not have to speak to anyone. You use the Internet to access the shop's website and then choose your goods or services from a computerised catalogue. You make the payment by entering your credit card details. The goods are then sent to you by a parcel firm or by post.

Buying your groceries on-line

In many areas of the country, Tesco (the large retailer) is using e-commerce, allowing customers to shop from home. Tesco packs and dispatches a customer's on-line orders from the nearest supermarket rather than fulfilling the order from large warehouses like other e-commerce companies. They charge a fee for delivery of the goods (currently £5) and also specify a two-hour slot so that you can be in when the goods arrive. So that you do not have to waste time ordering things you order every week, such as bread, milk, fruit, etc., these items are 'remembered' so it is possible to repeat that part of the order. The main advantage of the system is that busy people do not have to waste time shopping.

The Tesco e-commerce site can be found at:

`www.tesco.com`

RESEARCH TASK

Internet shopping
For this task you have to find out about ordering goods over the Internet.

1 *Produce a short questionnaire to give to friends, relatives and neighbours to find out whether they have ever bought anything on-line and how satisfied they were with the process.*

2 *Choose two websites for ordering goods and take a careful look at them.*

3 *Produce a form that can be used to evaluate each site and then fill it in.*

4 *Explain briefly why shopping over the Internet is ideal for certain groups of people.*

FIND IT OUT

A good way of finding out about a service such as ordering goods over the Internet is to try it out yourself. Failing that, you can ask others what their experiences have been like.

You could also evaluate certain sites, such as sites for ordering any of the following:

- *CDs*
- *books*
- *groceries*
- *flights*
- *holidays.*

Think IT THROUGH

To many people, ordering goods over the Internet is just a convenience. To people with mobility problems it is a godsend. They are no longer reliant on others to do their shopping for them.

Think about the ways that these services are useful to the disabled and older members of the community who have mobility problems.

Security of information on the Internet

Many people worry about using e-commerce sites. Their main worry is that their credit card number could fall into the wrong hands.

Most sites use encryption for personal details, including ten-digit credit card numbers. Encryption jumbles up the number as it passes to the receiver's computer system.

Unless credit card details are encrypted tapping could mean that they fall into the wrong hands

On-line auctions

In the past, if you wanted to buy an antique or a painting one of the best places to buy one would be at an auction. The problem is that auctions take place during the day when most people are at work, and they are often held only in main towns and cities. Now there are on-line auctions where you can bid on not just antiques and art, but also cars, houses, books, furniture and almost anything you can buy and sell. As with most e-commerce sites, you have to use either a debit or credit card to pay for your goods or services if your bid is successful. Take a look at the most popular auction site at the following web address:

www.ebay.com

Technical services

Many businesses provide technical computing services for other businesses.

Customised databases

For example, companies can set up customised databases for other businesses to use. This service is important since businesses do not always employ computer staff who have the necessary expertise to set up databases.

There are large savings to be made on the Internet. You can buy cars, CDs, books and electrical goods, take part in on-line auctions and so on. All this is fine, but you need one thing to take part: a valid credit card. A credit card gives you an electronic identity. If you do not have a credit card, then you will not be able to set up an Internet account with an Internet service provider, let alone buy goods or services.

Getting a credit card is not that easy. It is very hard if you do not have a job or have a bad credit history. Some members of society do not like using credit cards. They think that if you cannot afford it, then you do not have it.

The use of ICT means that there is less of a divide between work and home life. Companies give their staff laptops and mobile phones so that they can be more productive. Using these during non-work time for work-related tasks can cause friction at home. ICT should mean that it is possible to achieve more work in less time and so reduce the length of the working week.

Many people spend hours on the Internet chatting to people in chat rooms. These people may retreat into a cyber world where they are more at home meeting virtual people rather than people face to face.

Questions

1 *The use of ICT widens the gap between the 'haves' and the 'have-nots'. Briefly explain why this is so.*

2 *Not having a credit card can mean the difference between being able to access the Internet and not being able to access the Internet. Give one reason why a credit card is needed to access and also use the Internet.*

3 *ICT can cause problems in human relationships. Briefly describe a situation where this is so.*

Financial services

Financial services is the term used to describe those organisations that deal with the management of money. Financial services include banking, insurance, stockbroking (i.e. the buying and selling of stocks and shares), credit card companies, etc. Companies involved in financial services need to hold a lot of information about individuals. For example, they might need to know the financial history of a person applying for a loan. This means that they need to know whether they have had problems making the payments for previous loans or credit cards. This kind of information is essential to banks and loan companies, and such information is pooled so that other companies can use it.

Virtual banking

What does a bank do?

There are a number of things a bank does and here are the main ones:

- It keeps your money safe and allows you to withdraw it when needed.
- It issues you a cheque book so that you can pay bills and make other kinds of payments by post.
- A bank allows you to apply for loans and mortgages (mortgages are loans to buy a house).
- It issues you with credit cards.
- It allows you to take out money using ATMs. These are the 'hole in the wall' cash dispensers.
- You can set up standing orders and direct debits so that payments for bills are made automatically without you having to remember.
- It provides insurance services.

You may have noticed that many bank branches have recently closed. Banks are not closing because they have too few customers or because banking is not as popular as it used to be. Instead, they are closing because their customers are banking in a different way. Rather than visiting branches, they can bank from home by using either the Internet or a telephone. They find it more convenient to do so. They do not have to find somewhere to park for a trip to the bank and they do not have to wait in a long queue. Another big advantage is that they can bank 24 hours per day, 365 days per year.

Many banks have closed up to a quarter of their branches

Banking from home is called virtual banking because you do not attend a branch, and, in the case of Internet banking, you do not contact a member of the bank staff.

Virtual banking has changed the way people bank in many ways. In the past people opened a bank account when they first started work and stayed with that bank for their whole lives. Now the use of ICT has made it much easier to move your account, mortgage or loan. Many customers look at what other banks are offering and change their account if they find a better deal. Banks now have fewer loyal customers. It is common for credit card companies to entice new customers with offers such as zero per cent interest for the first six months.

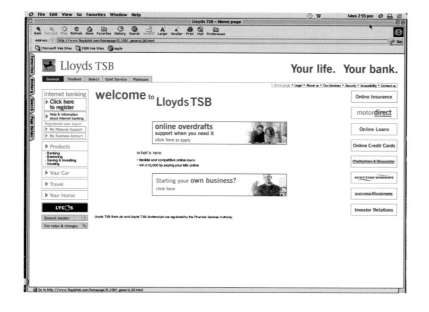

On-line banking – a page from Lloyds TSB website (reproduced by courtesy of Lloyds TSB Bank. ©Lloyds TSB Bank plc 2002. All rights reserved

There are some problems with virtual banking. Because there is no costly branch network for the banks to pay for, they can offer customers more interest, cheaper mortgages and loans. However, it is mainly people who are better off that are able to take advantage of the higher saving rates and lower borrowing rates offered. Poorer people may be more dependent on their local branch. Many welfare payments are made by cheque, and if their local branch shuts down these people may be forced to use cheque cashing services which often have high commission charges.

Travel

The use of ICT in the travel industry has led to a lot of changes. Here are some examples.

Travel information
The Internet is a huge source of information about public transport. In the past, if you wanted information about bus or train times, you would have had to find out from the library or train/bus station. Now you have access to all the timetables on the Internet.

Travel agents
Travel agents use computers all the time. They are used to check whether a particular flight or holiday is available. Once a holiday is found they can tell the customer the cost and book it for them. As well as booking holidays and flights, travel agents can also be used to book rail tickets and accommodation, hire cars, etc.

How the Internet may change the way that we book holidays
Using the Internet we can:

- check the availability and prices of some flights and holidays
- make savings when we book direct
- read reports written by people who have been on the same holiday that we intend to book
- arrange our own travel and accommodation
- find out about the resort before we go.

In the future, more people will book direct with the holiday company, as it will be cheaper because there is no travel agent's commission to pay. Travel agents may become a thing of the past. Some people think that the package tour will become less popular as more people are able to create their own holidays by booking travel and accommodation separately.

Call centres and customer enquiries

Many businesses make use of **call centres**. Call centres are used by companies to take and deal with enquiries made by the general public. Members of staff working in the call centre are equipped with a terminal and a headset. The headset allows the staff to use the computers at the same time as talking to a customer on the telephone.

Call centres are ideal for routine transactions. For example, they can be used for taking customer orders or for customers to pay bills using telephone banking. When a customer rings up the call centre, ICT (sometimes using voice recognition) is used to route the call to the person most able to deal with it.

THE JARGON DRAGON

call centre – a place where staff deal with enquiries from the general public. They make extensive use of ICT equipment

Call centres can be frustrating to customers but they are a cheap way for companies to operate

Advertising and marketing

Many organisations use ICT for advertising and marketing.

Advertising

Many companies do not do business over the Internet, but they do use the Internet for advertising their products or services. For example, car manufacturers do not sell direct to the public but they still use websites to let the public know about their latest models.

When surfing the Internet you may have noticed those adverts that occupy a thin strip at the top or bottom of the screen. These are called banner advertisements. If you click on one of these, it takes you to the company's website.

Marketing

People spend a lot of money on their hobbies and interests. They may be interested in travel and spend a lot of money on holidays. Football fans spend money on season tickets and kits. Keep-fit fans spend money on subscriptions to gyms. It is therefore important that organisations know how people spend their leisure time and what they buy or intend to buy during this time.

Everyone has certain characteristics that are of interest to commercial organisations. These characteristics include your age, where you live, details of your lifestyle, etc. If you are a regular customer of a particular shop, that shop will be interested in knowing about you.

Supermarkets ask questions like these about purchases made by each customer

Shops find out as much as they can about their customers. This is because they need to know why each customer shops at their shop and buys the products that they buy. Some shops use this information to send their customers information about special offers, and about new products which may interest them.

Toyota: reaping the benefits of banner advertising on the Internet

Toyota, the car manufacturer, put lots of banner adverts about their cars all over the Internet. Over a twelve-month period, around 152,000 web users typed in their names and addresses to request a brochure about a car. Toyota then used these names and addresses to see how many brochure requests resulted in the customer actually buying a Toyota car. The company did this by comparing the names and addresses it had collected with the details obtained when customers buy a car at one of their dealers. The management at Toyota were surprised at how many of these brochure enquiries actually resulted in sales. From the 152,000 brochure requests, the company had sold 7,329 cars. This meant that about five per cent resulted in sales. Because of the success of this advertising campaign, the Internet has now become the main source of sales leads for Toyota.

Questions

1   *What is meant by a 'banner advert'?*

2   *How did Toyota use banner adverts to try to sell their cars?*

3   *What is the main advantage to Toyota in advertising on the Internet rather than using adverts on TV or in magazines?*

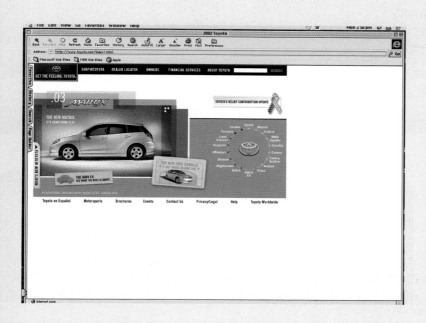

What you buy in a supermarket tells the supermarket something about you. It can then target you for details of special offers

THE JARGON DRAGON

processed – raw data is processed by a computer to give information; processing includes calculating, sorting, searching, storing and drawing

Other organisations need information in order to function. Sometimes organisations need to collect information for statistical purposes. The information collected by a school might be used to answer questions such as:

- How many students live beyond a five-mile radius of the school?
- How many disabled students are there in the school?
- Do girls do better at GCSE mathematics than boys?

In order to answer these questions, data needs to be collected. Once the data has been collected, it needs to be entered into the computer where it can be **processed**.

After processing, the output (results) is produced.

RESEARCH TASK

Market research
Companies like to find out as much as possible about their customers or potential customers.

Describe the ways that organisations can find out about the personal details of customers or potential customers.

FIND IT OUT

There are lots of ways organisations can obtain personal information about you.

Ask your parents, family, friends, etc. their experiences of companies and organisations

finding out about them and then pestering them for their business.

You may like to remind them of the following ways that organisations collect information:

- market research surveys (these are often carried out by people with clipboards who stop you on the street and ask you questions)
- questionnaires sent through the post with the chance of a large cash prize if you fill them in
- by people offering to enter you into a free raffle in exchange for information
- guarantee or warranty forms you send back to the company who made a product you have bought
- store loyalty cards (e.g. Reward cards, Clubcards, etc.).

Think IT THROUGH

Companies like to find out as much as they can about their customers. Some even sell the information they collect to other companies. There is a lot of profit in obtaining and selling information. They are not breaching the Data Protection Act because the customers have consented to having the details passed to others.

Here are some key words and concepts. You can use them to get further information by searching on them using the Internet.

- **database marketing** – only contacting those customers who are likely to buy

- **customer profiling** – understanding the buying behaviour of your customers and looking at the relationship between where they live and what they buy

- **mailshots** – promotional material sent through the post.

How ICT has affected work styles

ICT has affected the work styles of people in many ways. It has also had an impact on the locations and patterns of work.

In particular it has changed:

- the places where people work
- people's work patterns
- the hours that people work
- the ICT skills and training required
- the social aspects of work
- the way people interact at work
- the types of jobs available.

The places where people work

In the past people had to work away from home at the place where all the facilities were for them to do their job. In the office, for example, they had their filing cabinets, photocopiers, rooms for meetings, desks, etc.

In some jobs, people are now able to work from home. All they need to do their job can be stored on the computer and there are communication links between the main computer of the organisation they work for and the computer at home. Telesales is an example of a job that could easily be done at home.

Working from home

The ICT developments that have enabled more people to work from home include:

- e-mail
- **fax**
- the Internet
- **data warehouses** (where all the organisation's data is kept in a huge, single database)
- **videoconferencing** (a way of seeing other people at a 'virtual meeting' making use of cameras and computers)
- high-speed data links (e.g. fibre optic cables, satellite communication links, etc.).

THE JARGON DRAGON

fax – a machine capable of sending and receiving text and pictures along telephone lines

data warehouse – a computerised database system where all the data an organisation needs is stored

videoconferencing – using computer equipment to conduct a virtual face-to-face meeting

Working from home is called teleworking and it has many advantages to the employee, which include:

- in many cases you can be flexible regarding the times that you work
- you can live where you want to
- it is ideal for disabled people or people who have to look after young children
- there are no expenses involved in travelling, although household bills such as gas and electricity may rise
- time is not wasted travelling to and from work.

From the employee's point of view there are also some disadvantages in working from home which include:

- You are never 'off the job'. Because you sleep and work in the same place and are free to work your own hours, you may feel that you are never away from work and this could lead to stress.
- Increased stress at home. Teleworking could lead to arguments and stress in families since the teleworker may be expected to do household jobs since they are at home all day, or they may choose to work at times that do not fit in with the rest of the family.

Even the places in which people work have changed since the introduction of ICT. In the past, everyone who worked in an office was given their own desk, filing cabinet, etc. This is wasteful in terms of space and resources because not all desks are used at the same time. Using networks it is not necessary for a person to always sit at the same desk because you can access databases from anywhere there is a terminal. Many organisations use 'hot desking' where an employee arriving at work simply picks a desk or terminal that is not being used. Money is saved because:

- smaller offices can be used which are cheaper to rent or buy
- fewer desks are needed
- fewer workstations are needed.

People's work patterns

The way people work has changed due to the introduction of ICT. They are a lot more productive because they can use laptop computers, mobile phones, e-mail, etc. to work while travelling on planes, trains, etc. The use of mobile phones means that they can be contacted at any time such as during their lunch break, while visiting customers' premises, etc. By giving employees the latest equipment firms are benefiting by allowing their employees the opportunity to work more. The employees are usually happy to use the new equipment as it allows them to do their jobs better.

The hours that people work

The use of ICT has changed the hours that people work.

Call centres, where people take telephone orders for goods and services, need to be staffed during the times when people need them, which in some cases is 24 hours a day. This means that the staff in these call centres have to work shifts.

"It might be my girlfriend but it could be work, so shall I answer it?"

As more people work from home, there is blurring between work and home life

Businesses often operate throughout the world, so because of time differences they need to have staff who work around the clock.

Companies that operate world-wide need office staff available twenty-four hours a day

1 A company has asked some of its staff if they would like to telework. Explain what teleworking means.
2 What equipment would the company need to supply to enable an employee to telework?
3 Teleworking is not suitable for everyone. Write down three advantages and three disadvantages of teleworking.

ACTIVITY

The ICT skills and training required

The use of ICT continually changes the way in which a job is done. This means that people will need to re-train to make sure that their skills are up to date. The skills that are needed include the following.

voice recognition – the ability of a computer to ' understand' spoken words by comparing them with stored data

Keyboard skills

Keyboards are the most popular input device for the computer. Everyone who uses a computer should know the layout of the keyboard and be able to type with reasonable speed and accuracy. Many people are put off using keyboards and they may instead prefer to use **voice recognition** where they can simply say commands and dictate documents straight into the computer.

Technical skills

Technical skills would typically involve:

- installing new software (i.e. putting new software onto a computer and getting it to work)
- adding new hardware such as extra memory, printers, scanners, etc.
- networking groups of computers together
- configuring software to suit the user's needs.

Because technical expertise can be expensive, many computer users choose to learn the above skills themselves via magazines, books, videos, college courses and the Internet.

Design skills

In the past, if you wanted a poster or leaflet to be designed you would have gone to a printer for their expertise. After asking some questions, the printer would recognise your needs and produce some designs for you to choose from.

Using desktop publishing or wordprocessing software it is possible for a person with limited design skills to produce an eye-catching poster, leaflet, etc.

Because people produce documents for others to use, design skills have become very important and people need to know about the presentation of different kinds of document.

The social aspects of work

There are many ways in which the increasing use of ICT has changed society as far as work is concerned. In many ways, ICT has led to greater stress in the workplace and there are a number of reasons for this.

Motivation changes

Teleworkers (people who work from home) have to be self-motivated as they no longer have a boss looking over their shoulder all the time. If they want to get up at 11.00 a.m. they can, but they will have to catch up with their work. When you work in an office, you know what time you start and when you finish. Telework blurs work and home life, and this can be stressful for some people who cannot motivate themselves.

A greater risk of job loss

Computers are more powerful than they used to be and can be used in many new ways. They may be used to do jobs that were previously done by people. Employees live with the threat that there may be some new development in ICT that could replace them, and this is stressful.

Jobs which could be at risk from new technology include:
- postal workers – as more e-mails are sent, although the number of packages and parcels could increase with the use of e-commerce
- people who work in video libraries – as more and more people use cable and their credit cards to book films
- shop staff – as more and more people order goods on-line.

Less security at work

Call centres have to operate 24 hours per day and they need staff to cover the whole period. Shops are open long hours (24 hours per day in the case of certain supermarkets) and they need staff who are flexible about when they work.

All this has led to a huge growth in part-time work and shift work, with a drop in the number of full-time posts. Full-time staff preferring to work 9–5 may feel pressurised by their employers who may want them to be more flexible. Often the employers get round the problem by offering new workers a more flexible contract that says they can work any hours of the day and at any location. Many staff are given short-term contracts (say for one year), so if the employers need to get rid of them after that time, they can. This makes it hard for employees because they find it difficult to get a loan for a car or a mortgage if they do not have a permanent job.

Reduced social interaction at work

As people spend a lot of time at work it becomes a major part of their lives. They work with the same people and also meet new people all the time, so work provides companionship. It is this companionship that people miss when they retire. Work provides an opportunity to make friends and people to go out with. Employers often encourage their workers to spend time together socially, so they subsidise social activities such as meals out, holidays, sporting events and other social activities.

As teleworking increases then the opportunities to interact with other people at work decrease. Many people find this one of the most negative aspects of working at home.

Changes in leisure time

Some staff who work in administration have seen a drop in their working hours due to the efficiency of ICT. Others have found they can only get part-time work, and although they have more time on their hands they probably do not have the money to enjoy it.

The timing of leisure time has changed. People are working different hours so they may be off during the morning or afternoon. Some people prefer this arrangement, but others do not, yet are given no choice.

Stress caused by the fast-changing pace of ICT developments

Nothing stays still in ICT. Things are constantly changing and people have to learn new skills all the time. This can be frustrating, because as soon as you have mastered one software package another is released that you have to learn. All this adds to the stress of modern life.

The way people interact at work

The way people interact at work has changed with the introduction of ICT. People are more likely to communicate information via e-mails rather than paper. E-mail gives people the ability to send the same message to many different people, and this saves a lot of time.

The types of jobs available

ICT has automated many traditional manufacturing jobs such as paint-spraying, welding, picking and packing goods in warehouses, etc. It has also changed many jobs in offices, particularly those of typists and admin workers. Some jobs, such as the delivery of internal mail and filing, may no longer exist.

On the other hand, there are many jobs that have been created by ICT. These jobs include network engineers, website designers, hardware and software engineers. Other jobs, such as delivery drivers, have increased due to a rise in home shopping using the Internet.

A magazine article says that the use of ICT has made life more stressful for workers. Say whether you agree or disagree with this. In your argument you need to give the reasons for agreeing or disagreeing with the statement.

Legislation

Life has changed a lot since the use of computers, mobile phones and other technologies have become widespread. However, introducing this technology has produced new problems, and legislation (another name for laws) has been passed to deal with them. The main items of legislation dealing with ICT are outlined here and although you do not need to know the details of the laws themselves, you do need to know the reasons why they were introduced.

THE JARGON DRAGON

Data Protection Act 1998 – a law that restricts the way personal information is stored and processed on a computer

Data Protection Act 1998

As more and more information about ordinary people and their lifestyles is held on computers, there has become a need to control the way that this information can be collected and used. The use of large databases that are able to cross-reference data and look for trends, and the widespread use of networks to connect systems together, led to the introduction of the **Data Protection Act 1998**.

The Data Protection Act's main purpose is to protect the privacy of ordinary people.

Before we look the DP Act, we will look a little at database marketing and how it is used.

Database marketing

Everyone is affected by database marketing, mainly because any organisation that we deal with keeps details of what we have bought and when.

Imagine you are the boss of a catalogue company that sells goods by mail order. You have a decision to make. You have 10,000 catalogues to send out (you only have this number because they are expensive to produce) and you have a database of 30,000 past and present customers. Who do you send the catalogues to? You want to send the catalogues to those customers who are most likely to order from them.

You might use special database marketing software which would look at your customers to identify a profile (age, postal area, job, etc.) of the customers most likely to order. This software may look at what each customer has ordered before and their response to previous catalogue mailings. The software would use this information and give you a mailing list of the customers who are most likely to respond by placing orders.

To be able to target likely customers it is important that you know as much about them as possible. The problem with this is that people do not like giving detailed information to companies. There are some companies that collect information about their customers, and sell databases containing this information to other companies who can then use it. You may think that this is illegal but it isn't, provided that the customer has not objected to the information being used like this.

You can now see that a customer's personal data isn't very private at all.

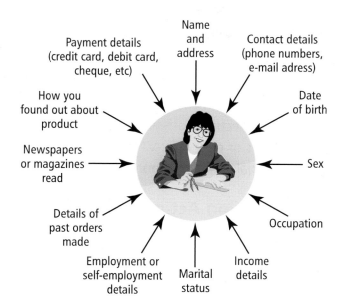

When you place an order, the company may be interested in knowing these details about you

The main purpose of the Data Protection Act 1998 is to prevent the misuse of personal data and to give some rights to the person to whom the data refers.

Under the Act, the person to whom the data refers is able to look at the data to see if it is correct and if it isn't they can insist that it is changed or deleted. This means that decisions will not be based on wrong information. If the information is wrong and it can be proved that the company collecting the information did not take enough care and caused some damage to the person, then the company can be sued for damages in the courts.

All organsiations that hold personal data must register their use. They must say what personal data they hold, how the data will be used and also the details of anyone to whom the data will be disclosed. There is a very large fine for organisations that do not register.

Is it necessary for everyone who uses personal data to register?

If you keep a list of your friends' personal details (e.g. names, addresses, telephone numbers, e-mail addresses, favourite groups/singers, etc.) then you do not need to register because the data is being held for personal or household affairs.

Can I see the personal data held about me?

Organisations such as your school, your GP practice, your video club, etc. will all hold personal data about you and they must register their use. You are allowed to see the data held about you to check its accuracy. However, not all organisations have to allow you to see the data – there are some exemptions. You may be denied access to your personal data if the data is being used for any of the following purposes:

- the prevention or detection of crime
- catching or prosecuting offenders
- collecting taxes or duty (e.g. VAT)
- medical or social workers' reports in some instances.

The Data Protection Act website
Full details of the Data Protection Act 1998 can be found on the following website:

`http://www.dataprotection.gov.uk/`

Computer Misuse Act 1990

As computers and communication over networks became more popular, some people started to misuse them. Existing laws did not cover these misuses so a new law called the Computer Misuse Act 1990 was passed covering the following:

- deliberately planting **viruses** in a computer system to cause damage to program files and data
- copying computer programs illegally; this is called software piracy
- using computer time to carry out unauthorised work
- **hacking** into someone's computer system to see the information held or to alter it
- using the computer to commit certain frauds.

One of the problems with the Act is that to prosecute a person it is necessary to prove that they intended to do one of the above things. 'Intended' means that they set out with the aim of doing the illegal act. If they did it by accident, they are not found guilty.

THE JARGON DRAGON

virus – a program that has been created to do damage to a computer system

hacking – the process of a person trying to break into a secure computer system

Copyright, Designs and Patents Act 1989

The Copyright, Designs and Patents Act 1989 makes it a criminal offence to copy or steal software. It protects the money the software developer makes from the sale of software. A lot of effort goes into the creation of new software and it is only fair that the developer/manufacturer is rewarded for their efforts.

The Act also makes it an offence to run a piece of software on more computers than the software licence allows. For example, a school may buy a licence to run Microsoft Office on 40 computers. If they then use it on 50 computers, they are committing an offence.

Usually, if you have a desktop computer and a laptop computer, the software licence allows you to run the software on both at no extra charge.

Health and Safety at Work Act 1974

Under the Health and Safety at Work Act 1974, employers have to make sure that their employees have a safe place to work and, as far as possible, have a safe system of work.

Wherever people work there are hazards. When you are at work you need to know about these hazards to avoid accidents and make a safe place for others to work in.

Hazards in the workplace may include:

Large quantities of paper lying around, particularly if people are allowed to smoke in the office

Wedging a fire door open which should be kept shut at all times

Wires trailing across the floor which people might trip over

Overloaded power sockets, which can cause fires

Not lifting properly (back should be kept straight with legs bent)

Get into the habit of sitting like this when you are using your computer

Notice the following in the diagram:

- The chair should have five castors otherwise it might tip up.
- The height of the chair seat should be adjustable.
- The back of the chair should be adjustable too.
- Feet should be firmly on the floor if a footrest is not available.
- Upper arm should be at right angles to the forearm.
- Wrists should be kept straight.

Health and Safety Regulations 1992

The Health and Safety Regulations 1992 cover working with VDUs (visual display units). People who work with computers a lot may experience some health problems which include:

- eyestrain
- stress
- backache or joint aches.

Eyestrain

Eyestrain causes blurred vision and headaches. Refocusing your eyes between paperwork and the screen can cause eyestrain. Another cause is reflections off the screen preventing you from seeing the screen properly.

Eyestrain is common with computer users and the older you are the more likely it is that your vision will be affected. If you work with computers a lot then your employers (i.e. the people you work for) are required to pay for eye tests and for any glasses you might need.

Stress

I SEE BILL IS HAVING TROUBLE WITH HIS COMPUTER AGAIN!

Working with computers can be very stressful

Using computers can be stressful. Losing an important file or discovering that there is a virus on your machine is a very stressful situation. If you are using new software and can't work out how to do a simple task this is also stressful. These things tend to be more stressful when you have to complete work to an important deadline. To reduce stress, try to get into the habit of not leaving things to the last minute.

Backache or joint aches

Backache can occur if you slouch in your chair while using a computer. Try to sit upright with both feet flat on the floor. If you do not adopt this correct posture then it may lead to backache in the future.

People who spend long periods typing at the keyboard may develop a medical problem called repetitive strain injury (**RSI**). This is caused by repeatedly using the same muscles in the hands, arms and neck, causing pain in the joints.

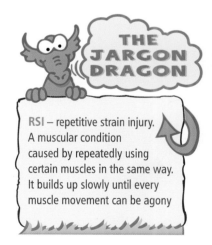

THE JARGON DRAGON

RSI – repetitive strain injury. A muscular condition caused by repeatedly using certain muscles in the same way. It builds up slowly until every muscle movement can be agony

The Health and Safety Executive is a government body responsible for enforcing the regulations. Further information about health and safety aspects of using VDUs can be found at:

`http://www.hse.gov.uk/pubns/indg36.htm`

FIND IT OUT

What are the main points of the Health and Safety Regulations 1992?

The people who you work for are required by law to:

- look carefully at the terminal/workstation where you work to see if there are any health and safety risks. If there are any, they must be fixed immediately
- plan work so that there are changes in activity or breaks
- arrange eye tests and provide glasses if they are needed
- provide health and safety training.

We will now look at the practical implementation of these regulations.

Inspections

Employers should periodically inspect the workplace environment and the equipment being used to make sure that it complies with the regulations. Any shortcomings in working conditions, working practices or equipment should be reported and corrected. Desks, chairs, computers, etc. should be inspected to ensure there are no risks to workers' eyesight and to avoid physical and mental stress problems.

Training

All employees should be trained in the health and safety aspects of their job. They need to be told about the correct posture for the use of keyboards etc.

Job design

Jobs should be designed so that workers have periodic breaks or changes of activity when using computers.

Eye tests

For computer users there should be regular free eye tests, with free glasses provided if necessary, at the employer's expense.

The law also lays down certain minimum requirements for computer systems and furniture. All new and existing equipment bought should now meet the following requirements:

Display screens

These must be easy to read and therefore have no flicker and be very stable. Brightness, contrast, tilt and swivel must all be adjustable and there must be no reflection off the screen.

Keyboards
These must be separate from the screen and tiltable. Their layout should be easy to use and the surface should be matt in order to avoid glare. There must be sufficient desk space to provide arm and hand support.

Desks
Desks must be large enough to accommodate the computer and any necessary paperwork and must not reflect too much light. An adjustable document holder should be provided so as to avoid uncomfortable head movements.

Chairs
Chairs must be adjustable and comfortable, and allow easy freedom of movement. A foot rest must be available on request.

Lights
There should be a suitable contrast between the computer screen and the background. There must be no glare or reflections off the computer screen, so point sources of light should be avoided and the windows should have adjustable coverings such as blinds to eliminate reflections caused by sunlight.

Noise
Background noise should not be loud enough to distract attention and disturb speech.

Software
This must be easy to use and should be appropriate to the user's needs and experience.

Other matters
Heat, humidity and radiation emissions must be kept within reasonable limits.

What can you do to reduce the risks to your health when using ICT equipment?
- Make sure that there are no reflections off the screen. If sunlight is coming in, take time to adjust the blinds. Doing this will reduce eyestrain and prevent headaches.
- Use a copy-holder to hold documents rather than read them from the surface of the desk. This means that you will not have to move your neck awkwardly when looking at the papers and then the screen.

- Adjust your chair to the right height for you. Do not simply accept the position the chair is in.
- Alter the brightness and contrast of the monitor to suit you.
- Sit up straight. Do not slouch in your chair as this can lead to back problems in the future.
- Use special keyboards and wrist guards to minimise the likelihood of developing RSI.
- Make sure that your screen is clean.

Regulation of Investigatory Powers Act 2000

Sometimes it is necessary for the police, MI5 or Customs and Excise to intercept communications such as e-mails, telephone conversations, network links, radio links, etc. This is so they can collect evidence for the purposes of national security or fighting crime.

Some people are worried about this Act because it gives a lot of powers to the government. For example, it gives them the power to monitor all electronic communication (telephone, Internet, etc.) in the hope of catching someone committing a crime. This is just like them being able to open and read every letter you send in order to possibly catch someone committing a crime. They are also able to monitor your movements as you go about your day-to-day business. Did you know that it is possible for someone to find out where you are every time you make or receive a mobile phone call or send a text message?

Obviously the government must have powers to deal with terrorists and criminals, but people are worried that the Regulation of Investigatory Powers Act gives them too many powers. Here are some of the things the Act allows the government to do:

- They can order telecommunications companies to intercept your communications (e-mails, telephone calls, text messages, voice mail, etc.).
- They are able to target everyone in the hope that they will catch some people doing something illegal.
- They can monitor a person's use of the Internet for any purpose.

- They can demand that if you use encryption, you hand over the key so that they can see what you are doing. They can do this without you even knowing.

The Internet Code of Practice

The Internet is not owned by a person or company. The Internet is owned by everyone who is connected to it. This means that people are free to put on it what they like (provided their government does not block their access in some way). Most of the time there are no rules and regulations, except for **Internet service providers**. Because of this freedom, people worry that there should be some guidelines about its use. They do not want to see laws banning certain things on the Internet because freedom of speech is so important. Instead, there is the Internet Code of Practice (ICOP). This document is constantly changing (because the way we use the Internet is constantly changing). The ICOP is simply a guideline for everyone involved in using the Internet.

THE JARGON DRAGON

Internet service provider – a company that provides you with a permanent connection to the Internet

The main items in the Internet Code of Practice are:

- Children's sites should contain only material suitable for children.
- Any pages that are likely to offend should have a warning first.
- Links to other sites should be checked to make sure they are not connecting people to sites they might find offensive.
- People should not send unsolicited e-mail (this is mail the recipient has not asked for) called SPAM.
- Adverts on the Internet should be honest.
- Extra charges such as VAT, post and packing should be clearly shown.
- The name of the advertiser should be clearly indicated.
- Advertisers should not be able to substitute goods (i.e. send goods in place of those a person has ordered).
- To use copyright material, people must have permission to use it in all countries throughout the world.
- Files such as images, audio clips and video clips should be compressed to reduce download times.
- Private data such as names, addresses, telephone numbers, credit card details, etc. should not be disclosed

to another person without permission of the data subject (i.e. the person who the data is about).

- Information should not incite or promote illegal acts.
- Information should not deliberately mislead the user.
- Programs downloaded by users from a site should be checked by the site owner to make sure they do not contain viruses.
- E-mail should not be used for hoaxes, chain letters or SPAM.
- Internet service providers (ISPs) should display and enforce the code of practice with their subscribers.

A full copy of the Internet Code of Practice is available from: `www.internet.org.uk/icop.html`

International fraud

The growth of ICT systems and the ease with which money can be passed around the world has led to a huge increase in fraud. With a reduction in the use of cash to make payments, criminals are instead focusing on other areas such as credit card fraud. Credit and debit cards are used to buy goods and services over the Internet. Although encryption is used to scramble credit card details as they are passed over the Internet, some people have managed to intercept them. Once these people have the details, they can then order goods and services using someone else's credit card.

Bogus companies have also been set up on the Internet with the sole purpose of parting you from your money. These companies offer goods and services, but after you have paid for them they never arrive. Many of these bogus companies are set up in other countries so it is hard for them to be investigated.

The misuse of personal information

Some Internet sites are able to drop a 'cookie' into your web browser each time that you visit the site. These cookies are used to identify you and to find out what other websites you have visited. This is useful information to anyone who wants to find out about a person's interests and buying habits. However, most people see this as a serious infringement of their privacy.

How ICT has affected personal communications

ICT has affected the way in which people go about their everyday lives. In this section we will look at how various aspects of our daily lives are affected by ICT.

THE JARGON DRAGON

terminal – a computer on a network, or a keyboard and monitor connected to a mini computer

The Internet

The Internet is a huge network of networks. Each time you log on to the Internet you are increasing the size of the Internet by one **terminal**. Almost any kind of information or person can be found on this network. As ICT students you will find a wealth of information on ICT applications along with information on some of the problems caused by ICT use. Anyone can put information on the Internet, so check who has provided it before you accept its authenticity.

Using the Internet means that you have access to e-mail. You can use e-mail to send people documents that they can then print out if they need to. With e-mail there is no delay while the document is 'in the post'.

The way information is stored and accessed has improved with the use of ICT. In the past you would have spent ages in the library looking up information, but using the Internet this can be done in minutes.

The impact of the Internet

The Internet has been one of the most important developments in ICT. Ten years ago hardly anybody had heard of it let alone used it. Now it is as much a feature of modern life as a television or telephone.

It is important for everyone to understand what the Internet is and how it can be useful to them. There are benefits in using the Internet but it also presents some threats and you need to be aware of these. Here is a case study that outlines just one of the threats.

The main advantages of using the Internet are:

* People have a wide range of products and services to choose from. You are no longer restricted to the choice of goods in the shops near to where you live.

case study

Internet chat-rooms

This is a summary of a newspaper article that appeared in the *Daily Mail* on 16 August 2001:

Two schoolgirls were lured by older men who they met in chat-rooms on the Internet. A girl of 15 spent the night in a hotel with a 31-year-old man she met on the Internet and another girl of 13 spent three days with a 17-year-old. Both of these incidents occurred in Cheshire and the police warned parents of the dangers that lurked in chat-rooms.

The police said 'we always warn our children about talking to strangers but this is exactly what they are doing in chat-rooms'.

The police gave the following advice. Never give out:

- your e-mail address
- your home address
- your telephone numbers
- the name of your school.

The dangers lurking in chat-rooms were highlighted in the TV programme Coronation Street where teenager Sarah Louise Platt (age 14) was lured to a house by a middle-aged man who posed as a 16-year-old boy in a chat-room.

Questions

1   *One feature of the Internet is chat-rooms. What is a chat-room?*

2   *Give two pieces of information you should never give in a chat-room.*

3   *Explain two dangers that chat-rooms pose to young children.*

Don't believe what people say in chat-rooms

- You can access the websites of companies throughout the world. The goods you want to buy may be cheaper in another country and you can take advantage of this.

- You can order on-line using the Internet and have the goods delivered straight to your door.

- There are special Internet-only offers on goods and services. These offer discounts only if you buy over the Internet.

The lack of control over the Internet

The Internet is for everybody. There is no control over the content of material on the Internet. Neither is there any control over the people who can access the Internet. This means that unless special software is used, children can easily gain access to pornographic or violent images.

The lack of control of the Internet means that often information is not checked to make sure it is accurate. It is therefore up to the users to check the suitability and accuracy of any information they obtain from the Internet.

Here are some tips about using material off the Internet:

- One way of checking information obtained from the Internet is to compare it with that obtained from other sources such as reference books, encyclopedias, magazines, etc., or you could ask someone, such as your teacher, a librarian or a parent, who has specialist knowledge of the subject.

- You could check the material against the same material obtained from books. Of course, books can contain incorrect information, but as books are normally written by experts in their field, this is unlikely. If sites produced by experts are used for information, then these are usually accurate.

- If you have thoroughly researched your information then it could be just as accurate as a well-known site. However, established sites such as the BBC are likely to be well researched and accurate.

RESEARCH TASK

Here are some topics of interest to many people:

- computer crime
- the Internet causes more problems than it solves
- ICT causes too much unemployment
- ICT developments always benefit the rich
- children are spending too much time on the Internet.

Choose one of the topics from the above list and research people's opinions of it by asking them to fill in a questionnaire that you have produced.

FIND IT OUT

When you are doing your research, remember that you can always ask people you know for their opinions. If you do this, you should quote them accurately and also say who they are and what age they are.

Questionnaires are very useful for collecting opinions. You can then categorise people's answers according to their age, sex and occupation. By doing this you may notice certain patterns that you can mention in your research. Remember that statistical analyses (e.g. finding means, modes or medians) and producing charts (graphs, bar charts, pie charts, etc.) can be done using spreadsheet software.

The availability of offensive, illegal or unethical material on the Internet

There are a lot of pornographic images/videos on the Internet. There are laws in the UK covering the production and distribution of this material, but because much of this material comes from countries where it is legal, there is not much that can be done to stop it.

The main worry adults have is that young children could accidentally access this material. Special software is available that can filter out sites that contain illegal subject matter or which are unsuitable for children, but it may not be completely effective.

What is really worrying is that paedophiles use the Internet for distributing pornographic pictures of young children and they also lure children into meetings with them after they have spoken to them in chat-rooms. You therefore need to be extremely careful if arranging a meeting with someone you have only spoken to on-line.

Almost everybody finds pornographic material offensive, but material does not have to be pornographic to be offensive. An image of a pack of hounds attacking a fox may not be offensive to the members of a hunt but it would be offensive to people who want to ban hunting. Whether material is offensive or not depends on the individual.

Illegal material

Some material is illegal, such as instructions on how to make bombs, where to buy drugs, racist material, etc. The problem with material that is illegal in the UK is that it may be perfectly legal in another counry. The providers of such material can escape prosecution by moving to a country where it is legal.

Unethical material

Ethics is about behaving properly towards others. Unethical material may be perfectly legal yet morally wrong. For example there may be a site on 'blagging'. Blagging is trying to get everything without paying for it. You could go into a restaurant and put a hair in your meal so that you get it for nothing even though you have eaten most of it. There are sites on the Internet promoting this practice, and material like this is certainly unethical.

Starting rumours

It is easy to spread rumours using the Internet. You only have to tell a few people in a chat-room and the rumour will rapidly spread. Normally, if someone starts a rumour that is untrue and causes another person distress, then the person starting the rumour can be sued. However, when rumours are started over the Internet it is difficult to identify the person responsible. They may live in a different country so it is difficult to involve the police. The Internet is not checked for the accuracy or content of information, so you should never believe something you read on the Internet unless it can be verified by another source.

Mobile phones

There has been a huge change in the way that people communicate with each other. The use of mobile phones means that people can be contacted anywhere and at any time. The use of text messaging means that you can still contact them if they are busy and do not answer the phone.

Here are some situations in which a mobile phone can be useful:

- Your train is delayed and someone is waiting at the station to pick you up. You need to ring them to tell them you will be late.
- There has been a serious accident along a quiet country road. You need to contact the emergency services.
- Your car has broken down. You need to ring for help.

The advantages of mobile phones

- Personal security – you feel safer if you know you can contact someone in an emergency situation.
- You can access the Internet (provided you have a WAP phone).
- People who are constantly on the move can be contacted by their base (e.g. lorry drivers, repair staff, company reps/salespersons, etc.).
- It removes the problem of needing to find a public phone that works when you want to make a call.
- It can avoid the need to make expensive calls from phones in hotel bedrooms.
- You can send and receive e-mail.
- You can send and receive text messages.

The disadvantages of mobile phone use

- People sometimes forget to turn their phones off during concerts, lectures and in libraries. If it rings it can be distracting to others.
- People can become obsessed with using their phones.
- They can be a nuisance in public places (restaurants, bars, trains, etc.).
- People can be contacted at any time, even when it is inconvenient.
- People use mobile phones in cars without hands-free kits, which is very dangerous and can lead to accidents.
- Using mobile phones can be very expensive.

Entertainment and leisure

Leisure activities have changed. Many people use computers for their entertainment and spend hours on the Internet or playing games. Most people enjoy watching television, and the use of ICT has enabled a huge increase in the number of channels.

ICT has had a huge influence on how people spend their leisure time. Many people are now turning off their televisions and using the Internet instead. They use the Internet to keep in touch with family and friends, or to contact people who have the same interests. If you have a specific problem, such as a medical problem, you can contact a support group for help and advice.

Computer games are very popular, and some people enjoy editing photographs obtained from their digital cameras, or desktop publishing.

ICT has also changed the way that we obtain music. Being able to choose what music to listen to, and when to listen to it, is important to many people. It is therefore also important that the device they use is small. You will all be familiar with portable CD players. There are now also Mini Disc players and Mini Disc recorders.

download – to copy files from a distant computer to the one you are working on

Mini Disc recorders are very small and allow you to record music from a CD player or to play music that has been **downloaded** from the Internet. Some Mini Disc recorders have a huge storage capacity of 128 MB and can record five hours of music. Because they are digital devices, the sound quality is very high. Mini Discs look like small music discs, except that they are in a plastic cover something like a floppy disk cover.

The latest development in portable music is the Digital Audio Player (DAP). A DAP allows you to play back music that has been stored on a computer. The music file on the computer will usually have been downloaded from the Internet. Because music computer files are very big, it is necessary to compress them so they occupy less space on a disk. This also means that they take less time to download.

An Intel Digital Audio Player that can record and playback MP3 files

For information about Digital Audio Players contact:

`http://www.intel.com/home/audio/`

FIND IT OUT

case study

Napster

You may have heard of Napster. Napster is an organisation that provided a way for users to share music files across the Internet. The music industry was very unhappy about this because it made it easy for copyrighted work to be copied. In America the music industry took legal action against Napster and won, and now Napster has to filter out any copyrighted material. The Copyright Designs and Patents Act protects artists against having their work copied. There are big fines for anyone caught doing this. Users can no longer copy copyrighted music using the Napster site. They are only able to copy non-copyright material or material where the owner has given their permission.

Information about the Napster site can be obtained from:

`http://www.napster.com/`

Questions

1   *If you were an artist and had a Number 1 hit, why would you be worried about your work being copied?*

2   *If you were an up-and-coming artist and wanted to become more widely known, why might a site such as Napster be able to help you?*

3   *Explain what the term 'copyrighted material' means.*

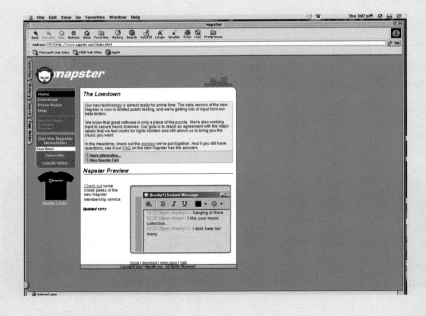

Education and lifelong learning

ICT provides opportunities for people, whatever their location. If you live in a remote part of the country you may find it hard to have access to a university or college, particularly if your mobility is limited.

You can now take various courses using CD-ROMs and DVDs. You can also use the Internet to take on-line courses. If you miss the companionship of other students who are taking the same course, you can 'meet' and chat to them in a chat-room that has been specifically set up for that purpose.

Your local college or university will only offer a limited range of courses. It may not run the course you are interested in and it may be too far to travel to somewhere that does. Taking a course using the Internet may be the answer in these circumstances.

Active citizenship

What is active citizenship about?

Active citizenship means caring about your country, believing that you can make a difference and involving yourself in the democratic process (e.g. voting at elections and writing to elected representatives about the things you feel strongly about).

Active citizenship involves caring about what goes on around you. It involves caring about what happens to your fellow humans wherever they are in the world.

Politicians and world leaders are worried that fewer people are involving themselves in the democratic process, and this shows itself by fewer and fewer younger people voting in local and general elections. It may be that they simply cannot be bothered to vote, or perhaps they feel that their vote is not important.

Active citizenship is important because there are many social problems that it can help solve such as violence, drugs, crime, poverty and pollution. If these problems are to be solved then it will need active participation by everyone.

Cyber elections

In the general election of 2001, in some constituencies 80 per cent of pensioners voted compared with less than 40 per cent of people aged under 25. In the country as a whole the average was below 60 per cent for the under-25 age group.

What is going wrong? Do young people not care who is elected?

Why is it that the pensioners voted while many younger people did not?

Perhaps if people could vote using the Internet, then more of them might vote. Putting crosses on bits of paper in a church hall or a school may not appeal to some people.

If the weather is bad then it is found that the turnout (i.e. the number of people who actually vote as a percentage of those who are eligible to vote) is low. If people could vote using the Internet then they could vote without leaving the house.

One of the problems with cyber elections is that it is difficult to make sure they are fair. Each voter could be given a PIN (personal identification number) but these could be given or sold to others. Also not everyone is on the Internet so you would still need traditional polling stations.

Cyber elections have some big advantages that include:

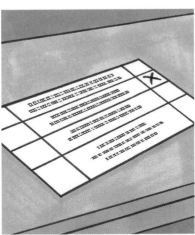

- Voters could vote from anywhere in the world
- It eliminates the need to print paper ballot forms
- Votes could be counted much faster and more accurately

Cyber elections also have disadvantages which include:

- not everyone has access to the Internet so polling booths would still be needed
- the system is more open to abuse by hackers, fraudsters, etc.
- some people may not understand the new system.

In one of the counties in California, USA e-voting was used for the presidential election in 2000. £10 million was spent making it an all-electronic voting county. This was a lot of money, though £1 million would normally have been spent just printing and distributing the ballot papers. The system made use of a touch screen where the voter touched the part of the screen for the candidate they wanted to vote for. The voters still had to go to a polling station to vote because the touch screens were situated in kiosks at the polling station. This meant that voters still needed to make an effort to vote. If they could have voted from the comfort of their own homes, then many more of them may have voted.

In the future it is hoped that voting could be done remotely. Mobile phones or digital TV could be used to place a vote. The main problems with this are privacy (i.e. keeping who you vote for private) and security (i.e. making sure that you only vote once and that others cannot interfere with your vote).

Questions

1 What is meant by the term 'e-voting'?
2 Although the equipment for e-voting is expensive it can be used for many elections. Why does this make it cheaper in the long run?
3 Give two advantages of the e-voting system.

Civil rights issues

Civil rights are given to people to stop them being discriminated against in some way. These legal rights protect people and guarantee them certain freedoms such as freedom of speech, freedom of assembly (this allows peaceful protests to take place), freedom of worship (i.e. people are free to have any religion), the right to the due process of the law and the right to vote. Civil rights issues arise when people disagree about these rights.

Not all countries have all these civil rights and in some countries you are not free to protest about the government and can be sent to prison with no reason having to be given. In the next section we will look at how the Internet helps the people in countries whose governments abuse their civil rights.

Don't we live in a free country?

The Internet is not owned or censored by anyone. Newspapers, magazines, television and radio programmes, books, etc., on the other hand, are all owned by someone. Usually it is the owner or, in some countries, the government who decides what is to be put in them. This means they are censored. If a news item could damage big business, then the owner of the newspaper may decide not to include the article. The Internet belongs to everyone who is connected to it and is an uncensored mass of material.

Some governments around the world are corrupt and anyone who tries to oppose them will almost certainly be killed. The Internet allows a free flow of information to and from these countries so that evidence of the abuse of human rights can be gathered and suitable action taken.

Here are some facts that might surprise you:

- In Burma an ordinary citizen is not allowed to own a personal computer with networking facilities unless it has been authorised by the government.
- At present, in Iraq, there is a total ban on Internet access.
- In the United Arab Emirates you need a licence from the police if you want to access the Internet.
- In Vietnam and China political content is monitored on the Internet and the governments block access to certain sites.
- In South Korea you can be prosecuted for trying to access a North Korean web page, and if you meet someone from North Korea in a chat-room, then you must report to the police within seven days.

RESEARCH TASK

Freedom of speech is important to everyone. Some countries do not enjoy the same freedoms as we have in the UK. Your task is to do some research and produce a short essay on how countries prevent freedom of speech on the Internet.

FIND IT OUT

There is a website set up by an organisation called 'Human Rights Watch' and on this you will find details of all the human rights abuses around the world. The web address of this site is:

`www.hrw.org`

Take a look at the site to see the extent of human rights abuse in other countries.

There is also a site that looks at the rights and liberties people should enjoy when using the Internet. The site is:

`www.cyber-rights.org/`

Think IT THROUGH

Use search conditions with various search engines to find other websites that cover human rights and the Internet. You could use a multiple search condition like this: "human rights"AND"Internet". If you find any good sites, then write down their web addresses and include them in your work.

Encryption: for and against

There are many arguments for and against the use of **encryption**.

For the use of encryption

- Freedom of speech is a fundamental right. Encryption means that people who are denied this right are free to say what they like without fear.

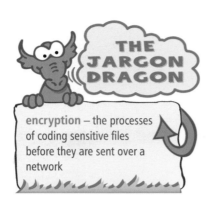

encryption – the processes of coding sensitive files before they are sent over a network

- Encryption is important for the transfer of confidential information such as credit card numbers.
- Encryption means that information about abuses of human rights in some countries can be freely sent to other countries around the world.
- For many people who have been punished over the years for fighting for their right to freedom of speech, personal privacy is very important.

Against the use of encryption

- 'Those who are innocent have nothing to hide'. Many people hold the view that only criminals wish to hide information.
- People should not be able to send what they want over the Internet.
- It makes it more difficult for the police and MI5 to collect evidence against people who are committing crimes.
- Offensive material, such as child pornography, can be freely distributed without the worry of discovery.
- A ban on encryption would be very difficult to enforce.

RESEARCH TASK

Carry out some research to find answers to the following:

1   *What is encryption?*
2   *Why is encryption needed?*
3   *Give the name of an application where encryption would be used.*
4   *Describe a situation where encryption would be considered to be a bad thing.*

FIND IT OUT

The use of ICT affects all of us even if we do not use ICT equipments ourselves.

Privacy and encryption applies to each one of us. To find out more about encryption, take a look at the following site:

http://www.animatedsoftware.com/high-tech/philspgp.htm

This site contains an interview with the author of PGP (pretty good privacy) which was broadcast on a radio show. It explains about how the program works and how it is important that we are all allowed freedom of speech without interference from governments, etc.

This site contains a free version of the latest PGP program that you can download to see how it works:

```
www.pgpi.org/
```

How ICT is used in community activities

The use of ICT can bring communities together. In many areas members of the community keep in touch using the Internet. Communities often set up a website and these typically contain material such as:

- lists of what's on (discos, lectures, bingo nights, sports events, etc.)
- local history – young people are able to contact older people about what life used to be like in the area
- school reunions – older people can get in touch with people who they went to school with and have now lost touch
- lists of playgroups
- volunteer bodies
- support groups – these offer residents the chance to help and advise each other
- courses at local schools and colleges.

Public access to the Internet

In order for the members of the community to gain the benefits of the Internet, they need to have access to it. This might not be possible in some areas where few people can afford computer equipment.

In many of these communities, the problem has been solved by offering people free or very cheap access to the Internet. Access is obtainable at public places such as shopping centres, libraries, community centres, etc. This type of access is ideal for people who do not have access to the Internet at home or at work.

Cybercafés

Cybercafés are coffee shops that also offer computing facilities. You can access the Internet, scan in material, print out material (sometimes in colour) and have a coffee and a cake while you are doing it. Cybercafés are springing up in all the major towns and cities in the UK and they provide comfortable surroundings in which to use computers. You can find cybercafés in many public places such as high streets, shopping centres, libraries, airports, train stations, etc. They provide a cheap way of accessing the Internet. Many cybercafés, though, have quite old hardware and software, so it is not always possible to read the latest websites or even pick up all e-mail attachments.

THE JARGON DRAGON

cybercafé – a coffee shop that also offers Internet access as well as the use of other computing facilities

Public transport and travel information

The Internet provides a huge store of information about public transport. For example, you can find out when a particular flight is due to arrive at the airport before you set out to pick up someone. There is even a website where you can find complete information about a particular flight (when it took off, its current speed, height and position, its expected landing time, etc.).

Using the website:

`http://www.flytecomm.com/trackflight.html`

you can follow the progress of a particular flight in the USA. All you need to know is the flight number.

The picture at the top of the next page shows the position of a flight from Chicago to Manchester.

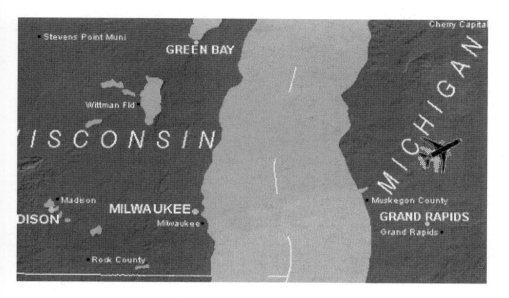

Taxis

If you want to hire a taxi, you usually have to ring a local taxi firm and the radio operator uses the radio to find out which taxi is nearest to you. The closest taxi driver then radios back to confirm that they want the job. The details of the job, including the address, are then given by the operator.

The problems with this system include:

- interference on the radio can sometimes make the instructions unclear
- taxis occasionally go to the wrong address or arrive at the wrong time
- taxis sometimes get lost and arrive late.

Many taxi firms now have a new system, which makes use of global positioning. This system enables the taxi office to pinpoint a taxi that is free and nearest to the caller. The details of the pick-up are displayed on a small screen on the taxi's dashboard so the driver no longer has to rely on voice messages. The system can also provide detailed instructions on how to get to both the pick-up and drop-off points.

Some of these new systems can even allow payment to be made using credit cards.

Information on these new taxi systems can be obtained from the manufacturers at:

`http://www.taxitronic.net/` and
`http://www.alephcomputer.com/html/cadtx.html`

The computer fits on the dashboard of the taxi

Air traffic control

Information about National Air Traffic Services, the company who provide all the air traffic control in Britain and some other countries, can be found on:

`http://www.nats.co.uk/about/technology.html`

Using ICT to find your way: using satellite positioning systems

Satellite positioning systems are able to locate the position of any object on the Earth's surface. These systems can be used to locate the position of an aircraft or ship or even a person. Some cars are equipped with a similar system so that the driver can locate their position on a map on a small screen inside the car. The driver can then use the system to obtain directions to their destination. Some systems give the directions (turn left, turn left, etc.) on a screen whereas others give the driver verbal directions as they approach junctions and turns.

Hand-held satellite positioning systems are available and are used by people walking in isolated regions such as mountains or deserts.

Satellite positioning systems use information from a host of satellites to determine where the driver is located, and a small computer is used to provide the maps. As well as giving details of roads, the system can also provide information on the locations of airports, banks, hotels, restaurants, etc.

Tracking stolen cars using satellite positioning systems

A more sophisticated version of a satellite positioning system can be used to track a stolen car. The car has a tracking device installed in it. When the owner reports the car as stolen, the tracking response centre can see where the car is on a large road map on a large computer screen. They can then watch the position of the car as it travels along the roads. The response centre can then send this information to the police who are then able to intercept the stolen vehicle.

Information services

Information kiosks

An information kiosk is a small structure, usually with a computer and monitor in it, that displays information for the public. They are often located near the entrances of shopping centres where they provide information about the shops in the centre. Kiosks are also used to provide points where tourists can get information such as maps, places to visit and accommodation details.

Information kiosks often make use of **touch screens**.

Information on touch screens and their uses can be obtained from:

http://www.magictouch.com/applications.htm and
http://inventors.about.com/library/inventors/
bltouch.htm.

THE JARGON DRAGON

touch screen – a computer display screen that is sensitive to human touch, allowing a user to interact with the computer by touching pictures or words on the screen

Finding a venue

If you decide to go on a night out you might need to consult the local paper to find out what's on. If you don't have one, then you would need to go out and buy one. Instead of doing this, you could access the Internet for details of concerts, plays, gigs, films, etc. You could find out where the events are and their start times. Many websites also allow you to book tickets on-line using your credit card.

Information services in libraries

Many libraries offer on-line access to a newspaper and journals database called INFOTRAC. This allows users to search and access 40 newspaper titles and over 6,000 journal titles. As well as the current issues, you can access past issues too, so this database is a very good source of information.

The National Health Service (NHS)

The National Health Service provides free healthcare to everyone in the UK. To provide a suitable level of care requires a lot of money. Any money the NHS saves can be used to employ more doctors and nurses and to take up the latest treatments.

NHS Direct Online

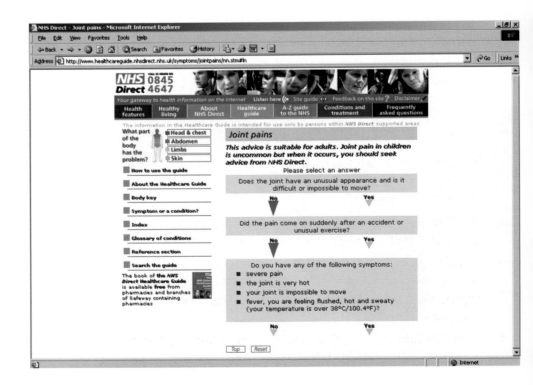

A screen from NHS Direct. Notice the way it asks you questions on your condition so that it can assess whether a trip to the doctor is necessary

NHS Direct Online is a new website that provides information on non-serious conditions such as coughs, colds, sore throats, etc. Doctors spend a lot of time with patients who have non-serious conditions that would clear up by themselves after a couple of days. Patients can now get advice on these conditions over the Internet, or over the telephone from qualified nurses. This frees up GPs' time for more serious cases.

Take a look at the website on: `www.nhsdirect.nhs.uk`

The police

The police force is considered a community service. One of its tasks is to make links with local communities in the fight against crime.

The police force is not simply there to catch criminals, it is also there to prevent crime. Here are some ICT developments that have helped prevent crime:

- Speed and red-light cameras deter drivers from committing offences and make the roads a safer place. Some of the latest digital cameras send an image of the car to the police computer that then looks up the registration number and sends the registered keeper a warning or a fine.
- Computerised camera systems monitor the areas around shopping centres, bars and other areas where people congregate to deter would-be criminals.

Here are some ICT developments that have helped detect crime:

- Police force websites where members of the public can inform anonymously on people they know who have committed an offence.
- A national computer system called the Police National Computer (PNC) which all police forces can access.
- National fingerprint collection on computer enables fingerprints found at the scene of a crime to be compared and matched with all those kept on the computer.
- DNA profiling, where DNA samples are compared and matched with samples taken from suspects or criminals.

On-line discussion forums

There are many websites on the Internet where people with similar opinions and interests can discuss matters that are important to them, such as health or political issues.

After topical or controversial television programmes, websites are often advertised where you can find further information on the subject raised.

Pressure groups are groups of people who try to change legislation or public opinion over an issue they feel strongly about, such as fox hunting or testing drugs on animals. There are many pressure groups that promote environmental issues, such as a group called Greenpeace.

It is important that issues raised by pressure groups are actively debated. There are always two sides to an argument. On-line discussion forums enable people with both points of view to debate the matter.

ACTIVITY

1   What is meant by the term 'pressure group'?
2   Explain what is meant by 'on-line discussion forum'.
3   Use the Internet to find some discussion forums and websites for pressure groups. Write a summary of how these forums and websites can be of use to people with the same interests or views.

ICT and people with special needs

There are many ways in which ICT can help people with special or particular needs. Disabled people have needs that depend on the nature and extent of their disability. ICT can present these people with many new opportunities and make their lives more fulfilling. We will now look at how ICT can help improve the quality of life of people with various disabilities.

People with a sensory impairment

People with a sensory impairment include those who are blind or partially sighted. It also includes people who are deaf or who lack clear speech. If a person is blind then ICT can help through the use of a talking computer. Instead of appearing on screen, the text is 'spoken' as it is typed in by the user or output by the computer. For people who are partially sighted, computer screens are available that use very large characters.

Blind people can also use a special Braille keyboard to put data into a computer (see page 179).

For partially-sighted users, there are keyboards with large coloured keys that are easier to see. Each key is about 2.5 centimetres square (see page 179).

There are also printers that can print in Braille using raised dots, so the output can be read by someone who is blind. Braille monitors use raised pins which the user moves their fingers over to read.

People who have a physical disability

A physical disability usually affects a person's mobility. For example, it could mean that they are unable to use their arms or hands or they may be unable to walk. In some cases the mobility problem can be so severe the person is almost completely paralysed.

People who are unable to write because of their disability can use voice-activated systems to put data into a computer.

People who have a learning difficulty

Someone who has learning difficulties finds it harder to learn than the majority of people in the same age group. This can affect their ability to read, write and recall important information. ICT can help make things easier to learn for these people by using the following hardware and software:

- **Multimedia** – some people find it hard to listen. Multimedia makes use of more then one sense to help reinforce learning.
- **Overlay keyboard** – these keyboards make it easier for a user to select a certain key.

- **Spellcheckers** – spellcheck software can help people with dyslexia to check the spelling of words.
- **Touch screens** – users can select options by touching part of the screen rather than having to use the keyboard or mouse.
- **Speech recognition systems** – instead of typing in text or making selections using the mouse, the user can create text or give commands using speech.
- **Predictive wordprocessors** – these wordprocessors can predict the ending of a word after you have typed in the first few letters. This is helpful for people who are slow at typing.

People with multiple disabilities

Unfortunately some people have multiple disabilities and experience more than one of the problems described above. There are huge numbers of ways in which ICT can help people with individual needs, and here are just some of them.

If mobility is a problem then just a simple trip to the corner shop is difficult, and a trip to the local library might be a major undertaking. Now, books, newspapers, magazines, films, music and software can be accessed using the Internet without the person having to leave their home. The Internet can also be used to order taxis and book seats for concerts.

If a person cannot speak or their speech is not clear, then they have a problem communicating with others. Sometimes they are misunderstood and this can be very frustrating for them. There are ICT systems where the user can type in messages and the computer turns them into speech.

People with multiple individual needs often need a carer to help them with their daily activities. In some cases the carer has to be with the person almost all the time. This causes problems if either the person being cared for, or the carer, wants to be more independent. The use of mobile phones, which both people can have with them at all times, means that the carer is only a phone call away if they are needed or if they want to check that the person they are caring for is all right.

Some people with individual needs have problems opening and closing doors and windows. They may have problems operating lights or central heating systems. With the use of voice activation, they can issue commands to operate these devices.

Some people with medical problems need constant access to medical equipment. For example, someone with kidney problems may need regular dialysis. This makes it very difficult for these people to go out to work in a regular 'nine-to-five' job. With the use of ICT equipment and the Internet, it is now possible for many such people to work from home.

Specially adapted hardware and software

Induction loops

If a person has hearing problems then the problem can be solved by them wearing a hearing aid. Hearing aids are simply amplifiers that fit in one or both ears. But as well as amplifying the sounds the person wants to hear, the hearing aid also amplifies any unwanted sounds. This can make it difficult for someone who has hearing problems to use the telephone in, for example, a busy office where there is a lot of background noise.

An induction loop allows sound to be transmitted from the phone to the user's ear through a magnetic field rather than through the air. This means that there is no background noise picked up along the way, and the sound received is clear. The induction coil is fitted into a hearing aid, and it enables people with hearing problems to lead normal lives and to have the same employment opportunities as everyone else. For an induction loop system to work, there needs to an induction coil in the listener's hearing aid and also an induction loop fitted in the place of work or entertainment. Both are needed for the system to work.

Induction loop systems can be found in many public places such as churches, cinemas, service counter windows and telephones.

Environmental control systems

People with special or particular needs feel they are restricted in the amount of control they have over their surroundings. For example, they may not be able to open windows if it is too hot. They may be unable to use the small switches to turn lights on or off or to alter the volume on a radio or TV.

Environmental control units can control the environment in which a person lives. They can be tailored to people's needs to ensure that they are able to operate them easily. An occupational therapist assesses a person's requirements and then the control unit is specially designed so that they can use it. In some cases, large buttons are used to input instructions, while others may be operated by simply bending a finger. Where a person is severely disabled, the system can accept commands by blowing or sucking on a tube. It is also possible to issue voice commands to control the environment.

Speech synthesis systems

Speech synthesis is the production of an electronic voice as the output from a system. Using one system, called a Braille'n Speak notetaker, a person types in notes using a simple Braille keyboard. The notes are stored in the memory of the notetaker. The notes can then be played back using speech synthesis.

Speech synthesis systems can also read out information from other computers, floppy disks or the Internet.

Videoconferencing

Videoconferencing allows two or more individuals situated in different places to talk to each other and see each other at the same time. They are also able to exchange electronic files with each other.

THE JARGON DRAGON

videoconferencing – using computer equipment to conduct a virtual face-to-face meeting

Videoconferencing systems can be used to assist people with dementia and their carers living in remote areas. Dementia is an illness which impairs memory, orientation, comprehension, language, judgement, emotional control and social behaviour. Using videoconferencing, the carer is able to seek professional help directly it is required.

ICT and older people

You may think that the latest technology is only used by younger people. This is not true, and it can bring benefits for all members of society. People are retiring much earlier than in the past and so they may have a lot of time to fill. As people get older they have more time to think about what is important in their lives, such as family, friends, their local community, etc. More and more people are living longer and older people are making up an increasingly large portion of society. When people get older they have more health and mobility problems, and they will sooner or later have to cope with the death of a partner. The use of the Internet can help them overcome the problems that these events can bring. There are many advantages of ICT for older people, and these are summarised here.

What are the advantages of ICT for older people?

Many older people are realising the benefits of using ICT. Using ICT they can:

- keep in touch with grandchildren and other family members who may be located all over the world
- learn new skills using the computer
- communicate with people who share the same interests using chat-rooms
- explore their family history (this is called genealogy)
- gain access to the vast amounts of information on the Internet, from health to gardening
- form self-help groups to deal with problems such as serious illness, bereavement, etc.

RESEARCH TASK

For this task you are required to produce a presentation on how ICT can be used to help older people in their everyday lives. Your presentation is to be given to a group of senior citizens who are all thinking of buying computer equipment.

You will need to cover the following:

- *what they can use the equipment for*
- *how other groups of senior citizens have made use of ICT.*

For your presentation you can either produce the presentation yourself, or use presentation software.

As part of your presentation you will need to produce a handout that contains some of the information covered in your talk. Try to make this as interesting and as lively as possible. Make use of diagrams, photographs, clip art, etc.

When you are doing your research, as well as the text (i.e. what you are going to write) you should also research diagrams, photographs, clip art, etc. These will not only brighten up your report or presentation, but also make it more interesting.

FIND IT OUT

If you spot a picture or diagram on a web page that you would like to use, move the cursor onto the diagram and click on the right mouse button. Select Copy from the menu displayed and this will put a copy of the picture or diagram on the clipboard. You can then go into your document (wordprocessor or DTP) and paste it into a suitable position.

You should also consider producing some of your own photographs using a digital camera, or scanning in artwork from books and magazines.

Think IT THROUGH

If you intend to produce a presentation using presentation software then you will need to consider the following:

- *animation – moving text and pictures*
- *sequencing – putting the slides in a logical order*
- *timing the slides – making sure that the slides remain on the screen long enough for the text to be read by the slowest reader.*

You should always show your presentation to someone else to make sure that the content can be understood and that your timing of the slides is right.

The future: human–machine links?

In the future, it may be possible to send signals between the human brain and a computer. This means that you would have access to all the information stored in the computer. You wouldn't need to add numbers up in your head as the computer could do this for you. You wouldn't even need to tell the computer what numbers you wanted to add up; just thinking them, and thinking that you want to add them up, would be enough.

ICT developments are only available to those people who have the money to pay for them. Computer equipment and access to the Internet is a luxury for many people, and for some an impossible dream.

In Scotland a large grant has been allocated to make ICT available to the more disadvantaged members of society. ICT facilities will be provided in libraries so that everyone, from toddlers to senior citizens, can use them. The money will also be used to:

- widen Internet access by using wireless technology in mobile libraries
- develop local community websites with links to government services, job opportunities, events, etc.
- increase access to specialist software and hardware for people with special needs.

Launching the fund in 2001, Ms Baillie said:

"Only 14 per cent of households in Scotland have access to the Internet at home. With computers increasingly conditioning the kind of country we live in, it is crucial that we widen access. Libraries are an ideal access point for everybody in the community.

"Internet services such as local government, banking and supermarkets are starting to make a real difference to people's lives. New technology is also opening up learning opportunities by allowing people to fit study or skills training comfortably in their daily schedule.

"But this technology must not be allowed to create exclusion. We simply can't afford to leave people outside this information loop. This funding will help to ensure that everyone has high quality access to digital technology and information.

"We are determined to accelerate the number of households in disadvantaged areas with access to the Internet, and to have universal Internet access by 2005."

case study

Access to ICT for deprived communities

Questions

1 *Why do you think it is important to widen access to the Internet in deprived communities? Write a sentence to explain your answer.*

2 *The case study mentions access to digital technology. Give the names of three applications of digital technology.*

3 *Describe three things a senior citizen might want to do using the Internet.*

Communication across the Internet could be done using thought signals alone. Imagine how powerful our brains would be if they had all the information on the Internet available to them. And if we can communicate with the Internet by using thought, then it could be possible to communicate with each other simply by using thought. Speech as a way of communicating may no longer be needed.

If there is the possibility of linking the human body to a machine, then life as we know it will be a lot different in years to come. It may be possible to make the blind see or the paralysed walk using this future technology.

FIND IT OUT

There is a good site with information on virtual reality and nanocomputers (very small computers) at:

`www.transhumanism.org/`

Here is a brief summary of a newspaper article that appeared in the *Guardian* on 5 December 2000:

When the Internet first started it promised so much. Many people thought that it would change our lives forever. Books, films, shopping and banking would all be virtual. Our high streets would become deserted as everyone shopped or banked from home.

Do you think that this has happened? I don't think so. Some people who had the Internet have given up using it. Two million people in the UK have given up using the Internet. It is interesting to note that the teenagers, the very group who new technology should appeal to, are leaving in greater volumes than any other age group.

One commentator said 'they have looked at what the Internet has to offer and have decided that there is more to life in the real world'. He went on to say 'people really want real books and to watch movies with other people and to communicate with real people'.

Questions

1   The writer of the article suggests that it is the end of the digital dream. Do you agree? Support your answers with one example.

2   Give one reason why people may have left the Internet.

3   Do you see high street banks and shops being completely replaced by virtual banks and shops? Give a reason for your answer.

Glossary

Absolute referencing: in this type of referencing, a particular cell is used in a formula and when this formula is copied to a new address, the cell address does not change. *Compare with* relative referencing.

Access: to obtain data from a computer.

Address book: a list of the names and e-mail addresses of people to whom you are likely to send e-mail.

ADSL (Asymmetric Digital Subscriber Loop): a broadband service that provides greater bandwidth for the downstream data traffic (i.e. the data from the site that you are visiting) than for the data travelling in the other direction.

ALU: *see* arithmetic and logic unit.

Application: what a computer can be used to do.

Application software: software designed to do a particular type of job.

Applications package: a program or a set of programs designed to carry out a particular application, such as accounts or payroll.

Arithmetic and logic unit: part of the central processing unit. It performs all the arithmetic and logic operations.

ATM (automated teller machine): a cash dispenser which performs many of the tasks previously done by bank clerks. You can obtain cash, statements, make deposits, etc.

Automation: the automatic control of a process or system, i.e. one that does not require a human operator.

Backing storage: storage outside of the computer (i.e. it excludes ROM and RAM).

Backing store: memory storage outside the CPU. It is non-volatile which means the data does not disappear when the computer is switched off.

BACS (Bankers' Automated Clearing Service): an organisation set up by all the main banks to deal with standing orders and direct debits. Both of these involve making payments direct into bank accounts.

Back-up file: a copy of a file which is used in the event of the original file being corrupted (damaged).

Bandwidth: the factor that determines how fast data can be passed along a communication channel.

Barcode: a series of lines on labels on items such as goods, luggage, etc. used to encode information about the item.

Barcode reader: an input device used to scan a barcode.

Bit: a binary digit; 0 or 1.

Bitmap: an image represented by patterns of tiny dots called pixels.

Bitmap graphics: graphics formed by a pattern of pixels. The whole picture is stored as a series of dots.

Broadband: a very high-speed Internet connection (usually cable).

Bug: a mistake or error in a program.

Bullet point: an indented paragraph or section of text that has a symbol placed in front to make the section of text stand out.

Byte: the amount of memory needed to store one character, such as a letter or a number. *See also* kilobyte and megabyte.

C++: a general purpose programming language which is easier to understand than assembly language but runs almost as fast. It is a development of the programming language C.

CAD (computer-aided design): the use of computers to produce designs.

Call centre: a place where staff deal with enquiries from the general public. Call centres make extensive use of ICT equipment.

CAM (computer-aided manufacture): the use of computer-based systems to control the machinery in manufacturing processes.

CD-ROM: compact disk read-only memory. A compact disk containing data and programs in read-only memory.

CD-RW: compact disk read/write. A CD that can be used in a similar way to a floppy disk (i.e. you can store and alter data on it many times).

Cell: an area on a spreadsheet produced by the intersection of a column and a row in which data can be placed.

CPU (central processing unit): the computer's 'brain'. It stores and processes data. It has three parts: the ALU, the control unit and the memory.

Character: any symbol that you can type from the keyboard.

Check digit: a number placed after a string of numbers that is used to check that they have all been correctly input to the computer.

Chip: an integrated circuit etched onto a thin slice of silicon.

Clip art: predrawn computer artwork that is available for people to use.

Computer Misuse Act 1990: a law that covers the misuse of computer equipment.

Configuration: the hardware that is needed to set up a certain computer system.

Copyright, Designs and Patents Act 1989: a law making it a criminal offence to copy or steal software.

CPS (characters per second): a measure of the speed of data transfer between hardware devices.

Credit card: a plastic card containing a magnetic stripe that is used to make purchases. You are given a limit, called a credit limit, and you are not allowed to go above this.

Cybercafé: a coffee shop that also offers Internet access and other computing facilities.

Data: information in a form that a computer can understand.

Database: a series of files stored in a computer that can be accessed in a variety of different ways.

Data capture: the way a computer obtains its data for processing.

Data compression: taking files on a disk and using software to reduce their size so that they take up less space on the disk.

Data logging: a system that automatically collects data over a certain period of time. Remote weather stations use data logging.

Data processing: doing something with raw data to produce some form of useful output.

Data Protection Act 1998: a law that restricts the way personal information is stored and processed on a computer.

Data warehouse: a computerised database system where all the data an organisation needs is stored.

Debit card: a plastic card with a magnetic stripe on it. It can be used to make purchases. The money is instantly transferred from your account to the store's account.

Debugging: removing all the errors from a program.

Desktop publishing: combining text and pictures on a screen to produce posters, newsletters, brochures, etc.

DFD (dataflow diagram): a diagram showing the information flows in an organisation.

Digital: a device (including most computers) that works using data represented by numbers.

Digital camera: a camera that takes a picture and stores it digitally.

Disk: a storage medium used to hold data.

Document: a text file produced by a wordprocessor.

Documentation: the paperwork that accompanies an information system explaining how the system works. The manuals that accompany a program or software package.

Download: to copy files from a distant computer to the one you are working on.

DPI (dots per inch): the term used to describe the resolution of printers. The sharpness of the printed image depends on the DPI.

DSL (Digital Subscriber Loop): a broadband service that combines separate voice and data channels over a single cable.

DVD (digital versatile disk): disk with a larger storage capacity than a CD-ROM. It is set to replace CD-ROMs. Recent models allow the user to write data to the disk.

e-commerce: conducting business by making use of the Internet.

e-mail (electronic mail): e-mail messages and documents can be created, sent and read without the need for them to be printed out.

EDI (electronic data interchange): a network link that allows companies to make payments electronically.

Edit: to change something stored on a computer.

EFT (electronic funds transfer): the process of transferring money electronically without the need for paperwork or the delay that using paperwork brings.

EFTPOS (electronic funds transfer at point of sale): where funds are transferred electronically at a point-of-sale terminal.

Encryption: the process of encoding sensitive files before they are sent over a network.

EPOS (electronic point of sale): a computerised till which can be used for stock control.

Ergonomics: the science of designing work equipment and working environments so as to maximise the efficiency of the people working with or in them.

Evaluation: the process of determining the quality of software or hardware.

Fact finding: investigating a system prior to performing a feasibility study.

Fax machine: a machine capable of sending and receiving text and pictures via telephone lines.

Feasibility study: a study carried out by experts before a new system is developed to see whether it will be able to do the job required, within budget, etc.

Fibre optics: thin strands of glass along which light signals pass for communication purposes.

Field: a space in a database used for inputting data. For instance, there might be fields for surname, date of birth, etc.

Field check: a check performed by a computer to see if the data is of the right type to be put into a field. For example, It could check that only numbers are entered into a numeric field.

File: a collection of data stored under one name; for example, a student file could contain details of all the students in a school.

File attachment: a file that is attached to an e-mail.

File server: a network computer used for storing all the users' programs and data.

Flat-file database: a database that is able to use only one file at a time, unlike a relational database, which is able to use two or more files at a time.

Floppy disk: a magnetically coated disk used to store data. The 3.5 inch disk is inside a hard case.

Flowchart: a flow diagram. A chart or diagram used to break down a task into a series of smaller parts.

Font: a style of type.

Footer: text placed at the bottom of a document.

Form: a screen used to enter data into a database. It can also be a document that is used to collect data.

Function: a predefined formula for making a certain kind of calculation.

Gateway: the computer link that translates between two different kinds of computer networks.

GIGO (garbage in garbage out): the idea that if you put rubbish into a computer then you get rubbish out.

GIS (Geographical Information System): database arranged spatially using a map.

Grammar checker: a program (usually part of a wordprocessing package) that checks a document for grammatical errors and suggests corrections.

Graph plotter: a device that draws by moving a pen. It is useful for scale drawings and is used mainly with CAD packages.

Graphics: diagrams, charts or graphs either on a screen or printed out.

GUI (graphical user interface): a way of allowing users to communicate with a computer that makes use of icons and pull-down menus. Windows is a GUI and Macintosh computers use a GUI.

Hacking: the process of a person trying to break into a secure computer system.

Hard copy: printed output from a computer which can be taken away and studied.

Hard disk: a rigid magnetic disk which provides more storage and faster access than a floppy disk.

Hard drive: a computer unit containing a hard disk.

Hardware: the parts of a computer system that you can touch and handle, including the visual display unit, processor, printer, modem, etc.

Hash total: a meaningless total of numbers used to check that all necessary numbers have been entered into a computer.

Header: text placed at the top of a document.

Health and Safety at Work Act 1974: a law to ensure that employees have a safe place to work.

Health and Safety Regulations 1992: laws which cover working with VDUs.

HTML (Hypertext Markup Language): a language used for the development of websites.

Icons: symbols displayed on a computer screen in the form of a menu.

Immediate access store: storage in the memory of the central processing unit (i.e. RAM and ROM).

Implementation: the process of converting to a new system.

Information: what we get from a set of data.

Information retrieval: the process of recovering information after it has been stored.

Information technology: the application of a combination of computing, electronics and communications.

Ink-jet printer: a printer that works by spraying ink through nozzles onto paper.

Input: data fed into a computer for processing.

Integrated circuit: semiconductor circuits inside a single crystal of semiconductor.

Interactive: a program or system that allows a user to respond to questions from a computer (and vice versa) and immediately acts on the answers.

Interface: the hardware and software used to enable devices to be connected together. (e.g. an interface would be needed to connect a joystick to a computer)

Internet: worldwide network of computer networks. The Internet forms the largest connected set of computers in the world.

Invoice: a bill.

ISDN (Integrated Services Digital Network): a communications standard for sending voice, video and data over digital telephone lines. It is much faster than sending data using modems.

ISP (Internet service provider): a company that provides a connection to the Internet.

Jaz drive: fast, removable and high-storage disk drive. It is used for backing up hard drives.

Joystick: an input device used instead of the cursor keys or mouse as a way of moving around a computer screen.

K: kilobyte, or 1024 bytes. Often abbreviated to KB. A measure of the storage capacity of disks and memory.

Keyboard: a computer keyboard consists of the standard typewriter keys plus calculator keys and some special function keys.

Key-to-disk: a way of inputting data directly into a computer and onto disk using the keyboard.

LAN (local area network): a network of computers on one site.

Laptop: a portable computer small enough to fit in your lap. Laptop computers use rechargeable batteries.

Laser printer: a printer which uses a laser beam to form characters on paper.

LCD (liquid crystal display): a flat screen which looks similar to that on a calculator except it is much bigger and can also be in colour.

Magnetic media: media such as tape and disk where the data is stored as a magnetic pattern.

Magnetic stripe reader: reads the data contained in magnetic stripes, such as those on the back of credit cards.

Mail merge: combining a master file with a secondary file containing variable data such as names and addresses to produce multiple documents such as mail shots.

Mailing list: a list of people and their e-mail addresses.

Mainframe: a large computer system with a number of 'dumb' terminals attached.

Mainstore: memory inside a CPU.

Master file: the main source of information and the most important file.

Medium: the material on which data can be stored, such as magnetic disk, tape, etc.

Memory: area of storage inside silicon chips. ROM and RAM are two types of memory.

Merge: to combine data from two different sources.

Megabyte: one million bytes.

Megahertz (MHz): one million cycles per second. The speed of the internal clock which controls the speed of the pulses in the computer is measured in megahertz. Chip design and clock speed determine the overall performance of the CPU.

MICR (magnetic ink character recognition): method of input that involves reading magnetic ink characters on certain documents. MICR is used on cheques by banks.

Microcomputer: a cheap, relatively slow computer that can work on only one program at a time. The memory is usually limited.

Model: a computer program that mimics a real situation.

Modem: MODulator/DEModulator. A modem converts data from a computer into a form that can be passed along a telephone wire.

Monitor: another name for a VDU.

Mouse: an input device which, when moved over a flat surface, moves the cursor on a computer screen. Buttons on a mouse are pressed to make a selection from a menu.

MP3: a file format for music files that makes use of compression.

Multimedia: software that combines more than one medium for presentation purposes, such as sound, graphics and video.

Network: a group of computers which are able to communicate with each other. *See also* LAN and WAN.

Network interface card (NIC): a card which slots into the motherboard of the computer and is used primarily to reduce the amount of cabling in a network.

Notebook: a small portable computer.

OCR (optical character recognition): a combination of software and a scanner which is able to read characters into a computer.

OMR (optical mark reader/recognition): a reader that detects marks on a piece of paper. Shaded areas are detected and the computer is able to interpret the information contained in them.

On/off-line: when a device is under the control of the computer it is said to be on-line; otherwise it is off-line.

Operating system: the software that controls the hardware and also runs the programs.

Output: the results obtained from processing data.

Output device: a device used to output the results of processing.

Package: sometimes called an applications package. A set of programs, with documentation, used to perform a task or a set of tasks.

Password: a string of characters (letters and/or numbers) that the user (or the person who looks after the network) can select. It is used to authenticate the user to the system. Only if you type in the correct password will you be allowed access.

PDA (personal digital assistant): a small computer used mainly for organising a busy schedule.

Peripheral: a device connected to and under the control of a CPU.

PIN (personal identification number): a secret number that needs to be keyed in to gain access to a cash dispenser.

Piracy: the illegal copying and use of software.

Pixel: the smallest individual dot of light on a computer screen.

Port: an external connection point on a computer where input, output and other devices can be connected.

Presence check: a check carried out to ensure that a field in a database has data entered into it.

Presentation graphics: an applications package for producing slides, graphics etc.

Primary key: a field that uniquely defines a row in a table in a relational database.

Privacy: the rights of individuals to decide what information about them should be known by others.

Processed: raw data is processed by a computer to give information. Processing includes calculating, sorting, searching and storing.

Programmer: a person who writes computer programs.

Protocol: a set of standards that allows the transfer of data between computers on a network.

QWERTY: the arrangement of the letters on a standard keyboard.

RAM (random access memory): a fast, temporary memory where programs and data are stored while a computer is switched on.

Range check: a data validation technique which checks that the data input to a computer is within a certain range.

Real time: A real-time system accepts data and processes it immediately. The results have a direct effect on the next set of available data.

Record: a set of related information about a thing or individual. Records are subdivided into fields.

Regulation of Investigatory Powers Act 2000: a law that gives the government permission to monitor all electronic communication.

Relational database: a database that consists of several files. It is possible to use a single file to access data in several of the other files.

Relationships: the ways in which tables are related to each other in a relational database.

Relative referencing: when a cell is used in a formula and the formula is copied to a new address, the cell address changes to take account of the formula's new position. *Compare with* absolute referencing.

Remote sensing: the process by which sensors, such as environmental sensors, are connected via communication lines to the main computer.

Report: the output from software such as a database in which the results are presented in a way that is controlled by the user.

Robot: a machine or device that has been programmed to carry out a process (usually mechanical) automatically.

ROM (read-only memory): computer memory whose contents can be read but not altered.

RSI (repetitive strain injury): a painful muscular condition caused by repeatedly using certain muscles in the same way.

Scanner: a hardware device used to scan photographs or text into a computer system.

Screen dump: a printout of what appears on the computer screen.

Search: to look for an item of data.

Sensors: devices which measure physical quantities such as temperature, pressure, etc.

Simulation: an imitation of a system using a computer program (e.g. an aircraft flight simulator, or a simulation of how a country's economy works).

Smartcard: a plastic card which is 'intelligent' because it contains its own chip.

SMS (Simple Message Service): the service that mobile phones use to send and receive text messages.

Software: the programs used by a computer. *Compare with* hardware.

Source documents: the original documents from which data is taken.

Spellchecker: a program, usually part of a wordprocessing package, which checks the spelling of words in a document and suggests corrections.

Spreadsheet: a software package which consists of a grid used to contain text, numbers or formulae. Spreadsheets can be used to produce financial predictions.

Systems analyst: a person who studies the overall organisation and implementation of a business system.

Table: a structure used to hold data in a relational database.

Tape: magnetic media used to store data.

Tape streamer: tape drive used for backing up data and programs on a hard drive.

Telecommunications: the field of technology concerned with communicating at a distance (e.g. telephones, radio, cable, etc.).

Teleworker: a person who works from home by making use of ICT equipment.

Templates: electronic files which hold standardised document layouts.

Terminal: a computer on a network, or a keyboard and monitor, connected to a mini or mainframe computer.

Test data: data used to test a program or flowchart for logical errors.

Thesaurus: software which suggests words with similar meanings to the word highlighted in a document. Thesauruses are usually form part of a wordprocessing package.

Thumbnail: a rough design drawn on paper, or a small image of a page displayed on a computer screen.

Toner: the 'ink' used by laser printers consisting of tiny black plastic particles.

Topology: the layout of the components in a computer network.

Touch screen: a special type of screen that is sensitive to touch. A selection is made from a menu on the screen by touching part of it.

Update: the process of changing information in a file that has become out of date.

USB (universal serial bus): a fast external bus that supports the fast transfer of data.

User: a person who uses a computer.

Validation check: a check performed by a computer program to make sure that the data is allowable.

Validation rule: the rule governing a validation check.

Validation text: a message displayed if a validation rule is breached.

VDU (visual display unit): the screen on which data is displayed. Also called a monitor.

Verification: checking the accuracy of data entry.

Videoconferencing: using computer equipment to conduct a virtual face-to-face meeting.

Virtual reality: computer technology which creates a simulated multidimensional environment for the user.

Virus: a nasty program created to do damage to a computer system.

Voice recognition: the ability of a computer to 'understand' spoken words by comparing them with stored data.

WAN (wide area network): A network whose terminals are remote from each other and telecommunications are used to communicate between them.

WAP (Wireless Application Protocol): a mobile phone service that allows the phone to access the Internet.

Web browser: software used to help you search for information on the Internet.

Web camera: a digital camera used to capture still and video images.

Web server: a computer containing a website's information. Users can access the webserver using the Internet.

Website: a site on the World Wide Web which provides information or views about a person, products or services. There are often links to other websites.

WIMP (Windows Icons Menus Pointing devices): operating a computer using a graphical user interface (GUI) rather than by typing in commands at the command line.

Windows: a graphical user interface designed by Microsoft used on many desktop computers.

Wordprocessor: a computer application that allows text to be typed in, displayed on a VDU and edited before being printed out.

World Wide Web: a system of file servers on the Internet that supports special documents in a language called HTML. It also supports graphics, audio and video files.

Wrap: the process by which a computer automatically starts a new line.

Write–protect notch: a notch found on a 3.5 inch floppy disk which, when opened, will not allow data to be stored on the disk.

Zip drive: a high-capacity floppy disk drive. Disks are removable and can typically store 100MB.

Index

A4 paper size 115–116
absolute cell references 62–3
Access
    forming relationships between
        tables in 87
    loading 80, 92, 97
accounts department 135
active citizenship 287–93
addition 43
address book 33, 34, 228
ADSL (Asymmetric Digital
    Subscriber Loop) 236
advertising 113, 114, 185, 255–6
    case study 257
    Internet 277
air traffic control 296
align left 8
align right 9
Amazon, case study 132
animation 306
animation schemes 109–10
applications packages 118
applications software 4, 113–14,
    177, 205
    examples 178
arrows 198
Article Number Association (ANA)
    168
assignments 124
attachment see file attachments
auctions, on-line 250
automatic sensing 142
AutoNumber 72, 77
AutoSum 49
average 57, 59, 61

backache 273
backing storage 177
backup copies 123, 160
backup devices 191
backup procedures 170
    BACS (Bankers' Automated
        Clearing Service) 139
bandwidth 234
banking
    functions 252–3
    Internet 253
    virtual 252–4
barcode reader 166, 183–4, 222

barcodes 166–8, 183–4
blagging 283
blind people 301
BMW 5 Series cars, case study
    245–6
bogus companies 278
bold 7, 57
booking systems 148
    flowchart 195
    Internet 149–50
bookmarks 35–6
Boolean search 38
box 198
boys versus girls exercise 57–61
Braille 301
    keyboard 179
Britannia Airways
    benefits of ICT 163
    case study 162–5
    communication with cus-
        tomers, suppliers and staff
        162
    engineering system 164
    financial system 164
    forecasting 163–4
    management information sys-
        tems 164
    strategic planning 163–4
broadband 235, 236, 240
    applications 236
    main features 235
    see also ADSL; DSL
broadband services 240
    activity 241
bullet points 11
business, ICT use in 247–59
business documents 113–19
    accuracy 116
    clarity 116
    consistency 116
    design 113
    evaluation 118–19
    layout 115–16
    number of copies 116
    presentation 115
    producing 119
    research tasks 117–19
    software applications 118
    target audience 114

tone 115
types and their purpose 114,
    118

cable systems 240
cables 187
cache 37
CAD 109, 120–1, 170
    see also CAD/CAM
CAD/CAM 5, 120–1
CAL 158
calculations 41, 43, 49–50
call centres 255, 262, 265
CAM 120–1
    see also CAD/CAM
car park management systems
    146–7
car speeding systems 146
cartoons, website 32
cash flow forecasts 140
CD drive 190
CD player 285
CD-ROM 287
CD-RW (Read/Write) 190
CDs 243
cell presentation formats 64–5
cell references 62–3
cells 40
    aligning 64–5
    copying and pasting 48
    cutting and pasting 48
    formatting to match data types
        63–4
central processing unit (CPU) 186
centre text 9
chairs 126, 127, 272, 273, 275,
    276
charts 40, 44–8
    location 47
    options 46
    size 47
    sub-type 53
    title box 54
    type 46
    wizard 46, 53, 54, 55
chat-room 251, 283, 287
    case study 280–1
    North/South Korea 290
checkout information 169

children, checking in nurseries 185
chips 189
civil rights 290
clip art 15–19, 34, 122
clipboard 6, 7, 306
Clubcard 173
code, security 231–3
codes of practice 125–6
    Internet 277–8
college enrolment 200
college enrolment system (activity) 200–1
colour-coded keyboard 179
colour of text 8
colour schemes 110
columns 40, 42
    deleting 42–3
    inserting 42
communication 32–9
communications software 33
    features 35–7
community activities 293–300
    websites 293
compressing files 285
computer-aided design see CAD
computer-aided design/computer-aided manufacture see CAD/CAM
computer-aided learning (CAL) 158
computer games 285
computer graphics (exercise) 109
Computer Misuse Act 1990 126
computer requirements for publishing 30
computerised camera systems 299
computerised database see databases
computerised simulation 142
computers
    authorisation 290
    mainframe 170
    vs. television 285
control, research 121–2
copy and paste 48
copy-holder 127, 275
copying text 6–7
copyright 124
Copyright, Designs and Patents Act 126, 270–1, 286
correlation between amount spent on advertising and

appointments booked 54–6
Cozy Plastics, case study 213–17
crash testing, case study 245–6
credit/debit card 150, 167–9, 182, 232, 247, 250, 251, 278, 292, 295, 298
crime prevention 299
customer enquiries 255
customer information 258–9
customer targeting 268
customised database 250
cut and paste 48
cutting text 6, 7
cyber elections 287–8
    advantages and disadvantages 288
cybercafÇs 294
cycle optimiser 143

data
    definition 69
    types 71
data capture 185–6, 207
data controller 160
data entry form 96
    creating 97–101
data privacy 232–3, 277
data processing 186
    definition 258
Data Protection Act 126, 160, 268, 269
    website 270
Data Protection Commissioner 149, 160
data recording 123
data sources 204
data storage 154, 242–3
data storage devices 189–91
data type check 83
data warehouses 260
database 4, 65–101
    access 261
    advantages 69
    customised 250
    definition 154
    entering data 96
    estate agent 190–1
    extracting data from 92–6
    INFOTRAC 298
    opening 80–1
    patient 154
    personnel system 216
    primary key 71–2, 78, 82, 84, 89

relational 69, 72
    saving 74–5
    setting up 66–8
    sorting 66–7
    structure 70–1, 77
    tables 69–71, 74–9
    video hire store 220–2
database marketing 268–9
dataflow diagrams 198–201, 204
    example 198–200
day-to-day processing tasks 138–9
deadlines 124
    meeting 124
decimal places 57, 58
decimal point 57
decision boxes 194
dental records, security 160
dentist's practice
    administrative work 159
    case study 158–61
    stock control 161
departments 131
deprived communities, access to ICT, case study 307–8
design skills 264
design specification 203–5
desks 275
desktop publishing (DTP) 4, 5
    equipment 30–1
    hard drive 30
    memory 30
    screen size 30
    software 30
digital 240
Digital Audio Player (DAP) 285
digital broadcasting 240–1
digital camera 31, 34, 159, 184, 299, 306
Digital Subscriber Loop (DSL) 236
digital TV 289
digital X-ray camera 159
digitised photographs 191
direction finding 296
display screens 274
division 43
DNA profiling 299
document formatting features 10
documents see business documents
down scroll arrow 9
downloading 285
    times 277
    viruses 278

DVD 287
DVD disks 243
DVD drive 190
DVD read/write drive 243
dyslexia 302

e-commerce 248, 250
  home shopping 247
  NHS 156–7
e-mail 33–5, 171–2, 176, 222, 227
  advantages and disadvantges 229–30
  encryption 233
  file attachments 33–5, 229
  mailing lists 34
  off-line 227
  on-line 227
  preparation screen 33
  privacy 229
  reply 33, 227–8
  security 232
  unsolicited 277
e-mail addresses 33, 34, 228
e-mail facility 175
e-mail software 33
e-voting see electronic voting
EasyJet, case study 152–3
education 287
EFTPOS (electronic funds transfer at point of sales) 168–9
electric motors 187
electronic commerce see e-commerce
electronic data interchange (EDI) 159–60, 170
  examination entries 176
electronic fund transfer (EFT) 139
electronic mail see e-mail
electronic records 154
electronic school
  case study 174–6
  parents/carers access 176
  registers 174–5
electronic shelf labelling 169
electronic voting, case study 289
Emergency Vehicle Priority System 144
encryption 230–3, 250, 277
  arguments for and against 291–2
  definition 232
  e-mail 233
  problems 232–3
entering text 5–6

entertainment 285
environmental control sytems 303–4
environmental data 123
equals (=) sign 41, 43
estate agent database 190–1
ethics 283
European Article Number (EAN) 168
evaluation 210–11
events information 298
examination entries, electronic data interchange (EDI) 176
Excel 40–1, 125
  menu bar 40
  toolbars 40
Excite 38
eye strain 126, 272–3
eye tests 274

fact finding 203
favourite places 35–6
favourites 35–6
fax 260
fields 65, 70, 89
  definition 69
  description 77
  primary key 71–2, 78, 82, 84, 89
  selecting 72
file attachments 33–5, 229
file compression 285
file extensions 125
file management 123–7
file security 216
file server 226, 227
file storage 125, 216
filenames 125
files 65
  definition 69
filters 282
finance department 135
financial services 252–4
fingerprint collection 299
floppy disk drive 190
flowcharts 192–4
  symbols 192
  system 195
folders 125
font 8, 9
font size 9
foot rest 127
footers 10
forecasting 47, 139–40, 163–4

format menu 8
format picture screen 18
formatting text 7–8
formulae 41, 43, 60
  inserting 50
  printing 48
fraud, international 278
freedom of speech 291, 293
full-time posts 265
fully justify 9
functions 61–2

Gateway 188
general election 287–8
girls versus boys (exercise) 57–61
global positioning 295
grammar checkers 117
graphical methods 192–200
graphics images 15–16
  capturing 122
graphics software 122
graphs 40, 44–8
Groovy Movies, case study 218–23

hacking, definition 270
hand-held devices 241
hand-held satellite positioning systems 296
hard disk drive 189
hardware
  components 177, 221–2
  specially adapted 303–4
hazards, workplace 271
headers 10
Health and Safety at Work Act 1974 271–2
Health and Safety Executive 273
Health and Safety Regulations 126, 272–6
  implementation 274
  main requirements 274
health and safety rules 126
health risks, reducing 275–6
hearing aids 303
hearing problems 303
highlighting 6, 7, 13, 45, 57, 68
history list 36
holidays, Internet 254–5
home shopping 247
home working see teleworking; working from home
hospital appointments, case study 154
hot desking 261

hours of work 262
human–machine links, future 306
human rights abuse 290, 291, 292
hypertext links 37

ICT
  problems caused by 251
  systems design and implementation 201–23
  systems in organisations 128–76
  tools 113–14
  use in business 247–59
  use in organisations 120–3
IF function 57
illegal material 283
image manipulation 122
  research 121–2
induction loop systems 303
information, definition 69
information kiosks 297
information presentation 5
information selection in Internet 32–9
information services 297–9
information sources 204
INFOTRAC database 298
ink-jet printer 31, 187
input boxes 193
input devices 177–9
input requirements 205
inspections, workplace 274
interacting at work 266–7
interactive 240
interactive digital television 240
interactive program or system 230
International Air Transport Association (IATA) 163
international fraud 278
Internet 32–9, 122
  access ban 290
  access for deprived communities, case study 307–8
  access licence 290
  advantages 279
  advertising 277
  availability of offensive, illegal or unethical material 282–3
  banking 253
  booking systems 149–50
  connections 233–7
  definition 226

downloading 124, 240
electronic data interchange (EDI) 160
finding your way around 37
general use 285
history 36
holidays 254–5
home shopping 247
impact 279
information 294–5
lack of control 281
marketing, case study 152–3
medical advice 155
navigation 36–7
overview 279–93
political content monitoring 290
present status 309
public access 294
research 121–2
search engine 37, 38
searching 38–9
security 250
shopping, task 249
surfing 37, 237
terms and features 35–7
Tesco shopping service 172
times taken to deliver 1.5 megabyte file 236–7
tips concerning misuse 281
uncensored 290
voting 288
Internet Code of Practice (ICOP) 277–8
Internet Service Provider (ISP) 33–5, 38, 226, 228, 277, 278
ISDN (Integrated Services Digital Network) 234–5
italics 7

job availability 267
job design 274
job loss risk 265
joint aches 273
junk mail 230
justifying text 8

keyboard 5, 126, 179, 275, 276
  Braille 179
  overlay 301
keyboard skills 264
keywords 38–9

landscape 51
laptops 251

laser printer 31, 186–7
laser scanner 166
layout tab 18
learning difficulty aids 301–2
left justified 8
legend 55
legislation 125–6, 267–78
leisure 285
leisure time changes 266
lifelong learning 287
lights 275
links 35–6
  between tables 72
liquid-crystal shelf labels 169
local area network (LAN) 12
loyalty card 173, 182
Lycos 38

magnetic ink character recognition (MICR) 181
magnetic stripe reader 182
mail merge 19–30
  customize 23–4
  exercise 20
  preview your letter 29
  type a new list 22–3
  variable data 29
  write your letter 27
mailing lists 34, 228
main components see hardware; software
mainframe computers 170
management information system (MIS) 150, 164
many-to-many relationships 73
market research 258–9
marketing 256
  database 268–9
  Internet, case study 152–3
marketing function 140
mathematical operators 43
median 62
medical advice, Internet 155
medical records, security 155
merge, definition 19
Microsoft Office 5, 40, 101
Microsoft PowerPoint 5, 101, 107, 112
Microsoft Publisher 5
Microsoft Word 5
Mini Disc players 285
Mini Disc recorders 285
mobile phones 183, 237–9, 242, 251, 261–2, 289

advantages and disadvantages 284
tasks 239
useful situations 284
mobility problems 301–3
mode 62
modem 233–4
modem/terminal adapter 33
monitor 126, 186
monitoring
case study 141–7
physical and environmental data 123
motivation, teleworking 265
mouse 179
moving text 7
MP3 240
multimedia 4, 230, 301
definition 230
software 101–12
multiple disabilities 302–3
multiple search criteria 38–9
multiplication 43
music computer files 285
music selection 285

nanocomputers, website 308
Napster, case study 286
National Air Traffic Services 296
National Health Service (NHS) 298–9
case study 154–7
e-commerce 156–7
see also dentist's practice; NHS Direct Online
navigation 36–7
network interface cards (NIC) 188–9
network protocols 188
networks 154, 222–3, 261
definition 154
NHS Direct Online 155, 157, 298–9
noise 275

offensive material 282–3, 292
offset optimiser 143
older people 304
advantages of ICT for 305
presentation 305
one-to-many relationship 73, 90
one-to-one relationship 73
on-line, definition 155
on-line auctions 250

on-line bookings, security 150
on-line courses 287
on-line discussion forums 300
on-line shopping, case study 248
open rectangle 198
operating system 4
examples 178
software 177, 178
operations function 135
optical character recognition (OCR) 180
software 5, 31
optical mark recognition (OMR) 180–1
order processing 138
organisers 241
output 206
output boxes 193
output devices 177, 186–7
output requirements 204
overlay keyboard 301

paedophiles 283
Page Break Preview 67–8
paper-based school registers 174
paper sizes 115–116
part-time work 265
partially-sighted users 301
password 155
definition 155
pasting text 7
patient data, security 160
patient information 154
payroll processing 138
percentage 43
personal communications, overview 279–93
personal data
accessibility 269–70
privacy 268–9, 292
personal digital assistants (PDAs) 159, 241–2
personal information, misuse 278
personnel system
advantages and disadvantages of computerisation 214
case study 214
changes in working practices 216–17
computerisation 213–17
costs 217
data input 214–15
database 216
future trends 217

information requirements 214
main components 214–15
working practices 215
PGP (pretty good privacy) 293
physical disability 301
pictures 34
website 32
planning 124
police 299
Police National Computer (PNC) 146, 299
pollution monitoring 145
pornographic images/videos 282–3
pornography 292
ports 187–8
posters 113
PowerPoint 5, 101, 112
loading 107
predictive wordprocessors 302
presence checks 85
presentation
software 5, 101
structure 101
presentations
design 106
evaluating 306
producing 107–12
templates 106–8
presidential election 289
pressure groups 300
primary key 71–2, 78, 82, 84, 89
printed reports 206
printer 31, 301
printing
formulae 48
reports 106
spreadsheet 49–51, 68
printout 206
privacy 293
infringement 278
personal data 268–9
voting 289
process boxes 193
process control, case study 141–7
process requirements 204–5
production planning 169
promotional analysis 168
proof-reading 117
public access to Internet 294
public transport 294–5
publishing 30–2
design tips 31
features 31–2

planning your design 31
using templates 32
see also desktop publishing
(DTP)
purchasing 131

queries 87, 92–6
QWERTY keyboard 179, 242

RAM (random access memory)
189
range checks 84–5
read/write DVD drives 190
real-time system 142
recording, physical and environmental data 123
records 65
definition 69
sorting 104
referential integrity 90
Regulation of Investigatory
Powers Act 2000 276
relational database 69, 72
relationships 72
creating 88–91
setting up 86–7
types of 73
relative cell references 62–3
remote control systems 142
remote monitoring 147
repetitive strain injury (RSI) 273
reports 69, 206
creating 102–6
definition 206
printed 206
printing 106
producing 101
style 105–6
right justified 9
ROM (read-only memory) 189
rows 40
deleting 42–3
inserting 42
RSI (Repetitive Strain Injury) 127,
276
rumours 283

safety precautions 126–7
sales 131
sales analysis 168
sales-based ordering 169
sales information 167, 169
sales prediction 140
satellite positioning systems
296–7

sausage 198
scanner 31, 180
scanning 5, 34, 122, 166–8, 306
scattergraph 52–6
school *see* electronic school
school registers
electronic 174–5
paper-based 174
SCOOT (Split Cycle and Offset
Optimisation Technique) 142–3
screen reports 206
search engine 37, 38
searching
tables 87
using a phrase 38
using a single word 38
security
at work 265–6
code 231–3
e-mail 232
Internet 250
medical records 155
on-line bookings 150
patient's data 160
voting 289
selecting text 6
sensing, research 121–2
sensors 141, 142, 145, 185–6
sensory impairment 301
sequencing 306
service provider *see* Internet
service provider (ISP)
shift work 262, 265
sink 198
sitting position 272, 273, 276
skills requirements 263–4, 266
slides
design 110
sequence 112
setting up 108–12
tips 112
SMS (Simple Message Service)
237–8
social aspects of work 264–7
social interaction at work 266
software
requirements 275
specially adapted 303–4
software components 222
software packages 178
software systems 177
sorting
database 66–7
records 104

tables 87
SPAM 277
special needs 300–3
see also specific disabilities
speech disabilities 302–3
speech recognition systems 302
speech synthesis 187, 304
speed camera 146, 299
spellcheckers 116–17, 302
split optimiser 143
spreadsheet 4, 39–65, 140
appearance 42
basics 39–43
cells 40
design 42
layout 42
printing 49–51, 68
tips when using 41
standard ways of working 123–7
start boxes 193
stock control 135–8, 169
dentist's practice 161
stock levels 167
stock replacement 167
stolen cars, tracking 297
stop boxes 193
storage media 242–3
strategic planning 163–4
stress at work 264–7, 273
activity 267
structure diagrams 196–8
subtraction 43
sum 62
surfing the Internet 37
activity 237
system design, possible errors
208
system flowcharts 195
system implementation 205–6
systems, graphical representation
192

tables 11, 40
autoformat 13
creating 76–8, 82–3, 84
database 69–71, 74–9
height of rows 13
links between 72
number of columns 12
number of rows 12
sample formats 13
saving 78
searching 87
selecting 13

sorting 87
summary 12–14
width of columns 13
see also relationships
talking computer 301
taxis 295
technical services 250
technical skills 264
telecommunications, protocols 188
television programmes 300
television signals 240
television vs. computer 285
teleworking
activity 263
advantages and disadvantages 261
motivation 265
negative aspects 266
see also working from home
templates 32
advantages in using 32
presentations 106–8
selecting 108
user's comments 211
temporary pages 37
terminal, definition 279
Tesco
barcoding system 166–8
case study 166–73
communicating with customers 172–3
designing store layout using CAD 170–1
electronic data interchange 170
electronic mail 171–2
electronic shelf labelling 169
hardware 170
Internet shopping service 172
loyalty card 173
on-line shopping, case study 248
sales-based ordering 169
stock control 169
using checkout information for planning bakery production 169
warehouse systems 171
testing 208–9
planning 209
text effects 8
text file 33
text formatting 33

text messages 237–8
theatre, case study 148–51
theatre booking system, flowchart 195
theatre ticket printer 149
Thomson Holidays 162
thought signals communication 308
3D models 244
thumbnails 16, 31
ticket booking systems 148–51
timing the slides 306
top-down approach 197
touch screen 182, 243–4, 289, 302
definition 297
tourist information 297
Toyota, case study 257
tracking stolen cars 297
traffic control system
case study 141–7
remote monitoring 147
training 263–4, 274
travel 254–5
travel agents 254
travel information 254, 294–5
trends 47

underlining 7, 8
undo command 7, 41
unethical material 283
universal serial bus (USB) 188
user documentation 209–10
user guide 209–10
user requirements 202–3

validation 207, 216
validation checks 83, 85
validation rule 85
validation text 85
verification 207, 215
video hire store
case study 218–23
current system 218–20
future improvements 222–3
main components of new system 221–2
videoconferencing 184, 260, 304
virtual banking 252–4
virtual reality 244, 246
website 308
virus 191
checking 124
definition 270

downloading 277
voice-activated systems 301
voice mail 183
voice output 187
voice recognition 183, 264
voting, electronic, case study 289

WAP (Wireless Application Protocol) 238
warehouse systems 171
weather checks 185
weather forecasting 144–5
web address 37, 152
web browser 35
web camera (web cam) 184–5
applications 185
web pages 6, 35, 122
design 114
North Korea 290
web server 35
WebCrawler 38
websites 6, 122, 158, 162, 226, 281, 300
community activities 293
wide area network (WAN) 12
Windows 2000 4
Windows Millennium Edition 4
Windows XP 4
wizard 97–102
word-wrapping around images/objects 16
wordprocessing 5
wordprocessors 33
predictive 302
work location 260–1
work management 124
work patterns 261–3
work styles 266–7
working from home 260–1
see also teleworking
working hours 262
workplace
hazards 271
inspection 274
worksheet 39, 44, 47, 50, 52
World Wide Web (WWW) 35, 226
wrapping text around an image 17–19
wrist guards 276
wrist rest 126

X-ray pictures 159

Yahoo 38